Enrichment Activities for Able and Talented Children

Barry Teare

Published by Network Educational Press Ltd
PO Box 635
Stafford
ST16 1BF

First published 2004
© Barry Teare 2004

ISBN 1 85539 065 5

Edited by Dawn Booth
Design & layout by Neil Hawkins, NEP
Cover & additional illustrations by
Kerry Ingham

Printed in Great Britain by
MPG Books Ltd, Bodmin, Cornwall.

Contents

Acknowledgements

Many thanks to the 'team' at Network Educational Press for their support and hard work – Jane Phillips, Dawn Booth, Kerry Ingham and Neil Hawkins. A special thank you to Christina Teare for her encouragement and support generally, and for her particular work for the two pieces '2 Across, 4 Down', and 'Follow the Yellow Brick Road'.

Apart from pieces of work based upon actual historical events, the names and events are fictional and any link to real people is accidental and coincidental.

Introduction

Enrichment Activities for Able and Talented Children has been produced as a consequence of the coming together of five factors (listed below the grey box).

It should be clear that this book has been written to help those who find themselves with responsibility for running enrichment activities for able children.

However, much of the theory included in the book has real significance in getting good results with able children in the normal classroom. Moreover, the great majority of the book is devoted to materials for use with children. These resources can be used for lessons and homework as well as collectively for courses.

In this sense, the book has two overlapping and complementary purposes and target groups.

> **More simply, the book is designed to be of value to all teachers, advisers, co-ordinators and headteachers whose work brings them into contact with able children.**

ONE

There are many people throughout the country running enrichment activities for able children as a result of a heightened interest and specific initiatives. The gifted and talented strand of *Excellence in Cities* has looked not only at improved provision within the normal classroom but also at making available a growing number of activities outside the normal classroom. Education Action Zones have become involved in a similar way. Schools and authorities outside funded programmes for able children have been strongly influenced by those programmes. Money has been available to all Local Education Authorities (LEAs) to make bids for summer schools.

The result is a dramatic growth of teachers and advisers involved in provision of such activities.

TWO

The background and experience of those involved in running enrichment activities are very mixed. Some have a long history of such work; others have been thrust into the situation. There has therefore been an urgent request for advice and help from many areas.

THREE

The author has a substantial and lengthy experience of organizing enrichment activities for able children at both primary and secondary age:

- Some ten years, or more, of being the link person in the running of Saturday Club activities for the Greater Manchester branch of the National Association for Gifted Children. These activities were aimed at five- to thirteen- year olds.
- Involvement in special activities within the secondary school in Devon where the author was headteacher.

- The provision of a large number of weekend courses at Kilve Court Residential Enrichment Centre in Somerset.
- The ongoing provision of two-day residential and one-day courses for Devon LEA.
- One- and two-day courses for able children in many areas including Woolwich, Greenford, Swansea, Hull, Rotherham, Stoke, Stockton, Birmingham and Dorset.

This experience started in 1974 and is still continuing.

FOUR

The author's decision to spend less time travelling means that there is reduced availability to work as widely with children. Passing on the expertise and experience is a prime consideration of the book.

FIVE

The huge success of the four previous books on able and talented children for Network Educational Press has underlined the almost insatiable demand for enrichment materials.

Using this Book

This book is composed of two sections.

Section One

Section One is a concise, but important, exposition of theory on running enrichment activities successfully. There is an examination of a range of issues including:

- aims and objectives
- the selection of appropriate participants
- creating an encouraging atmosphere
- staffing
- flexibility
- pastoral concerns
- key elements
- patterns and rhythms
- monitoring and evaluation.

Section Two

Section Two of the book forms the majority of it and contains commentaries, advice, and a wealth of activities and new resources under six main headings:

- English
- Reading/Thinking Skills
- Mathematics
- Games/Thinking Skills
- Humanities/Thinking Skills
- Detective/Thinking Skills

These activities and resources have the dual purpose of content for courses and for use individually in the normal classroom.

Abbreviations and symbols

Abbreviations are used to avoid unnecessary repetition. Symbols have been designed to direct the attention of the reader to key points or cross-referencing.

Talking Point This symbol is used when an important issue is under discussion.

Remember The elephant refers to key messages.

Practical Points These give advice on delivery and teaching methods.

Verbatim This is normally an exact copy of what has been said to children. Teachers may well wish to change what they say but they have a reference point to work from. The verbatim symbol also occurs in Teaching Notes where it shows exactly what instructions should be read out to children at the start of an activity or piece of work. Again, teachers may wish to make changes.

This Book This indicates that the resource is printed in full in the book. The pupil sheets can be photocopied for use in the institution that has purchased the book.

Other NEP Books Comments are being made about pieces of work from the four previous books by Barry Teare on able and talented children for Network Educational Press.
EPATC   This refers to Barry Teare, *Effective Provision for Able and Talented Children*.
ERATC   This refers to Barry Teare, *Effective Resources for Able and Talented Children*.
MERATC This refers to Barry Teare, *More Effective Resources for Able and Talented Children*.
CRATC   This refers to Barry Teare, *Challenging Resources for Able and Talented Children*.

Other Materials Reference is made to commercial materials from other sources that have been used successfully on courses. There is special advice on securing copies of books that are out of print on page 30 of this book.

Time Activities and resources have this clock at the end of them. A time is given as a rough guide to the length of time needed for the activity. However, it is important to realize that such timings can only be approximate. A teacher may vary how much is said as an introduction (the level of previous knowledge and experience will affect the detail required). Very able pupils may complete a task in a very short time, especially where tasks such as matrix puzzles are used.

| 5 | 6 | 7 | 8 | |

Year Range The ruler attempts to give the appropriate age of children for the various activities and resources. The courses have been directed largely at Key Stages 2 and 3, with the optimum range being Y5, 6, 7 and 8. However, this is a very rough guide. The chronological and developmental ages of able pupils are very different. It is amazing what some very young children can achieve. In any case, open-ended materials can be tackled by a wide range of ages and abilities.

The example given here would indicate a target group of Y5, 6, 7 and 8. A plus sign at either end means that the range is extended, either younger or older, for that particular activity or resource.

Modular Design

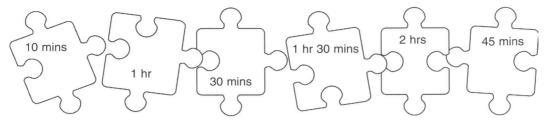

The pieces described in Section Two of this book cover a wide range of time requirements and types of activities. Think of them as jigsaw pieces. From them you can build jigsaws of different sizes, containing various types of pieces. You can build work periods of very different durations in the same way. Individual pieces can be as short as ten minutes and as long as two to three hours. Activities within long tournaments can be used individually as much shorter pieces. Using the pieces in this book you therefore have two-way movement – adding up units to make a longer session and breaking down long activities into shorter individual items, depending on where and when you wish to use them.

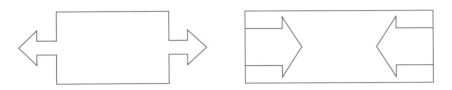

Curricular Flexibility

The activities and resources are set out under six main headings but this does not tell the full story. The following points should be noted:

1   English and Reading have been separated because of the courses led by the author. Clearly the materials can be interchanged. Some activities specifically concerning children's literature would give variety to more general English courses. There are writing outcomes in both sections. Wordplay is a key feature in both.
2   The Games theme has a strong mathematical content and that is why it follows the Mathematics section in the book. Some of the activities could be used as easily on mathematics courses or during mathematics lessons. Authors, such as Brian Bolt, are referred to freely. Logic features strongly. Word games also appear and the presentations enhance English skills.
3   The Detective theme plays strongly to the skills needed by the pupils in the humanities subjects. The code activities clearly link with mathematical thinking. Both logical thinking and lateral thinking feature strongly.
4   The teaching of one method of lateral thinking is explained fully in the Humanities section (page 205). However, lateral thinking can be employed in courses on many curriculum areas.
5   The teaching of logical thinking via the matrix method is fully explained in the Detective Section (page 247).

The Key Element of Thinking Skills

In *Excellence in Cities* documentation the government has quite correctly advised participating schools to put emphasis upon the higher-order thinking skills of analysis, evaluation and synthesis. The courses, activities and resources in this book have looked for a similar emphasis. 'Thinking skills' is the subtitle for many of the main headings in Section Two, underpinning *Enrichment Activities for Able and Talented Children*.

Section 1

Running Enrichment Activities and Courses Successfully

Aims and Objectives

What are the purposes behind enrichment courses? People have varying views, but aims need to be clear for an event to be successful. If the purposes are not properly thought out then outcomes may not fulfil expectations.

The following points are of great importance in the view of the author:

- ☞ The course is different from normal school – in setting, organization, timetable and content.
- ☞ The material is demanding and challenging. Participants have to think hard. Nobody will get everything totally correct.
- ☞ Participants learn new methods and techniques while at the same time learning about themselves.
- ☞ There is a great variety of activities.
- ☞ Content concentrates upon transferable thinking skills.
- ☞ The work is exciting and enjoyment is central to it.

The comment you most want to hear from children at the end of a course is something like: 'The work was quite difficult and challenging. I have learned a lot. I was made to think. It was very enjoyable. When is the next one?'

Children attending enrichment courses is fine, but how do they fit in with normal school?
This query should definitely be raised. Enrichment activities and courses have an important role to play as part of provision for able children; they are the 'icing on the cake'. The huge majority of children's learning takes place in the normal classroom. There is no point running enrichment activities and ignoring the rest, and the majority, of provision. Every effort needs to be made to have feedback from such activities to the mainstream providers so that the overall needs of the child are taken into account.

The Selection of Participants

The target group
For children to gain maximum benefit from an enrichment activity, one important factor is that the most suitable groups are assembled for the work to be undertaken. Setting percentages for the target group is likely to be too narrow and crude a method. The events described in this book are enrichment activities rather than masterclasses. Masterclasses would seem to be the correct name for a small minority of events aiming at incredibly talented children and given by a recognized leader in the specific fields: appropriate in areas such as music.

Enrichment Activities for Able and Talented Children © Barry Teare (Network Educational Press, 2004)

There is a wider target group here so that many able children can take advantage of the courses. This does not imply that the courses are suitable for everyone – far from it. Some open-ended materials provide opportunities for a wide range of abilities, but some of the contents are very definitely aimed at the able. A course that is well planned will cater for the exceptionally able within provision for a larger cohort of able children.

What do you do when the group turns out to be much more mixed in ability than was planned or expected?
The tutors need to do their best for all the children attending but they must not compromise the provision for correctly-selected able participants. Otherwise there is a repeat situation that some able pupils encounter in normal classes – that is, they are not given work appropriate to them because it would be unsuitable for other children in the class. This is, in effect, a disenfranchisement of able pupils. Strategies for dealing with this situation can be built into an enrichment course, for example, by using a proportion of open-ended materials and introducing an element of choice into the activities.

What happens if the children that have been selected are not what the organizers had in mind when planning the course?
This happens on some occasions and it is often the original information that is at fault. Mathematics provides a really good example. Mathematics is not just one subject. It is several, with different skills and abilities. The facility to compute well does not necessarily equate with ability to work in the abstract (algebra), to deal with spatial problems or to carry out successful investigations.

If the course is to concentrate upon a particular type of mathematics, then that needs spelling out in the advertising information, or you end up with inappropriate participants. Alternatively, the organizers need to ensure that different areas are covered so that children of different types of ability are all given an opportunity.

Be very specific about the contents or the course in the initial information. Stress the particular skills and abilities that will be needed.

Another reason for 'wrong' children being selected is that there is a lack of awareness of what is required among the staff making the selections. The answer here is for INSET to improve knowledge about the identification of able pupils.

Among the 25 to 30 children chosen for a course from several schools, there is a block of 15 or so from one school. Is this a problem?
In practice, this can produce problems. The general tone is dominated by the large group. They can gang together and be less outgoing. One aspect of enrichment courses is meeting new peers. A large group can fail to socialize widely or work with different children. It also makes it more difficult for children who are on their own to settle in.

Recruitment for courses takes place in a variety of ways. If a leaflet is sent out to a number of schools, the information must appeal to children but also explain to schools and parents the educational reasoning behind the course. Two examples follow on the next page.

1. Marvellous Mathematical Medicine

Pupils

Some people take a gloomy view that education, like medicine, does not do you any good unless it tastes nasty. They believe that mathematics, in particular, is hard, dull and boring. Nothing could be further from the truth. Come and be invigorated by 'marvellous mathematical medicine'.

IT'S FUN, IT'S ENJOYABLE, IT'S CHALLENGING. IT COULD BE JUST THE TONIC THAT YOU NEED!

The materials are very varied being drawn from the course tutor's own work as well as from the enchanting and magical work of mathematicians such as Brian Bolt, Carol Vorderman and Anita Straker.

Have a go at creating and playing the 'Spiral Board Game'. See how well you fare in the fast-and-furious tournament 'All Numbers Great and Small'. Employ a fun method to deal with factorials in 'The Year of the Dragon'. Tackle logical thought problems. There is something for everybody from 'Single Surprise', an exercise involving computation and following instructions, to mathematical novelties like 'Metamorphoses', to the maths coming out of games as in 'Par for the Course'. You will feel so much better when you have tasted your 'marvellous mathematical medicine'.

You need to bring writing materials, a lively mind and a desire to enjoy the delights of mathematics.

Parents and schools

The materials are challenging and enjoyable, but they also answer the demands of the National Curriculum and the Numeracy Strategy. Suitable participants will have ability in mathematics but not just in the narrow computational sense. The course has much practical content and 'fun' material that will appeal to those who have a love of numbers.

2. Super Sleuth

Pupils

Murder, mystery, baffling brainteasers, cunning clues, crafty codes, intriguing investigations, lateral and linear logic, perplexing puzzles, enigmatic evidence – these are the enjoyable and challenging ingredients of 'Super Sleuth'. Have you a clear, logical mind? Do you fancy yourself as Frost, Morse, Poirot, Sherlock Holmes, Miss Marple, Colombo, or any of the other great detectives from literature or television? Can you sort out the important from the unimportant and solve the case? Do you enjoy pitting your wits to unravel mysteries and to draw conclusions from evidence? Can you crack codes to discover vital information? If so, 'Super Sleuth' is designed for you.

The various materials, cases, problems and investigations are mixed in length and complexity. They include both real-life situations and fictional cases. Some need logical thinking, some clever hunches, others a look from a different angle. The situations vary from solving a theatre murder, to locating the farmer's treasure, to deciding upon the culprit in 'an arresting problem', to spotting the way into a complex code, and to taking on the mantle of Sherlock Holmes.

You need to bring writing materials and a 'razor-sharp mind'.

Parents and schools

This is a skills-based, cross-curricular course. It involves elements which are pertinent to English, mathematics, history and science, but its relevance is more general than that. With thinking skills and the ability to reason having important places within current educational thinking and planning, courses based upon logical thinking, lateral thinking and deduction have a significant part to play. More than that, education should be enjoyable and exciting.

- Information also needs to include the target group in terms of age.
- A further sensible statement to add is that 'participants should understand that the course involves sustained hard work and concentration'. It is important that participants realize that there will be great enjoyment, coupled with challenging and thought-provoking work.

It is surprising how important the presentation of courses is, including the title. **TITLES MATTER!** For example, a word-based course initially advertised under the title of 'Paronomasia' (meaning play on words) attracted little attention. The same programme under the title 'Raining Cats and Dogs' was oversubscribed.

Flexibility of Length and Content

Time
Different time-scales are possible; each has its own advantages and disadvantages.

- One-day courses cut down on administrative costs and avoid the complications of residentials. A problem is that longer activities cannot be included easily as they unbalance the programme.
- Two-day courses without an overnight stay in between can be held in many venues without the cost that a stay would entail. The loss of a residential experience is a drawback, but longer activities can be included.
- Two-day, one-night courses give plenty of time for a variety of activities in terms of length. The residential experience adds to the benefits for the children although homesickness can be a problem. It is a minority problem, but even one child in such a state can be unsettling. Costs are clearly higher than for non-residentials.
- Weekend courses, starting on Friday evening and finishing on Sunday afternoon, have the advantage of not affecting normal school time. They are high in costs due to two overnight stays and do not provide significantly more time than two-day, one-night courses. Longer activities are a 'must'.
- One or two weeks give the maximum possibilities for developing work programmes and being able to follow through. Major projects can be undertaken. The demands upon tutors and pupils are very substantial. Costs rise steeply, especially when the residential element is included.

Content
Tutors need to have available much more material than the time would appear to permit. There are two main reasons for this:

1 If it is a group of children not known in advance by the tutor, there may be problems over selection. Some of the group may not be as able as was anticipated. Alternative material should then be used without compromising the challenge to those who have been correctly chosen.

2 If you use material that is in a published form (as the author does with his own materials), it may be that some members of the group have already tackled certain pieces. Alternative items are required but they need to match the type of activity so that the overall balance of the programme is not adversely affected. For example, a new logical problem needs to be substituted for a logical problem that has already been covered by a minority of the group.

The initial programme is planned to have a variety of styles and outcomes. The planning also involves alternative items that will not upset the balance.

Staffing issues

The role of the tutor is crucial to the success of enrichment activity.

Key Characteristics of a Good Tutor

★ **Enthusiastic.** Many able pupils are perceptive. They possess good interpersonal skills. Obvious enthusiasm from the tutor provides a great stimulus to exciting pupil work.

★ **Flexible.** Changes of content or, sometimes, of order of events can be critical to success.

★ **Possessing stamina.** Enrichment activities are intense and demanding as the time available has to put to the best use.

★ **Having a sense of humour.** So many able children have an 'off-the-wall' sense of humour. They can be reached by staff who appreciate this mentality. Recent, more general findings have stressed the importance of this, particularly when dealing with boys.

★ **Having high expectations.** Too many people underestimate what able pupils are capable of doing. The danger is perhaps greater when young children are involved. Judgement comes with experience.

★ **Intervening as little as possible.** Teachers sometimes feel that they have to be engaged directly with children to justify their position. Non-intervention is very important with able pupils. The tasks are for them to sort out, not for the tutor. If the tutor steps in the moment that there is a difficulty then the child is never challenged and does not learn. Clearly, behavioural problems have to be dealt with and it is unhealthy for frustration to reach excessive levels. Having said that, if the children have been correctly selected and the materials and tasks are suitable, the tutor should be able to 'take a back seat'.

★ **Tough when required.** Championing the rights of able children does not mean 'being soft' with them – far from it. Just as with good parents, 'tough love' is what counts. If able children are under-challenged in lessons and obtain high scores easily, they can become intellectually idle. When more challenging work is encountered, able children do not necessarily 'jump for joy'. The tutor needs to take them through this barrier to enable them to work to their full potential. This approach works in the great majority of cases, providing immense satisfaction for both child and tutor.

★ **Risk taking.** If the tutor always plays safe, why should the children take risks? This is an unfair contract. The tutor must be prepared to use unusual resources and methods to stimulate the participants.

★ **Interesting.** The tutor should ask 'Why would anybody wish to be with me?' You cannot enrich the lives of able children without being enriched yourself. No matter how difficult it is to keep the balance between home, school, family, work and you, the part called 'you' has to be nourished and stimulated. Otherwise you become a dull and uninteresting person, and of no use to able children.

Possessing knowledge is only part of the formula for success. Developing vital personal characteristics is as, or even more, important.

Tutors for enrichment courses may have some concerns. Some teachers lack confidence and are quite frightened of the challenge. Others are concerned about the 'risks' involved; they do not want to 'put their heads on the block' as children cannot be programmed and results cannot be guaranteed.

There is a 'catch-22' situation. You cannot gain experience without taking on the role, yet some teachers feel that they cannot take on the role without the experience. Nobody starts off experienced. You learn along the way and you learn quickly.

Why put your toe in the water?

✔ There is enormous professional satisfaction to be gained. The 'buzz factor' is fantastic.
✔ You see children produce the most incredible work, doing and saying the most amazing things.
✔ The professional development has knock-on effects in the teaching of all children.
✔ Acting as tutor allows courses to run that satisfy the needs of able children, all part of the teacher's job.

Enrichment activities not only provide challenge and enjoyment for able children but also provide a major professional opportunity for teachers.

'Able children are demanding and challenging. What if I am not able to answer all their questions?'
Nobody knows everything. The tutor should not be viewed as the fount of all wisdom but the facilitator of discovery and learning. The tutor needs to know enough or able children will become disillusioned, but gaps in knowledge are only natural and the great majority of able children will accept that.

The Magic Ingredients

Thinking skills and beneficial working methods underpin the successful delivery of enrichment activities.

A Recipe for Success

Main Ingredients
Evaluation
Analysis
Synthesis

On a base of
Interesting content

With good helpings of
Problem-solving
Lateral thinking
Logical thinking
Creativity
Following instructions
Imagination
Wordplay
Deduction and inference
Effective data-handling

Whisked together with
Communication skills
Presentation skills
Brainstorming
Collaboration
Teamwork
Listening skills
Wise use of time
Perseverance
Application

Garnished with
Alternative methods
Prioritization
Empathy

Leading to
Transferability

Essential ingredient

ENJOYMENT

You don't have to be a wizard to produce magic. The ingredients are readily available for everybody to use.

Patterns, Rhythms and Styles of Working

Successful enrichment activities do not just depend upon interesting content but also the order in which that content is used and the care taken to get the best from the participants. Often such enrichment activities involve concentrated programmes. It is essential therefore to:

- ✔ alter the mood
- ✔ vary the styles of work
- ✔ look carefully at sequencing of activities
- ✔ create movement
- ✔ vary the length of pieces
- ✔ mix lighter and more serious pieces
- ✔ mix the inputs and expected outcomes to cater for varied preferred learning styles
- ✔ vary the working groups.

Working groups

It is beneficial to mix up the formats for individual pieces:

- **Individual challenges.** There is a place for a child to produce his or her own work.

- **A choice.** For some pieces the participants can choose between working as individuals or in small groups. Faced with a code, for instance, some children prefer to take on the task individually, whereas others prefer a joint effort. Wherever a group is the preferred choice, the golden rule is that all members of the group contribute to the joint effort. It must not be one person doing all the work and the rest of the group benefiting from that.

- **Teams or groups.** Tournaments, presentations, treasure hunts and the like need a team to work together. Collaboration and teamwork are important elements. In the outside world a large number of people work in teams. It is not the fictional detective, like Poirot, but a crime squad. There are individual designers, but more often there is a design team. Organizations, businesses, schools and hospitals are today so complex that a management team is required. Successful teams tend to have a mixture of personalities and skills. Working in teams on an enrichment activity is a valuable opportunity for children to meet new 'like minds' and to develop their collaborative skills.

- **As a whole group.** Enrichment activities work best with movement, change and varied styles but, even so, there is benefit in putting in teaching units on fascinating topics, such as the place of codes in history, or the importance of probability theory in consideration of strategies within games.

How you work, and who you work with, are as important as what you do.

Typical Templates for Enrichment Courses

A two-day, one-night residential scenario is detailed below as one example, but the thinking involved is relevant for the construction of programmes for all enrichment courses.

Day One

Morning Session One

Welcome

Introduction

Starter or Icebreaker
(word game, lateral problem, a mathematical discussion and so on)

Early items should give everybody a chance to contribute and 'get into' the course.

A major item

Break

Morning Session Two

A substantial piece

One or two shorter items

Lunch

Afternoon Session One

(normally a considerable stretch of time)

A long activity (such as a treasure hunt, working with 'spy' materials, or a murder trial)

An extended time slot needs movement, activity and practical elements

Afternoon Session Two

A solid and substantial piece, perhaps as an individual challenge

Between two major and very exciting events, it is sensible to introduce a 'quieter' piece.

Choice Time

Dinner

Evening Session

A long and dramatic activity
such as a tournament of several rounds

Enrichment Activities for Able and Talented Children © Barry Teare (Network Educational Press, 2004)

Day Two
Morning Session One
Recapitulation and lessons from Day One
Starter or Icebreaker

After a long, demanding day, working late into the evening, participants need to be 'recharged' and 'set off' again.

A substantial piece
Break
Morning Session Two
A challenging piece of work (as a group or individually)
One or two very short items
Lunch
Afternoon Session One

Feedback on previous pieces, including competition results

After a very challenging one and a half days, now is the time to use lighter items and give children choice.

A novelty piece
Choice Time
Break
Afternoon Session Two
Pulling things together, time for reflection
Short preparation of parental presentation
Presentation to parents
End of Course

Children live today in a 'sound-bite society' of little attention and concentration. Substantial pieces are required to maintain and develop span of concentration, a very important skill for able children.

A thinking skills day

Schools often request a general thinking skills day rather than subject-specific courses such as English or mathematics. This is easily put together by using elements from different parts of Section Two of the book, and units from elsewhere.

A typical pattern might be:

Time	Activity	Where it is found
Morning: Session One	Introduction	
	Word game such as 'One Word Leads to Another'	English
	Lateral thinking problems	Detective, Humanities
	How to solve problems using the matrix method	Detective
	A logic problem such as 'Field and Track' or 'Canine Avenue'	Detective
Morning: Session Two	'The 24 Game'	Mathematics
	'Centrally Heated Knickers', science poems by Michael Rosen from the book of the same name, Penguin, 2000	
	A code such as 'Lucky the Cat'	Detective
	Choice Time	See below
Afternoon Session	A presentation 'Brief Case'	Detective
	'Tangled Tales'	Reading
	'Fox, Rabbit, Rat'	Mathematics

Choice Time

Enrichment courses need to use time well and to challenge children through the main activities. They also benefit from periods known as 'Choice Time'.

There are two main reasons for Choice Time:

1 Able children are all different. Children have different ways of working, and differing preferences and varying abilities in the activities undertaken. The result is that some participants complete a task more quickly than others. It would be criminal for those that gain time to fritter it away as they wait for others to finish. In this situation, children make a personal selection from the Choice List. There is, therefore, never a time when any child has not got something worthwhile to do.

   One of the most-heard criticisms by parents, advisers and inspectors is that when able children finish tasks early and well, the time is often wasted with 'more of the same' or trivial tasks. The Choice List is here in relation to enrichment courses, but it is equally applicable to the normal classroom and its significance is greater there as the time involved is substantially more.

2 It is always pleasant to have a choice for part of the time. The Choice List has a real mixture of items, some taking an earlier exercise further, some giving the chance for creating examples of their own, and some introducing new topics. Early in a course the Choice List is bound to be short but it grows as the course progresses.

An example of a Choice List

(Taken from the mathematics course 'Snakes and Races, Squares and Quotients'.)

1	GO × SIX = UP × TEN	A new item, from Brian Bolt
2	'Punch and Judy'	A new item, from Giles Brandreth
3	Create your own sheet like 'FIVE' but for a different number	Own follow-up
4	Add information to your 'Snakes and Races, Squares and Quotients' board	Ongoing item
5	Do the later sections of 'Spots Before Your Eyes', including 'Harry's Hand'	Taking things further
6	Play the game 'Fives and Threes'	Additional activity, following up a set item
7	Try a more difficult Tsunami puzzle	Higher level
8	Design your own Tsunami puzzle	Creating own example
9	Play 'Submarines, Cruisers and Helicopters'	A new item, from Brian Bolt
10	Change the rules to 'Submarines, Cruisers and Helicopters' and play the game that results	Follow-up to a new item
11	Design your own 3D game based upon the principles of the one above	Creating own example

As new items are added to the list, a small introduction needs to be given by the tutor so that children know what the choices involve.

In this way no child is ever faced with a waste of time and real choice is given. This means that, by the end of a course, all participants have tackled the main pieces of work, but what else is done will depend upon how quickly they have completed tasks and their own personal selection.

Success Criteria for Individual Pieces of Work

Able children should always start a task knowing what would make their response a good one. It means that they can work effectively. Otherwise, if informed of this after a piece of work they may well say 'Why didn't you tell me all this before I started?'

An example of success criteria

(Taken from 'Brief Case', an activity described on page 252 of this book)

> **The Criteria by which your 'Brief Case' will be Judged**
>
> 1   The extent to which the members of the team work well together.
> 2   The appropriateness of the title for the case.
> 3   The degree to which the exhibits play a key role.
> 4   The creativity and imagination shown without making the case unrealistic.
> 5   The suitability of the case to be presented in court.
> 6   The quality of the presentation itself.

Other examples of success criteria are given as part of pieces of work in Section Two of the book.

The notion of success criteria, ahead of task, is just as applicable in normal lessons.

The Prize Box!

The discussion of rewards for able children is an interesting one. Many would argue that the greatest reward is to be given exciting and challenging work, rather than dull repetition and 'more of the same'. Enrichment courses should certainly be giving this type of reward. The author has employed a prize box of inexpensive but interesting and unusual items for the winners of team activities and individual challenges within courses. This has been a popular feature, and it has been heart-  warming to see the value placed upon such inexpensive prizes by a supposedly materialistic and sophisticated generation. Examples of prizes include: puzzles (physical and mental), magic tricks, stationery (pens, notepads, staplers, colouring pencils and felt-tip pens), magnetic board games (chess, draughts, Backgammon, Nine Men's Morris), paperbacks and balls.

NOTE: Care should be taken to praise effort and achievement that has not resulted in gaining a prize, with an emphasis placed upon self-evaluation and progress.

Creating the Right Atmosphere, Getting the Best Out of Children

Venue

An enrichment course is a very special event for the children. A venue that is pleasant and facilitates the work can enhance the whole experience.

A large, main work space can provide the flexibility to alter seating arrangements and furniture to create contrasting atmospheres for differing activities. For example, in 'Brief Case', described on page 252 of this book, the introduction and preparation time, which involves intense and often noisy group work, is followed by the creation of a courtroom with an entirely different atmosphere. The presentations by the groups in the form of court cases must follow the rules of a courtroom: nobody must speak during a presentation unless asked to do so. This activity helps children to appreciate appropriate behaviour for varying circumstances and places. In this respect, it is very helpful to have the facility to alter the physical appearance of the room to reflect the activity.

For treasure hunts and large-scale practical exercises additional spaces, such as the hall, are valuable, both for use by the children and to give the tutor a chance to set up special activities.

Display can also enhance the ambience of the course. For example, reading courses could find display materials to do with children's literature is especially helpful. Posters and balloons can be obtained from the Booktrust (see page 80 of this book for details), and, if space permits, an area with easy chairs for reading, sharing passages and discussion work is very beneficial.

Display sheets

A particularly useful feature is to have a flip chart and pin-board space around the walls. As each piece of work is introduced and completed a flip-chart sheet, describing its main features, is exhibited on the walls. Similarly, sheets of information, such as Success Criteria or the skills used in a particular piece of work, are displayed. The purposes of display sheets are:

★ to make the workroom more interesting
★ to immerse the children in the thinking skills being used
★ to remind participants of the activities to assist selection in Choice Time
★ to assist children during the parental presentation.

Settling children at the start of the course

Enrichment courses are organized in a number of ways. If children are taken off normal timetable and work together in their own school, the familiarity reduces initial concerns. Even so, it will not be the 'norm'. When four or five children from each of five or six schools form the cohort, the 'strangeness' is increased. This situation is heightened further for an individual child, on his or her own with nobody else there that he or she knows. If the venue is new to participants this can also cause concerns. It is important to reduce worries at the start and to encourage children to relax so that they can perform well.

Children attending an enrichment course for the first time may have some very confused ideas about what will be expected from them.

> Peter attended an English enrichment course in Devon. In his evaluation, at the end of the two days, he admitted that he had been both excited and worried at the start of the course. He had tried to predict what he might be asked to do and had decided, erroneously, that, as this was an English course for able pupils, he might be required to write a long story but only be allowed ten minutes to do so. As a result, he had lain awake at night constructing a plot to save time!

The sooner that such fears are dispelled the better. You may not stop children worrying in advance, although prior information to the participants may help, but you can certainly make every effort to reassure and relax them at the start of the course.

❝ Welcome to this enrichment course. I hope that you are excited to be here, but you may also be a little tense and concerned. That is perfectly natural. You might be worrying about what will be expected of you and whether you will cope. You may not know anybody else. Those of you who haven't worked with us before may be wondering about the tutors. Relax. Nothing terrible is going to happen to you. All of the tutors, including myself, have had a good breakfast this morning. We don't need to eat any children today!

The course will be challenging and should make you think. However, there is plenty that everybody can do. You have been chosen because you have ability in this curriculum area. You are all different people and, therefore, a piece that one person finds easy somebody else might find tricky, and vice versa. The programme has been designed quite deliberately so that different skills and abilities will feature at different times.

Don't expect to get everything right. At school you may get top marks much of the time. I don't see the point, do you? If you keep getting 20 out of 20 it only means one thing as far as I am concerned – the work is too easy. You need to progress, to advance, and grow. So don't worry about getting everything correct.

Let me tell you about a famous scientist called Sir Harold Kroto, who is quoted as saying 'Nine out of ten of my experiments fail and that is considered a pretty good record amongst scientists'. Sir Harold Kroto has won the Nobel Prize for Chemistry, one of the highest awards in the world. If he can afford to make mistakes, I am sure that you can, too. The key thing is to have a go and learn from your mistakes.

Now, I want you to listen carefully. Can you hear the sound of hammering? (pause) You look puzzled. You can't hear the sound of hammering because there isn't any. One of the reasons there isn't any is that I have not asked for a scaffold to be erected to execute anyone who makes a mistake during the course. The only people who do not make mistakes are those who do nothing or those who only ever attempt 'Mickey Mouse' tasks, and that is of no use either to themselves nor anybody else.

Are you getting the message? We want you to relax and do your best. You won't get everything right because if you did there would not be sufficient challenge. What is important is that you think hard and see how much you can do.

The other thing that you should know is that the course has been designed to be thoroughly enjoyable. It contains exciting activities such as a treasure hunt and a fast-and-furious tournament. Learning should be enormous fun.

These opening remarks to children are not reproduced verbatim to be learned by heart and repeated, but rather to give a detailed explanation of key points to help settle participants. It is better if tutors develop their own delivery to convey similar messages.

This delivery was especially designed for the start of an enrichment course. The sentiments about Sir Harold Kroto, making mistakes and 20 out of 20, are applicable to the teaching of able children at any time.

Work ethic

One ingredient for a successful enrichment course is application. For children to derive maximum benefit they should understand that positive effort is required from them. Many participants will be keen to do their best, but not all able children are naturally hard working. Able children do not form a homogenous group – they are a mixed lot! Some work normally within fairly low expectations and are not used to challenge, concentration, commitment and hard work.

> The tutor is unhappy about the lack of application of some participants. The level of effort could be higher for some children. Work is not flowing as one would hope.

Issues should never be ignored. When you are dissatisfied, tackle the problem. The author, at such times (which are fortunately few), stresses the need for the delivery of talent and ability. He has devised a short piece called 'Heroes and Heroines' which follows.

'Heroes and Heroines'

 I would like you to tell me your heroes and heroines. Who are the people you admire?

Responses are likely to include pop stars, footballers like David Beckham, other sports people such as Paula Radcliffe or Mohammed Ali, writers like Jacqueline Wilson or Philip Pullman, caring people like Mother Teresa or Nelson Mandela. Some children will give locally based answers. Others will name members of their own family. When asked why he had nominated his father, one Asian boy said that his family had started with nothing, but they were now well provided for because of the hard work of his father.

These people that you have named, are they successful or unsuccessful? Did you choose David Beckham because he can't kick a ball? Did you choose Paula Radcliffe because she cannot run? Did you choose Nelson Mandela because he was a poor leader?

At this point children acknowledge that they have chosen some of the most successful people in the world.

People say that children today do not value success; that it is not cool to succeed. I think that we have just disproved that. Now let us move on to something that is not so easily understood. The people whom you have named, are they hard working or idle?

There tends to be a pause as children consider this new statement, followed by agreement that they are indeed hard working.

The people you have named are not only very successful, they have also worked tremendously hard to deliver their ability and gain success. When Eric Cantona was at Manchester United many commentators regarded him as the most gifted player in the country. Who came off the training ground last? Eric Cantona. What do golfers like Tiger Woods and snooker players like Peter Ebdon do between events? They practise for very many hours. An older world-class golfer called Gary Player once said, 'People say that I am lucky. I've noticed a funny thing. The more I practise, the luckier I get on the golf course.'

Making it 'cool' to succeed is a vital element in successful provision for able children. Explaining that hard work is part of success is very important indeed.

Sustained effort

It is important that span of concentration and good working practices are developed so that able children, especially, can tackle more complex or difficult tasks both at school and in life. If children normally achieve success easily and quickly, it comes as something of a shock to the system to make a sustained effort. The dreaded saying 'I don't get this' are words that often come after only two or three minutes on a task.

'I don't get this' is a banned expression in this room. How can you possibly hope to get something when you have had barely enough time to read what is required, let alone solve it? The work is intended to be challenging. It certainly will not be completed in three minutes. Let us rethink our approach. Important and difficult problems are not normally solved without much thought and effort. This is a skill you need to practise.

Pastoral care

It goes without saying that to get the best from any children, including able children, they have to be cared for and their genuine concerns and needs taken into account. This is especially the case when children are on residential courses and may be away from home for the first time. Able children are individuals and what bothers them varies considerably.

One difficult situation for some able children to come to terms with is to realize that there are others more able than themselves. Some able children can be described as 'big fish in a little pool'. They star in their own class or school, especially where the school is small. Then they meet other able children from elsewhere and they realize not only that there are other big fish but some whales as well! Or, to mix metaphors, they are no longer top dog! This is a difficult situation to come to terms with and it sometimes takes a little time. They may struggle or 'give up' for a while and they need to be encouraged to recognize that they are still able, even if not 'the tops', and that they can achieve at a high level to their own potential.

Time is also a factor in being patient for results. Even able children do not always 'deliver' when they first encounter challenging materials and tasks. This is particularly true when their normal diet is limited, predictable and rather 'on tramlines'. Given time and encouragement to think for themselves the great majority respond very positively.

A boy, who has been accelerated not just one year but two years at school and who has travelled a long distance from home to attend an enrichment weekend, fails to make any great impression.

The tutor may well feel that the child's abilities have been exaggerated, perhaps by staff who are not very familiar with the work of really able children. The tutor does not expect to meet the boy again but just a few weeks later he attends another course. This time much more ability is apparent. Over the next three years and involving a number of courses the boy shows himself to be one of the most able children ever encountered by the tutor and, also, over a wide range of skills.

Was he just 'finding his feet' first time? Did he need to become more familiar with his surroundings and the style of the tutor? Was the situation eased when he made friends and attended further courses with those friends?

Not everything is immediate. Patience is often needed before activities deliver the expected results. This is equally true in the normal classroom when the teacher moves to more adventurous methods.

On the other hand, pastoral care can mean tackling negative attitudes. For idleness a tough approach is required. Just because able pupils can do very nicely on 60 per cent effort does not mean that such a level is acceptable. High expectations have to be maintained.

Children should be encouraged to resolve issues for themselves. Part of teamwork and collaboration, on enrichment courses and in the normal classroom, is negotiation, compromise and making allowances. Give children every chance to develop their skills and abilities to resolve their differences. Only intervene when it is absolutely necessary.

During the 20 minutes preparation for a presentation, one boy is almost in tears. When asked what the problem is, he says that others in the group won't accept his ideas. The tutor has been keeping a watchful eye on the group and he knows that this is a misrepresentation of the facts. 'You mean that they have accepted the first nine of your ideas and they won't accept the tenth.'

The tearful child is looking to the teacher to impose a solution. If he or she does, an opportunity is missed and the members of the group fail to tackle the important social issues involved in teamwork and collaboration. When told that the issue must be resolved internally and that only nine minutes remain to presentation time, the group find a compromise. The author has never yet had a group that has failed to present.

One of the advantages of able pupils coming together is that individuals no longer stand out, attracting the unfavourable attention of bullies. They can be themselves. However, bullying is not unknown, perhaps when a child realizes for the first time that he or she is not well ahead of everybody else. The answer, as it is in school, is to generate an ambience in which it is cool to succeed and in which one does not become jealous of others' achievements but, rather, celebrates their achievements with them.

The course is more than the content

Does one teach a subject or does one teach children? Teachers and tutors do both, in school and during enrichment activities. One of the opportunities of enrichment courses is for able children to meet together and share experiences with each other. During enrichment courses the tutor hears unsolicited comments about school – homework, bullying, expectations and much more. Responding, in general terms and without getting into discussion about individual teachers, is helpful. The tutor may also take a pro-active role and raise key issues as part of the course – work ethic, delivery of ability, tackling bullying, confiding in the 'right' people, asking for success criteria, it really is cool to succeed and many others.

It is very noticeable how seriously many participants respond to these issues. They listen intently and it is clear that they are weighing up these issues in their minds. Enrichment courses can provide opportunities for consideration and reflection. For individual children, helping them to come to terms with an issue may be as important as any of the resources used or any of the events of the course.

Parents

Schools have looked to build a partnership with parents. Although contact is more sporadic, the organizers of enrichment activities should be looking to do the same. One key area is to supply good, full information about the courses (see page 14). That information needs to include details about health and safety issues, and explain exactly who the tutors are.

A particularly important feature to promote, if feasible, is a presentation to parents at the end of the course.

Parental presentations

Rationale

- Parents wish to know what their children have done. Children often do not communicate well about what has happened. Parents are only too familiar with the scenario 'What did you do at school today?' 'Not a lot.'
- In many cases parents have contributed financially to enrichment activities. They have a right to know how their money has been spent.
- Parents should be given the opportunity to hear the theory behind the activities and an explanation of why particular materials have been used.
- There is an opportunity to get across difficult points. A good example would be not to want the child to keep getting top marks as that only indicates that there is insufficient challenge in the work. Some poor practices are not helped by parental pressure arising from such misunderstandings.
- Presentational skills are important for children to acquire. For those with ability in this area this is an opportunity to display their skills.

A possible format

1 The tutor gives a general introduction about the purposes of the course.
2 Certificates are presented to the children to celebrate their attendance and work.
3 Individual children, pairs or small groups talk briefly about the activities, helped by the flip-chart sheets displayed around the room.
4 The tutor gives a running commentary to the pupils' contributions, explaining why pieces have been used and how they play to higher-order thinking skills.
5 The representative of the local authority, cluster group, Education Action Zone, or individual school makes concluding remarks about the place of the course within planned provision for able children in the area. Details of future plans are given.
6 After the formal presentation, some parents seek advice on materials and on their own children's responses to the course.

 Preparation for the presentation should not be allowed to take precedence over the course itself. A brief group discussion allocating sections to be covered by some children where a particularly good piece of work has been done, or asking for volunteers to talk about a more general activity, with a short time for children to work out for themselves, or in discussion with the tutor, what they are going to say, is sufficient. In the author's experience children respond very well to this situation, especially as the tutor is on hand during the presentation to support if required.

Monitoring and Evaluation

What is success?

To answer this, reference needs to be made to the aims and objectives.

- ★ Have children been challenged and made to think?
- ★ Have participants moved forward and 'grown'?
- ★ Have children advanced their thinking skills and working methods?
- ★ Have children enjoyed the course?
- ★ Would participants wish to attend another course?
- ★ Do parents perceive that they are taking home happy, excited and fulfilled children?

Evaluation forms for children

A variety of formats are used to elicit responses from children. Below are questions often asked with spaces between for answers:

Did you enjoy the course? (Please tick the appropriate box)

Excellent ☐   Good ☐   OK ☐   Not very good ☐

(OR ring the appropriate face)

☺   ☺   ☹

(OR underline)

Very good   Good   Satisfactory   Not very good

How difficult did you rate the work? (Underline the word(s) you think describe it best)

Easy   Just right   Hard   Very hard

How would you rate your learning in the course?

☺   ☺   ☹

OR

What do you think you have learned from the course?

What activities and pieces of work did you enjoy the most?

Why did you enjoy them?

Which were your least favourite activities?

Why is that?

Would you like to attend another enrichment course? (Please circle)

Yes   No

Have you any comments to make generally about this course, or about possible future events?

....

....

....

Having set questions normally appears to narrow the responses. An alternative is to set prompts on the board, covering the same areas as above, and ask the participants to write an extended paragraph on those prompts or anything else that they wish to say.

This second method tends to generate more natural and flowing comments. However, it is less suitable when statistics have to be compiled.

What children make of the courses, reflected in their evaluation sheets, is:

THE PROOF OF THE PUDDING!

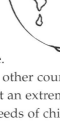

The comments also help to make improvements for the future.

Typical comments

The following clear patterns have emerged:

★ The overwhelming response has been extremely positive, almost surprisingly so given how honest children tend to be.
★ Virtually every child has said that they would like to attend other courses.
★ Favourite activities vary considerably, proving the point that an extremely varied programme and contrasting styles are needed to meet the needs of children, who are all different.
★ The reason for the choice of favourite activities is often given that they were particularly challenging. This is a gratifying response.
★ There is a high level of appreciation, and unsolicited thank yous are quite common.
★ Children often comment that their expectations turned out to be wrong and that the course was quite different from what they had anticipated. A number of unwarranted initial concerns are reported – a reminder of the need to reassure children at the start of a course.
★ As with all children, dramatic events such as treasure hunts, tournaments and murder investigations are extremely popular.
★ How they are treated pastorally is an important consideration for a significant number of participants.

Evaluation by staff

Staff observers attend some children's courses. This is partly because somebody needs to accompany visiting groups of children, but is mainly a form of INSET. Normally they do not complete an evaluation form but sometimes that occurs. Verbal comments are more common.

The four observations made more than any others are:

★ the very high expectations
★ the intense pace
★ the sustained concentration demanded of the children
★ the independence required of the children and lack of intervention by the tutor.

Parents' reactions

In general terms, parents have welcomed enrichment activities very strongly. Indeed, there is often demand far in excess of the places available. Not surprisingly, mathematics is of particular interest. There is, however, a sting in the tail! The more successful the courses are the higher the demand becomes. Many parents wish to see a planned programme over a period of time so that their children can attend on several occasions.

Evaluation of individual pieces of work

When one works with similar-aged children in various parts of the country, using a particular group of materials, it is obvious what works well. Also, the responses of different groups give a direct comparison in terms of performance. This level of performance may be due to relative ability, but it is often a consequence of the style of work that the children are used to. Pupils who work in a 'straight-down-the-middle' manner take time to adjust to more unusual materials. Pupils whose work has been closely supervised may take time to adjust to think independently. Conversely, children whose experiences are more varied in the classroom take readily to a wide range of deliveries and styles of activities.

Feedback to schools

Organizers of events vary in terms of giving feedback to the schools from which participants come, or, if the event is an internal one, to the teachers who normally teach the pupils. This is a practice that needs to be expanded as one of the aims of enrichment courses is to help inform delivery in the normal classroom.

The ultimate aim is that overall provision for able children becomes more effective, and enrichment is one part of that. They benefit from enrichment courses, but it is only part of the jigsaw and the normal classroom is where the great majority of time is spent.

In Conclusion

What is the reasoning behind running enrichment activities?

The children's perspective

★ They meet children of similar abilities and interests.
★ Transferable thinking skills are enhanced.
★ The variety of styles of work and outcomes extends their flexibility and range of skills.
★ Learning is enjoyable and exciting.

The teachers' perspective

★ Great personal and professional satisfaction.
★ The flexible timetable allows a more varied working pattern including lengthy activities.
★ Staff observing receive an unusual form of INSET.
★ Content is not prescribed.
★ There is a positive impact on other teaching.
★ Answers and responses assist the appreciation of what is quality work.

The parents' perspective

★ Their children are challenged.
★ The excitement and enjoyment created have a positive effect on the children's attitude to learning.
★ They gain a better understanding of what is required, and why.
★ They benefit from mutual support and sharing experiences.

The local authorities perspective

★ Parental satisfaction is increased.
★ Teaching staff awareness is raised.
★ Important information is gained about how expert schools are in the identification of the able.
★ Enrichment sessions help to deliver a target in the Education Development Plan (EDP).

Appendix

Obtaining commercially produced books

The majority of sources recommended in this book are available through the normal channels. Some may be out of print, but are such good resources that they are still recommended and worth tracing. There are a number of ways of setting about acquiring copies:

1   Second-hand books in general.
2   Bargain book shops – they often stock remaindered books.
3   Websites such as www.abebooks.co.uk which states that it is the world's largest marketplace for second-hand and out-of-print books.
4   Individual booksellers, who often provide a tracing service, for example, bookshop.exmouth@virgin.net

Section 2

English Courses, Activities and Resources

Introduction

The concentration within courses has been upon wordplay, vocabulary extension and writing in unusual circumstances. In that way, higher-order thinking skills have been employed. Varied activities, including treasure hunts, presentations and tournaments, have caused excitement and promoted considerable fun and enjoyment. Many able children have a particular sense of humour and they delight in puns, nuances and double meanings. That, too, has been an ongoing theme.

Some forms of enriching English activities would need week-long courses to deliver fully. Free creative writing of length has not featured although clearly such activities are extremely valuable, especially when conducted in the company of resident writers and poets.

This English theme is followed by a substantial set of activities involving reading and children's literature. They are interchangeable within courses and can, in any case, be used individually for normal classroom use. There are writing activities within that reading theme.

Possible Titles for Courses
'Raining Cats and Dogs'
'A School of Whales'
'Black and White and Red all Over'
'As Bright as a Button'
'While the Cat's Away'
'2 Across, 4 Down'

Part One: Starters, Icebreakers

Word games are particularly useful to help children think and work with each other. They loosen up the mind in preparation for other tasks. Many of them have a humorous style, and a few laughs are worth a great deal at the start of a course. The word games can be either written or verbal.

'Playing with Words'
Various versions of popular word games are passed from person to person and appear in many collections. 'Playing with Words' (page 39) has particular versions of six different games, namely, 'Tail, Mail, Post, Letter', 'What do you do in your Spare Time, Prime Minister?', 'Know them by their Names', 'One Word Leads to Another', 'Rhubarb' and 'Alphabetically Around the World'.

Time depends upon the number of examples used. Fifteen to 20 minutes allows a good feel for an individual word game.

| 3 | 4 | 5 | 6 | 7 | 8 | 9 | + | |

Books of Word Games

Good bookshops normally have copies of collections of word games. There is an enormous wealth of material to delve into. Recommended titles include:

David Parlett, *The Penguin Book of Word Games* (Penguin Books, 1982)

Graham King, *Word Games* (Harper Collins, 2002)

Giles Brandreth, *Everyman's Word Games* (Dent, 1986)

The Sunday Times, *Guide to Wordplay and Word Games* (Mandarin Paperbacks, 1993)

Tony Augarde, *The Oxford Guide to Word Games* (Oxford University Press, 1984)

Many newspapers contain word games on a regular basis. Saturday editions of the broadsheets are a particularly good source.

'A Cargo of Bread'

Cryptic clues lead to the identification of pairs of words that differ from each other by just one letter. That letter could be anywhere within the word. 'A Cargo of Bread' (page 43) is an example, and the two words are, therefore, 'load' and 'loaf'

Twenty-five to 35 minutes allows a good attempt to be made.

| | | 5 | 6 | 7 | 8 | 9 | | |

'Penguin'

The task is to identify 20 words from clues. Each of the words has 'pen' somewhere within it. 'Penguin' (page 45) is 'a flightless bird (7 letters)'.

Twenty to 30 minutes gives a reasonable time.

| | | 5 | 6 | 7 | 8 | 9 | | |

Other written word games

In previous books, there are a number of pieces that have been used either at the start of courses or in between longer pieces.

ERATC

'**Carp**' (page 44), homographs

'**Ant**' (page 46), homophones

MERATC

'**Tin Can**' (page 18), 20 words containing 'tin'

'**Nuts and Bolts**' (page 22), pairs

CRATC

'**Ram Arm**' (page 15), pairs of words with two neighbouring letters reversed

'**Work it Out to the End**' (page 17), 20 words and phrases containing 'end'

'**One Word from Two**' (page 19), cryptic clues on pairs of words leading to a third word

'**Bark up the Wrong Tree**' (page 27), pairing two definitions of homographs

Times vary, but around 30 minutes allows a good attempt to be made.

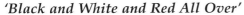

Part Two: Figurative Language

Words and figures of speech are fascinating and thoroughly enjoyable. They have a magic about them. Extension of vocabulary and enriching language are extremely valuable in improving the quality of children's writing and their appreciation of text when reading.

'As Bright as a Button'
Similes are the subject of this piece of work (page 47).

One hour 15 minutes for the complete piece, but it can be used as shorter sections.

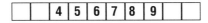

'Black and White and Red All Over'
The familiar title of this piece, (page 150), concerns the enchanting world of riddles.

As a complete piece over one hour is required, but the individual sections can be covered in much shorter time slots.

PROVERBS
Work on proverbs is very suitable for able children because of the abstract quality involved – something stands for something else. It is very welcome that the literacy framework emphasizes the importance of proverbs. Two pieces from previous books take different routes.

ERATC
'Doing the Proverbial' (page 52), uses cryptic clues to identify well-known proverbs and encourages children to create pictorial representations.

One hour 15 minutes allows proper feedback and discussion.

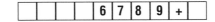

'While the Cat's Away' (page 37), requires identification of proverbs through ten short stories that illustrate them. A piece of writing is an optional extension.

One hour 15 minutes.

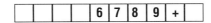

Even though proverbs have been included within the literacy framework, children are not familiar with them. As a consequence, lists of proverbs are included in both pieces of work, with the designated ones hidden among a larger selection.

COLLECTIVE NOUNS

This is another intriguing area of word play that was used more in the past but is still of great value in enriching language.

MERATC

'**A School of Whales**' (page 25), uses pictorial and written elements. Word humour is a key factor. Children have created wonderful examples of their own.

One hour 30 minutes in total, but individual sections can be fitted into short slots.

		4	5	6	7	8			

IDIOMS

The absurdity of some idioms delights able children, none more so than 'Raining Cats and Dogs'.

CRATC

'**Raining Cats and Dogs**' (page 31), the illustrated idioms are particularly popular and a large list is given to assist the children.

Individual sections can be covered in 20–25 minutes, but there is work for at least one hour 30 minutes.

		4	5	6	7	8			

Part Three: Written Outcomes

Philip Pullman criticized a writing exercise in the 2003 SATs that consisted of four pictures, badly drawn as far as he was concerned, and a time allocation of exactly 45 minutes. Fantastic creative writing results from a stimulating environment and the encouragement to 'let yourself go'. There is a place, however, for pieces that are more guided but with open-ended possibilities. The pieces referred to in this section are quirky and different.

'The Riddle in the Middle'

Children are presented with both the beginning and the end of a story (page 53). They have to write the middle section, using their powers of deduction and inference to deduce what happens. There are very definite success criteria.

Children need to know what would make a good piece of work before they start.

How long is a piece of string? Time is needed to take account of the beginning and end of the story. One hour is the minimum for a good response.

		4	5	6	7	8	9	+	

'Sensation'

Some parameters are set, via a picture (page 57), for this piece of creative writing.

Creativity is often assisted by some parameters, with space thereafter to develop in many different ways. A 'blank sheet' can be intimidating, even to able children. Don't miss the comments about 'The Mysteries of Harris Burdick' (page 84).

Times can vary with the ages of children. Forty-five minutes, or longer, is needed.

3	4	5	6	7	8	9	+	

'Every Word Counts'

This is a version of the mini-sagas that have become so popular (page 59). There is real pressure to write a story in exactly 50 words!

Forty-five minutes to one hour allows an introduction, examples given and time to work.

3	4	5	6	7	8	9	+	

ERATC

'*Mouthwatering*' (page 98), asks children to write menus for four different restaurants in such a way that they will appeal to their respective customers. Writing for a specific audience is an important skill. A variation of styles builds up versatility in children and an appreciation of apt approaches to particular circumstances.

Thirty minutes.

3	4	5	6	7	8	9	+	

FABLES

Fables are a particularly interesting genre to explore. It is useful to contrast famous examples with more modern, fun versions. There are many editions of Aesop's Fables in print. Choose, and read, some that particularly appeal. Next read *Squids will be Squids; Fresh Morals, Beastly Fables* by Jon Scieszka and Lane Smith (Viking, 1998). This fabulous book is one of a number of gems from these authors. They have written, and superbly illustrated, a number of absurd fables that cause able children to grin from ear to ear. A particular favourite is 'Straw and Matches'.

Children are then asked to write their own fable, either in the style of Aesop or in the crazy style of *Squids will be Squids*.

Forty-five minutes or more.

3	4	5	6	7	8	9		

Fables are another example of the abstract through second meanings where the story stands for a more general principle. This is a productive area to explore with able children.

Part Four: The Changing Language and Dictionary Work

LIPOGRAMS

Lipogram is the name given to a piece of writing with a particular letter banned; obviously, the more frequently used a letter is the more difficult the writing becomes.

ERATC

'**The Missing Letter**' (page 50), takes this method to the extreme by asking children to rewrite the first paragraph from a Sherlock Holmes story without using the letter 'E'.

There are good reasons for this type of exercise. All curriculum guidelines for English and Literacy require children to use a range of dictionaries, including a thesaurus, which are essential for this task. It is helpful to use a really big dictionary.

One hour 15 minutes is needed for this demanding piece.

			5	6	7	8	9	+	

You can 'bore for England' with a thesaurus or you can set a challenge for able children. Curriculum guidelines need to be delivered in challenging and enjoyable ways to engage and excite able children.

The Ultimate Alphabet

In this wonderful book, written and illustrated by Mike Wilks (Pavilion Books, 1986), 7,777 objects and concepts are painted in 26 alphabetically organized pictures. The 'S' page, that resembles a cross between a junk and toy shop, has 1,229 'S's' to spot. Children can design their own pages on a rather more modest scale. What wonderful dictionary work this is!

'A Giant Step'

English and Literacy guidelines present many exciting opportunities in the vocabulary section. One of these is the area of made-up words and the origins of words. 'A Giant Step' (page 61) is based upon Roald Dahl's brilliant book *The BFG* (Jonathan Cape and Penguin Books).

Thirty minutes gives a good start but more time could be usefully employed.

3	4	5	6	7				

'Wondrous Words in the Woods'
MERATC

This piece is also about made-up words (page 180). There are some delightful words to find and to interpret in 'Ian the Imp's Notebook'.

Thirty minutes for the main tasks, but extra time would be required for the extension.

3	4	5	6	7				

'Achilles Heel'
MERATC

Language is always changing; at one time, able children were very familiar with classical references but this is no longer true. 'Achilles Heel' (page 30) is amazingly popular with children. Perhaps that is not surprising as the stories behind the classical references are absolutely fascinating.

The teacher needs to give a good lead. Forty-five minutes covers many examples.

'The Full Monty'
ERATC
This piece (page 55) deals with the 'other end of the scale', or, words and phrases that are newly accepted into the language by the *Oxford Dictionary of New Words*. This makes a really good team activity.

One hour 15 minutes includes an introduction, the work itself and feedback.

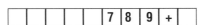

Able children, above all others, should realize that language is a living thing. It moves on, it changes, some words emerge and others go out of fashion.

Part Five: Longer Activities

'2 Across, 4 Down' – A Crossword Treasure Hunt
This unusual activity (page 63) shows children how to tackle cryptic crosswords and they are instructed on how to solve various types of cryptic clues. They then collect clues on a treasure hunt, try to solve them and complete the crossword.

Two hours 15 minutes for the lengthy teaching session on cryptic clues and then the treasure hunt itself.

Cryptic clues play to higher-order thinking skills and provide challenging work.

'Village Gossip' – An Event
'Call My Bluff' is a well-known and entertaining TV word game. 'Village Gossip' (page 67) is a version with significant amendments.

One hour or thereabouts gives time for an introduction, six rounds and the result.

'A Word to the Wise' – A Tournament
There are five rounds in the tournament (page 69).

Round One: 'Synonyms'
There is no pupil sheet as the questions are read out by the teacher.

Round Two: 'The Clue Cat'
Ten well-known expressions have to be identified from the pictures.

Round Three: 'Cluewords'
There are four chances to name the target word, but fewer points are scored as the information grows. There is no pupil sheet as the questions are read out by the teacher.

Round Four: 'The People of Britain'
A fun activity that involves wordplay and a map of Britain.

Round Five: 'Antonyms'
There is no pupil sheet as the questions are read out by the teacher.

Two hours are needed for the whole tournament, but individual sections can be used in shorter periods.

		4	5	6	7	8			

'Passing Sentence' – A Treasure Hunt
Children visit 30 sites to attempt to name a word at each (page 74). Coloured cards indicate whether the word is a noun, a verb, an adjective, an adverb or a preposition.

Thirty minutes introduction, one hour 30 minutes on the treasure hunt and 30 minutes feedback.

		4	5	6	7	8			

The treasure hunt can be shortened by having less cards and locations.

Even parts of speech can have some life put into them! Learning should be fun.

Playing with Words

Are you 'good with words'? Do you thrill at the nuances of language and find some words 'delicious'? Are you witty with vocabulary? Are you 'never short of a word' and can, therefore, respond quickly in verbal exchanges? If so, these word games are ready made for you!

Tail, Mail, Post, Letter

Work as a pair or, even better, in small groups. Go round in a clockwise direction. After each word the next person adds another word that either rhymes with the previous word or has an association with it. Try to work as quickly as you can.

Example

| Tail, | mail, | post, | letter, | vowel, | trowel, |
| spade, | made, | butler, | servant, | job, | rob |
| and so on |

Variation

If a word rhymes with the previous one, play continues in the same direction. If a word is associated with the word before, then change the direction of play.

'What do you do in your Spare Time, Prime Minister?'

You can work orally, as in 'Tail, Mail, Post, Letter' or you can write down examples individually. 'What do you do in your spare time?' is posed to famous people, either dead, alive or from literature. The answer must use his or her initials.

Examples

'What do you do in your spare time, **David Beckham?**'
'Dance Ballroom'

'What do you do in your spare time, **Paula Radcliffe?**'
'Pick Roses'

'What do you do in your spare time, **Robbie Williams?**'
'Race Wagons'

'What do you do in your spare time, **Tony Blair?**'
'Translate Bulgarian'

Know them by their Names

This is again about famous people, dead or alive, or characters from books. On this occasion you must use their initials to describe them appropriately. This can be done verbally in a group, or answers can be written down.

Examples

Michael Schumacher	Motoring Swiftly
Serena Williams	Serving Wonderfully
Gordon Brown	Generating Budgets
Florence Nightingale	Famous Nurse
Mickey Mouse	Making Mischief

One Word Leads to Another

In pairs, or in groups, you go round in clockwise direction giving a phrase or word of two syllables. The second syllable of the previous person becomes the first syllable of the following person. The two-syllable phrases and words must make sense.

Example

lost ball → ballroom

room key → key point

point right → right way

way out → outside

sideboard → board game

and so on

Variations

1   If you play collaboratively to achieve a long chain, each person tries to choose a second syllable that is easy to follow.

2   If you play competitively the reverse is true. In other words, each person tries to choose a second syllable that is difficult to follow.

The first variation is much more satisfactory.

Rhubarb

In this word game you will make use of homographs (words that sound the same, are spelled the same but have different meanings) and homophones (words that sound the same, are spelled differently and have different meanings). A sentence is constructed in which the word 'RHUBARB' is used at least twice in place of the homophones or homographs. Other players have to decide what 'RHUBARB' stands for.

Examples

1 'What a day! First the rhubarb at work was out of order and then I failed to get a rhubarb home'.
   Answer: lift

2 I got on the bus and paid my rhubarb to the rhubarb.
   Answer: fare and fair

Try these

1 On the way to the rhubarb, I saw a rhubarb tree.
2 The rhubarb asked rhubarb way to go.
3 After I have got the rhubarb from the butcher's, I will rhubarb you.
4 The girl rhubarb that the books were not rhubarb.
5 The athlete always caught the rhubarb when going to rhubarb.
6 The carpenter rhubarb a rhubarb in his tool box.
7 I went for a rhubarb along the rhubarb of houses.
8 The waitress with her hair in a rhubarb brought me coffee and a rhubarb.
9 Did you rhubarb that Jack is rhubarb at the party?
10 The traveller stopped to stay the night rhubarb the rhubarb.

Now, set at least ten of your own 'RHUBARBS'. Mix up examples of homophones and homographs.

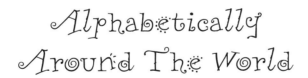

This is one of many games based upon progression through the alphabet. Each person is asked two questions: 'Where are you going?' and 'What will you do there?' The first person replies using the letter 'A', the second person the letter 'B', and so on.

Organize yourselves into small groups and see how far through the alphabet you can get.

Example

'Where are you going?'   'I am going to Australia'
'What will you do there?'   'I will assist aboriginal artists'

Variation

Instead of the second person going on to the letter 'B', each person answers using the letter 'A'. Then the game moves through the alphabet in the same way.

Teaching Notes

The six word games here represent a very large number that are available. They are excellent warm-up activities but clearly they can be used in other ways. They also answer some of the contents of the vocabulary extension section of the literacy framework.

Key Elements

- ❖ mental agility
- ❖ vocabulary extension
- ❖ homographs
- ❖ homophones
- ❖ rhyming
- ❖ word association
- ❖ word humour
- ❖ alphabetical order.

Contexts

'Playing with Words' can be used in a number of ways:

- ❖ orally in the normal classroom
- ❖ written versions in the normal classroom
- ❖ as starters or 'icebreakers' during enrichment sessions
- ❖ during 'Choice Time' within enrichment sessions.

Some Comments on the Word Games

'Tail, Mail, Post, Letter'

This is designed to be a verbal delivery. The players should attempt to respond as quickly as possible. The variation adds to the mental alertness required.

'What do you do in your Spare Time, Prime Minister?'

Answers are not so instinctive and immediate. This favours, therefore, some time and, as a consequence, a written format.

'Know them by their Names'

Some thinking time is required. Although word games are enormous fun, sensitive able children do sometimes give much more serious answers such as 'Awful Human' for Adolf Hitler and 'Anonymous Fugitive' for Ann Frank.

'One Word Leads to Another'

Both oral and written versions work extremely well. Pairs of children take up a private challenge, during Choice Time, to see just how long a list they can compile.

'Rhubarb'

This generic game appears under various names. It is particularly appropriate for literacy work because of its dependence upon homophones and homographs.
The 'Ten to Try' are:

1	beach and beech	**2**	witch and which	**3**	meat and meet
4	knew and new	**5**	train	**6**	saw
7	drive	**8**	bun	**9**	hear and here
				10	in and inn

NOTE: If children give alternative answers that are appropriate, then credit should be given. Children delight in creating their own examples.

'Alphabetically Around the World'

A quicker version is to allow each member of the group to tackle the first letters of the alphabet that are considerably easier to use. You can, of course, go out of order and put in Q, X or Z ahead of their designated time, as a real challenge. Answers from individuals tell you about them personally and add to your knowledge.

NOTE: With all these activities, a large amount of enjoyment can be derived from sharing good examples. This is especially true when the work has been undertaken in a written form.

A Cargo of Bread

There are many words that differ from others by just one letter.
'LOAD' and 'LOAF' form an example that could be described by the clue:
'A cargo of bread' (4),
where (4) indicates the number of letters in the word.

Your Task

From the clues, identify the pairs of words described below. Each pair has just one letter different, but this letter could be anywhere in the word.

CLUES

1 A mix-up over the pool of water (6)
2 The sharp, repeated sound of the time instrument (5)
3 The stupid person sees a young horse (4)
4 Close to being tidy (4)
5 Change the tree (5)
6 The sadness may be short (5)
7 A small package causes a noise (6)
8 To darken the fern (7)
9 To eat in a row (4)
10 The side of the mountain is a known thing (4)
11 This mixture may stop you from seeing (5)

12 A very wise story of heroic achievement (4)
13 Despatch and repair (4)
14 A charge for the playing object (4)
15 A coloured bar (3)
16 Unpleasant or delicious? (5)
17 Take it easy in the team race (5)
18 Could be tall and heavy (6)
19 Not in an athletic condition in the dark area (5)
20 A fast call from the duck (5)
21 Genuine book activity (4)
22 Secure the footwear (4)
23 Very dry corrosive substance (4)
24 Strong but uneven (5)
25 An attack on part of the fence (4)

Extension Tasks

1 Make your own collection of pairs of words that differ by one letter. Include examples where the letter is different at the start, in the middle and at the end.
2 For each pair, write a clue that defines both words.

A Cargo of Bread

Teaching Notes

Key Elements

- ❖ wordplay
- ❖ vocabulary extension
- ❖ dictionary work.

Contexts

'A Cargo of Bread' can be used in a variety of ways:

- ❖ as extension work to other exercises on vocabulary
- ❖ as enrichment work for those who have completed other tasks
- ❖ as a differentiated homework
- ❖ as an activity during an enrichment day, weekend or summer school.

Solution

1 muddle and puddle
2 click and clock
3 fool and foal
4 near and neat
5 alter and alder
6 grief and brief
7 packet and racket
8 blacken and bracken
9 dine and line
10 face and fact
11 blend and blind
12 sage and saga
13 send and mend
14 bill and ball
15 red and rod; tan and ban
16 nasty and tasty
17 relax and relay
18 height and weight
19 unfit and unlit
20 quick and quack
21 real and read
22 lock and sock
23 arid and acid
24 tough and rough
25 raid and rail

NOTE

These are the intended responses, but children may find others that are appropriate for which they should be given credit.

Penguin

Penguin is one of a large number of words that contain the letters 'PEN'. It could be identified through the clue:

'A flightless bird' (7)

where (7) refers to the number of letters in the word.

Your Task

Identify the 20 words below from the clues. Each word contains the letters 'PEN', but they are not necessarily at the start as in 'penguin'. 'PEN' could be in the middle of the word, or at the end. The difficulty of the clues varies!

CLUES

1   Uncover (4)
2   Last but one (11)
3   Repay (10)
4   Thoughtful (7)
5   Exhausted (5)
6   Repressed or held in (4–2)
7   A worker in wood (9)
8   A luxury flat (9)
9   A retiring sum of money (7)
10 Reliable (10)
11 A hanging ornament (7)

12 A coin for a girl (5)
13 A salary paid for services (7)
14 Expressing sorrow (8)
15 A strip of land jutting out into the sea (9)
16 A fine or punishment (7)
17 To hang (7)
18 A writing or drawing implement (6)
19 Inclination or tendency (10)
20 Upright, at right angles to plane of the horizon (13)

Extension Tasks

1   Find 15 more words that contain 'PEN', five at the start (that's the easy bit), five in the middle and five at the end.
2   Write definitions for your 15 words and give them to somebody else to try to identify.

Penguin

Teaching Notes

'Penguin' involves vocabulary extension and dictionary work. It encourages pupils to look for clues in terms of the tense or part of speech involved (to get the correct number of letters in the clue).

Contexts

'Penguin' could be used in the following ways:

❖ as extension work to other exercises on vocabulary

❖ as an enrichment activity for those who have completed other work quickly and well

❖ as a differentiated homework

❖ as an activity during an enrichment session.

Solution

1	Open
2	Penultimate
3	Recompense
4	Pensive
5	Spent
6	Pent-up
7	Carpenter
8	Penthouse
9	Pension
10	Dependable
11	Pendant
12	Penny
13	Stipend
14	Penitent
15	Peninsula
16	Penalty
17	Suspend
18	Pencil
19	Propensity
20	Perpendicular

As Bright as a Button

The quality and effectiveness of writing is improved by using descriptions that are not just straightforward. One method is to use a comparison with something that is similar in one essential way, but which may be very different in other ways. This comparison is known as a **simile**.

It is normally introduced by 'as ... as ...' OR 'like ...'

Examples: 'as pale as a ghost', 'cry like a baby'

Your Tasks

Part One
At the top of the page there is, in fact, an illustrated simile: 'as bright as a button'. Below, ten well-known similes are shown as illustrations. Can you identify them? Then draw your own illustrations of, at least, five other similes.

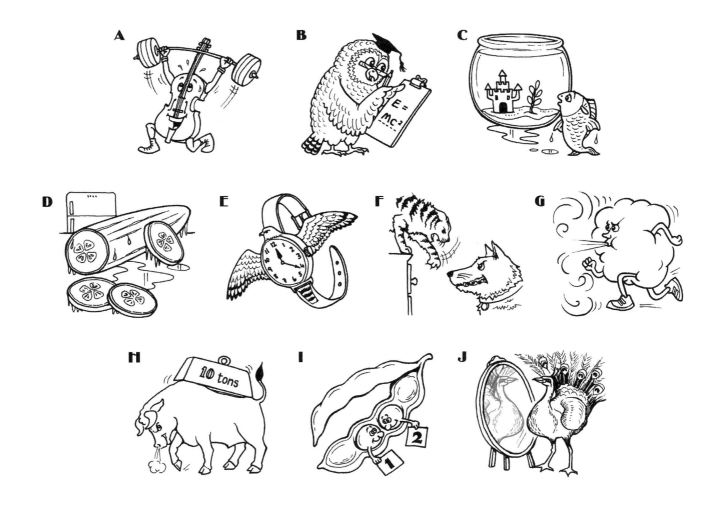

As Bright as a Button

Part Two

What words are missing in these well-known similes?

A	as ... as grass	**F**	as ... as lightning
B	as ... as a mouse	**G**	as ... as leather
C	as ... as nails	**H**	as ... as a church mouse
D	as ... as the hills	**I**	as ... as toast
E	as ... as a bee	**J**	as ... as brass

Part Three

Which similes are associated with the following?

A	a bone	**B**	a March Hare	**C**	a lamb	**D**	an eel	**E**	a bat
F	a fox	**G**	a lark	**H**	mustard	**I**	rain	**J**	thieves

Part Four

The number of similes is always growing as new examples are used.

Two lesser-known examples are:

as dead as a holiday resort in winter
as short as a British summer.

Make up some similes of your own based upon the following words:

A	comfortable	**B**	angry	**C**	bored	**D**	frightened	**E**	sensible
F	rare	**G**	popular	**H**	nervous	**I**	miserable	**J**	lonely

You can use either form of simile – that is, 'as ... as', or '... like ...'.
Try to make them imaginative. Remember that the best similes tend to be short and snappy.

Part Five

Many similes are sarcastic and say the opposite of what they really mean – for example:

- as useful as a chocolate teapot
- as entertaining as a bowl of cold porridge
- as exciting as watching paint dry
- as subtle as an enraged bull.

Make up ten similes like these. Let your imagination go – they can be great fun!

Part Six

You could use famous people or well-known television characters as the subject of ten more similes. They can be straight examples or sarcastic ones – for example:

- as sophisticated as the Simpsons.

Part Seven

Most writers use similes in their work.
Try to find examples in novels and poems and make comments upon how effective they are.
Look for both forms – that is, 'as ... as', and '... like ...'.

As Bright as a Button

Teaching Notes

Similes appear in literacy frameworks in a number of ways. They are one of many devices used by writers to increase the impact of their work. Appreciation of text involves locating the use of similes. Vocabulary extension includes the investigation of figures of speech from everyday life. The quality of children's own writing is improved by the inclusion of similes and other figures of speech. 'As Bright as a Button' visits a traditional area of work but opens up opportunities for more personal interpretation, creative work and appreciation of text.

In some other materials, the author uses an additional sheet to assist pupils, for instance, including a sheet listing well-known examples when working on proverbs and idioms. In those cases, interpretation was still required by the pupil. If a similar sheet was to be included with 'As Bright as a Button', it would be too simple a task to find the answers for Parts One and Two. Some children may not be as familiar with well-known similes as was once the case. Credit should be given for sensible and appropriate answers even if they are not the standard response.

Key Elements
- wordplay
- creativity and imagination
- vocabulary extension
- word humour
- research (especially for Part Seven)
- appreciation of text
- pictorial representation.

Contexts
'As Bright as a Button' can be used in the following ways:
- in normal classroom lessons where differentiation by outcome will occur
- as extension material to other work on vocabulary and literary terms
- as an enrichment activity for those ahead on standard work
- as differentiated homework
- as an activity within a word-based enrichment session, summer school or cluster day
- as an open-access competition
- as an activity for the English Club or Society.

Answers

PART ONE
A	as fit as a fiddle	E	watch like a hawk	I	as like as two peas in a pod
B	as wise as an owl	F	fight like cat and dog		
C	like a fish out of water	G	run like the wind	J	as proud as a peacock
D	as cool as a cucumber	H	as strong as an ox		

PART TWO
A	green	E	busy	I	warm
B	timid/quiet	F	quick/fast	J	bold
C	hard	G	tough		
D	old	H	poor		

PART THREE
A	as dry as a bone	E	as blind as a bat	I	as right as rain
B	as mad as a March Hare	F	as cunning as a fox	J	as thick as thieves
C	as meek as a lamb	G	as happy as a lark		
D	as slippery as an eel	H	as keen as mustard		

NOTES
1. Answers for Parts Four, Five and Six will include a number of possibilities. Quality depends upon suitability and creativity.
2. Part Seven opens up a different area. The examples chosen will provide information about the pupils. They could also provide profitable points for discussion, especially as to why they are particularly effective. Poems should be encouraged as a source.

EXTRA!!! Daily Times EXTRA!!!
Black and White and Red All Over

'Black and White and Red All Over' is an example of a riddle and a particular type of riddle. The answer is a newspaper or a book and the example depends upon a pun – a jokey play on words so that 'red' stands for 'read'. There are many other types of riddles as you will see.

Task One
What is a riddle? Try to define what is meant by the word riddle.

Task Two
Below there is a list of ten statements or questions. They are riddles that have been passed on from person to person and nobody knows the author. Work out what they mean.

1 What runs all day and all night but never stops?
2 What has four legs and a back but can't walk?
3 Riddle me, riddle me, riddle me ree,
   I saw a nut cracker up in a tree.
4 Over the water and under the water and never touches the water.
5 If you feed it, it will live
   If you give it water, it will die.
6 What gets wet when drying?
7 What comes once a minute, twice in a moment, but not once in a thousand years?
8 The more you take, the more you leave behind. What are they?
9 What goes into the water red and comes out black?
10 What kind of ear cannot hear?

Task Three
Try to write your own riddles to fit the following:

1 A cow
2 The wind
3 A box of matches
4 Green
5 A bad mood
6 A butterfly
7 Thunder
8 Number eight
9 A flag
10 The letter 'z'

Task Four

There are some examples of riddles in famous pieces of literature, including the works of William Shakespeare. Try to find some. In particular, read *The Hobbit*, chapter five, where Bilbo Baggins' riddling contest with Gollum is described.

Task Five

Some riddles are set in pictorial form. For example:

This is   (stick – tick = 's')   +   (ice cream – ice   = 'cream') =   'scream'.

Now draw some of your own picture riddles.

Task Six

One particular type of riddle involves following a pattern of 'my first', 'my second' and so on. Here is an example.

My first is in dog but not in log,
My second is in band but not in bind,
My third is in nut but not in rut,
My fourth is in goat but not in boat,
My fifth is in bend but not in bond,
My sixth is in car but not in cat.
My whole means that you should take care.

The distinctive letters spell out **DANGER** which is described in the last line.

Write some riddles of your own in this format.

Teaching Notes

Riddles are very popular with children. They play to the particular word humour and sense of the absurd that many able pupils possess. The devices within them contribute to vocabulary extension and appreciation.

Key Elements

❖ wordplay

❖ word humour

❖ engagement with text

❖ creativity and imagination

❖ puns or double meanings.

Contexts

'Black and White and Red All Over' can be used in the following ways:

❖ as extension work to vocabulary extension material

❖ as enrichment work for those who have completed other tasks

❖ as differentiated homework

❖ as an activity for an enrichment day, weekend, summer school or cluster day

❖ as an activity for the English Club or Society

❖ as an open-access competition.

Some Answers

Task One

The *Oxford English Dictionary* defines the word 'riddle' as:
'A question or statement intentionally worded in a dark or puzzling manner, and propounded in order that it may be guessed or answered, especially as a form of pastime; an enigma, a dark saying'.

Children's answers will be less formal, but key elements to be referred to should include the disguised form of presentation: the puzzle within.

Task Two

1 a river or time or circulation of the blood
2 a chair
3 a squirrel or woodpecker or a nuthatch
4 a person with a pail of water on his or her head crossing a bridge.
5 a fire
6 a towel
7 the letter 'M'
8 footprints
9 a red-hot poker
10 an ear of wheat

Task Three

The ten items have been chosen deliberately to be varied in nature and therefore promote different types of responses.

Tasks Four, Five and Six

These tasks allow for individual answers from the children. Tasks Five and Six are useful together as they facilitate pictorial responses and then written examples.

THE RIDDLE IN THE MIDDLE

Zita Malik turned the papers over and over in her hands. Her face wore a puzzled look. Here was the story written some time ago for the magazine but some of the pages were missing. Only the beginning of the story and the ending were there. What had happened to the missing sheets? A thorough search of the room failed to produce the pages that contained the middle section of the short story. Zita thought about rewriting that middle section but then she had a better idea. Why not challenge the readers of the magazine to provide a link between the two remaining passages?

Your Task

Put yourself in the position of one of the readers of the short story magazine. Read the two passages below – the beginning and the end of the story. Answer Zita's challenge by writing the middle section so that the story is complete. You will need to study both passages carefully to pick up all the clues that should inform your writing.

PASSAGE ONE: THE BEGINNING OF THE STORY

ON THE ROCKS

Colin peered despondently through the window in the hotel lounge. He had come to his beloved Cornwall for a quiet break and the chance to play golf on the renowned local links course. For three full days the wind and rain had battered the north Cornish coast making golf, if not impossible, certainly very difficult and uncomfortable. Now, at last, on the Tuesday afternoon the rain had slowed and finally come to a stop, the wind had moderated to a stiff breeze.

It was too late to play a round of golf that day, but Colin was impatient to rescue his clubs from their unwanted temporary retirement. Just along the road from the hotel was a large grassy area used for 'Pitch and Putt' during the season, a favourite practice ground for local players during the quieter months of the year.

Colin opened the boot of his new car, patting the gleaming metal affectionately. From his golf bag he drew out a number 7 iron – more than adequate he felt. With the club in his gloved left hand and a tube of old golf balls under his arm he strode eagerly along the path to the swathe of inviting green grass.

With the main rush of visitors some weeks away, the pitch and putt course was uncut and unprepared. There was a profusion of daisies and dandelions, their white and yellow heads clearly visible. Tufts of darker green grass grew in zig-zags and even the plateau areas used as rough and ready greens were overgrown and unkempt. It was hardly St Andrews, but to Colin, deprived of his pleasure and his exercise, it looked like paradise.

He decided to hit the balls diagonally to make maximum use of the confines of the field. The balls, released from their dull-white tube, lay invitingly on the ground, a mixture of colours – a rag-bag collection retained only for practice purposes. Colin felt somewhat stiff and out of condition. He had played very little during the winter months. A few practice swings at the leaves lying on the ground loosened him up.

PASSAGE TWO: THE END OF THE STORY

The following week the local paper carried a short, sad passage. There were new guests now at the hotel and they read the brief account with limited interest:

DOUBLE TRAGEDY ON CORNISH BEACH

Enquiries are taking place into the two deaths which occurred within 24 hours of each other at Whipsiderry Beach, near Newquay. Miss Diane Waring was found drowned on Wednesday morning, her face badly marked by buffeting on the rocks. She had recently been diagnosed as having a terminal illness and a suicide note was discovered in her flat.

Later that day, the body of a holidaymaker, Mr Colin Frazer, was recovered from the same beach. His death is still a complete mystery. Police have ruled out any connection between the two tragedies.

Success Criteria

The quality of your work will be judged on:
- the notice taken of the title
- the degree to which the main body of the story fits the two given passages
- the extent to which clues have been lifted from the two given passages
- the level of appreciation of style and genre
- the imagination and creativity displayed within the given parameters
- the quality of the writing.

Extension Task

Create your own 'riddle in the middle', by writing the start and the end of a short story, and then ask somebody else to construct the middle section.

THE RIDDLE IN THE MIDDLE

Teaching Notes

'The Riddle in the Middle' provides a creative writing opportunity with a number of parameters but also with considerable open-endedness and challenge.

Key Elements

- ❖ creative writing
- ❖ deduction and inference
- ❖ analysis of text
- ❖ appreciation of style and genre
- ❖ individuality of response and therefore differentiation by outcome.

Contexts

'The Riddle in the Middle' can be used in a number of ways:

- ❖ as general classwork where differentiation by outcome will apply
- ❖ as enrichment work for those who have completed other tasks
- ❖ as differentiated homework
- ❖ as an activity during an enrichment day, weekend, or summer school
- ❖ as an open-access competition
- ❖ as an activity for the English Club or Society.

An Answer

Below is given a possible (only one of many) 'middle' to complete the story.
Credit should be given for many possible successful outcomes that satisfy the success criteria. This version could be read, in full, to the children who have participated in the work. They could be asked how the piece had been put together – the whole story was written and then a decision was taken as to the 'cut-off' points for the beginning and the ending. Pupils attempting the extension task may wish to adopt the same strategy. Cut-off points should be chosen to give sufficient clues but allow for a large number of interpretations.

THE MISSING PASSAGE

The first shot was well struck. The bright yellow missile flew upwards and landed a pleasing distance away after a straight, successful path. Colin pulled down the sides of his sweater, a sure sign that he was contented with his initial effort. It was not, however, an accurate foretaste of what was to follow!

A large divot landed some 20 feet ahead of him. The grim look on his face was the result of the next ball not having gone much further. A few shots were sweetly struck but the majority of the balls lay haphazardly over the field, a testament to the inconsistent swing and his fluctuating level of technique.

It was a hunched and rather dejected figure who set off to retrieve the balls. Initially this was not too difficult as some had travelled an infuriatingly short distance. Colin pressed the clicka-tube face downwards on the offending objects but the task soon became more difficult. The large number of white and yellow daisy and dandelion heads made spotting balls deceptive. Feathers from the local population of gulls added to the confusion. He was deceived frequently, marching confidently to the next blob of colour only to find that the intended target was of a more natural origin than compressed rubber.

As the harvesting continued, Colin became more and more irritated. A very indifferent practice session was being compounded by a lengthy, and often unfruitful, search. Some balls had run into the hedgerow. He was sure of their destination at the time of impact, but now they had disappeared into the mixture of vegetation and stones. Nowhere could he see the welcoming glint of yellow or white. It was as though the balls had never existed.

After a long and increasingly annoying hunt, Colin set off back to the hotel. The void in the upper reaches of the tube acted as a reminder of his wayward play. It was a disillusioned man who trudged along the narrow track. At one point there were only four feet of grass and moss between the path and the cliff edge. He stopped and looked down at the magnificence of Whipsiderry Beach. It was a wonderful sight – the empty expanse of golden sand, the crashing breakers rushing in. In the centre, proud and defiant, stood the jutting, dark mass of rock known as Black Humphrey. The frustrations of the last hour evaporated. Colin's heart melted. This part of the north Cornish coast never failed to move him.

He put his spare hand into the pocket of his bodywarmer. His fingers closed around a smooth, hard object. Colin removed his hand and opened the palm. Nestled against the lined flesh was the oldest, dirtiest golf ball. It was dull with wear, the surface worn and cracked. Why he had kept it at all he couldn't think.

On an impulse he put the battered ball down on the grass near the cliff edge. He scanned the beach to check that nobody was about. Drawing a blank from his search, his attention went back to the ball lying expectantly at his feet. Colin took the club and settled himself, running through the familiar coaching routines in his head. He felt comfortable and for once he was confident that the strike would be a good one. The club went back a slow, smooth curve, then downward, making perfect contact. The follow-through was excellent and Colin felt exhilarated as he saw the ball soar out over the beach. It was a long hit – the ball cleared the jagged edges of one face of Black Humphrey, disappearing from view. As it did so a loud and piercing shriek rang around the cliffs. The gulls it seemed were not as appreciative of Colin's drive as he himself was.

★   ★   ★   ★   ★   ★

That night in the bar, Colin was in conversation with Vernon, the proprietor's son, who was on duty serving drinks. Vernon too was a keen golfer and he listened sympathetically to his guest's account of the disappointing practice session. When Colin finished by relating the final drive over Whipsiderry Beach, another guest remarked rather petulantly that such an action was quite irresponsible and even dangerous. The talk passed on to other matters but the comment stuck in Colin's mind. He felt strangely anxious and unsettled. However, as the evening wore on and the number of brandies increased, Colin's sense of well-being returned.

★   ★   ★   ★   ★   ★

The next day dawned bright and clear. Colin was early into breakfast looking forward at last to a full round of golf. He read his newspaper contentedly for a while but then became more and more conscious of a conversation taking place just outside the dining room. The voices were serious and dark. Fragments pierced his assimilation of the sports pages until Colin's full attention was concentrated upon what was being said. He could not hear everything but he grasped enough to alarm him: 'woman's body'; 'this morning'; 'Whipsiderry Beach'; 'blow to the head'.

Colin's mind was racing, the pieces of a frightening and threatening jigsaw fitting together in a relentless way. That piercing cry – had it really been sea-gulls disturbed by something not normally within their experience? Or was there another, more sinister, explanation ... ?

★   ★   ★   ★   ★   ★

The plans for golf long abandoned, Colin sat in the hotel lounge, his mind in turmoil. An iron band of fear fitted tightly around his forehead, contracting little by little, increasing the pressure that was sending waves of pain through his head. The feeling was unbearable. He felt like screaming out loud, but instead he sat still, paralysed with fear and foreboding. He sank deeper into the depths of despair, consumed by guilt and self-loathing for the consequences of a moment's recklessness.

Lunchtime passed with no acknowledgement from the stricken guest. Food and drink were irrelevant. As the afternoon wore on, Colin rose finally from his sedentary position. He walked slowly but purposefully to the cliff and descended the 89 steps, so familiar to him, at a mechanical robot-like pace. He crossed the beach towards the water's edge, past the foot of Black Humphrey, on into the shallows and then further, further, further... .

★   ★   ★   ★   ★   ★

Sensation

This was the scene of a mysterious episode that captured the imagination of people far and near. Of great significance in those happenings were the tree on the viewer's left and the pond in the foreground. The families who lived in the cottages never forgot those incredible days.

Your Task

Write a story based upon the information given above.

Success Criteria

Your story will be judged according to the following criteria:

★ the extent to which it justifies the title
★ the degree to which the tree and the pond are significant elements
★ the explanation of the phrase 'those incredible days'
★ the creativity and imagination displayed.

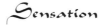

Teaching Notes

Children are required to take note of particular points and to take into account the success criteria. However, the interpretations that result are very varied.

Key Elements

- ❖ following instructions
- ❖ creativity and imagination
- ❖ appreciation of genre
- ❖ a combination of parameters and open-endedness
- ❖ deduction and inference
- ❖ hypothesizing.

Contexts

'Sensation' can be used in a number of ways:

- ❖ as a normal classroom activity where differentiation by outcome will apply
- ❖ as differentiated homework
- ❖ as an enrichment item when a child has completed set work ahead of others
- ❖ as an activity during an enrichment day, weekend, summer school or cluster day
- ❖ as an open-access English competition.

Some Interpretations by Children

1. 'Sensation' used not as 'incredible and dramatic' but as sensory pleasures associated with the pond and the tree.
2. A criminal case involving three sons, an inheritance, missing pearls, 'dirty deeds' and an accidental drowning.
3. A treehouse inhabited by a witch who cannot fly away as she has lost her broomstick. When this is restored to her, she plays a trick and deposits a child into the pond.
4. A fantasy tale with a strange fish that had a whistle inside it. The whistle, when blown, summoned a number of mysterious herons. They disappeared leaving many questions.
5. A ghost story examined many years later by a scientist.

EVERY WORD COUNTS

(with acknowledgement to Brian Aldiss and the *Daily Telegraph*)

'Words are cheap' is a saying that indicates that actions are important. Words are not so cheap if you only have 50 of them to use! That is the situation facing you in 'Every Word Counts'.

Your Task

You are asked to write a story of exactly 50 words in length, not 49 and not 51. Even with that restricted number of words, you are expected to tell a story that has a beginning, middle and end.

PARTICULAR RULES

1   The main story is exactly 50 words in length.
2   The words in the title are outside the 50, but they cannot exceed 15.
3   Hyphenated words count as one word. Numbers like sixty-three fall into that category.

AN EXAMPLE

A Day in the Life

As the clock strikes ten in the morning, the mayfly emerges. Twelve hours later dusk descends and the mayfly settles for the night. As the clock strikes ten on the following morning, the spent mayfly is gobbled hungrily by the rising brown trout.

A day's life has come and gone.

Barry Teare

Additional Advice

Anybody can write a story of 50 words. It can be completed very quickly. However, you need to think hard about the quality of the story. Write out a rough version and cross out and amend where appropriate. Even when you have hit the 50-word target exactly, don't be satisfied. Look to see if better, more descriptive or effective words can be substituted into your story without changing the total.

Write out a neat version so that you can check more easily that you have met the rules.

... 46 47 48 49 50

Teaching Notes

This piece is based upon the genre invented by Brian Aldiss, the distinguished author best known for his science fiction. Having written some long books, Brian Aldiss thought it might be fun to write a story in exactly 50 words. The idea was taken up by the *Daily Telegraph* as a competition.

This is an activity that can be used with all children but, clearly, able children will take particular advantage of the opportunity.

Key Elements

- ❖ differentiation by outcome
- ❖ creativity and imagination
- ❖ appreciation of genre
- ❖ following specific instructions
- ❖ careful use of words.

Contexts

'Every Word Counts' can be used in the following ways:

- ❖ as a piece of classwork when differentiation by outcome will come into play
- ❖ as differentiated homework
- ❖ as an enrichment activity for those ahead on other tasks
- ❖ as an individual challenge during an enrichment day, weekend, summer school or cluster day
- ❖ as an activity for the English Club or Society
- ❖ as an open-access competition within school.

Before children start work on their own stories, it is helpful for them to hear some examples. There is one on the pupil sheet and three more in the teaching notes. The *Daily Telegraph* publishes collections resulting from their competition. Get copies and read out a selection – commended entries, commissioned stories from famous people and children's entries.

Some Responses

NOTE:

The example on the pupil sheet concerns the mayfly, an insect that only lives for one day once it reaches that stage of its development. In that sense, the story really does have a beginning, middle and end.

I Wonder Why!
I opened the curtains. They fell down. I cooked the breakfast. It burnt. I brushed my hair. It fell out. I put on my shoes. They broke. I got on the bus. It blew up. I went to work. It was shut. I wonder why. Friday the 13th! I wonder!

James, Year 6

The Snake Charmer
The snake woke. The tune starts playing. The snake moves to the rhythm and its eyes are focussed. It stares at me determinedly. It suddenly leaps in the air. I crouch in fear. In fear that it'll strike me. It slithers past and rustles out of the market square silently.

Juliet, Year 6

The Magazines
1990   Dear Diary
      Today was the worst day of my life. Mum was going to throw my magazine collection away. She said they were rubbish.
1999   Dear Diary
      Today I chucked out my magazine collection. They were rubbish. I was trying to clear out mum's magazines too. Mum went crazy.

Sarah, Year 6

A Giant Step

One of Roald Dahl's most famous and loved books is *The BFG* (published by Jonathan Cape and Penguin Books), where the initials stand for 'Big Friendly Giant'. A fascinating characteristic of the BFG is that he uses many words that do not exist. Funnily enough, Sophie, the heroine of the story, and, indeed, the readers understand nearly everything the BFG says.

Have you stopped to wonder why? If not, let us take 'A Giant Step'.

Your Task

1 Study the list that records just some of the made-up words used by the BFG.

2 Explain what the words mean in 'normal' language.

3 Classify, or group, the words according to the reasons why we understand them. If you want a little help, try thinking about prefixes, onomatopoeia, combinations, homophones, homographs and spoonerisms. (You might need to refer to a dictionary!)

The List

scrumdiddlyumptious	notmuchers	maggotwise
hipswitch	dory-hunky	babblement
flungaway (places)	fibster	mintick
jipping and skumping	rotsome	chiddlers
gun and flames	langwitch	plexicated
catasterous disastrophe	snitchet	pibbling
uckyslush	gogglers	a ringbeller
buzzburgers	barking up the wrong dog	

Extension Task

Try creating some made-up words of your own and explain what they mean and how they are constructed.

Special Task

If you have not already done so, read *The BFG* by Roald Dahl.

If you have read it, read it again. It is a very special book.

Teaching Notes

The vocabulary extension section of the literacy framework requires teachers to get children 'to invent words using known roots, prefixes and suffixes' and 'to experiment with language'. The targets for other terms include onomatopoeia, a range of suffixes and the identification of word roots. Work on Roald Dahl's *The BFG* is therefore not only great fun but helps to deliver the literacy framework.

Key Elements

- ❖ vocabulary extension
- ❖ wordplay
- ❖ word humour
- ❖ made-up words
- ❖ prefixes and suffixes
- ❖ onomatopoeia
- ❖ classification
- ❖ creativity and imagination.

Contexts

'A Giant Step' can be used in many ways:

- ❖ as normal classwork in Literacy
- ❖ as extension work to vocabulary extension
- ❖ as differentiated homework
- ❖ as an activity during an enrichment day, weekend, summer school or cluster day
- ❖ as an activity for the English Club or Society, or the Reading Club.

Some Answers

Responses will not be exact but certain patterns could be expected:

- ❖ Onomatopoeia has examples such as 'uckyslush'.
- ❖ There are spoonerisms, but not quite pure examples, 'gun and flames', 'dory-hunky', 'catasterous disastrophe', 'jipping and skumping'.
- ❖ 'Langwitch' is a form of homophone.
- ❖ 'Barking up the wrong dog' is based upon a homograph.
- ❖ There are combinations, such as 'mintick' (minute and tick, indicating a very short time), 'plexicated' (complex and complicated, meaning difficult to understand), 'chiddlers' (children and tiddlers, indicating small children).
- ❖ Prefixes give the meaning in 'fibster' (liar), 'rotsome' (horrible), 'babblement' (talking) and 'notmuchers' (people of little account).
- ❖ 'Flungaway (places)' and 'snitchet' are more dependent upon the ending, or suffix.
- ❖ 'Hipswitch' clearly means straightaway, 'gogglers' are eyes, 'a ringbeller' is a fantastic idea, 'buzzburgers' are thoughts and 'pibbling' replaces piddling (of little account).

2 ACROSS, 4 DOWN

You may have seen members of your family, or friends, doing the crossword in their newspapers. Here is your chance to do the same – but not by sitting still in a chair!

Your Tasks

1. Listen carefully to the explanation about how cryptic clues work. A reminder of the main points is given on a separate sheet.
2. Go round with your team and locate all the clue sheets. Clues across are on yellow sheets. Clues down are on blue sheets. Green sheets refer to clues that have both down and across elements.
3. Work out as many clues as you can and enter them on your blank crossword grid.

CRYPTIC CROSSWORDS AND HOW TO SOLVE THEM

In cryptic crosswords the normal type of clue is where part of the clue is a definition of the answer and the other part of the clue, using cryptic hints, helps you to work out what the answer is. Part of solving the clue is to work out which part is the definition and which part is the cryptic help. Cryptic crosswords need a mixture of logical and lateral thinking.

1. Sometimes the cryptic clue is an anagram (that is, the answer is shown as mixed up letters). You are normally given a hint that it is an anagram with words such as 'could be', 'off', 'unusually', 'bad', 'mixed', 'mixture', 'various', 'poorly' or 'unfortunately' included in the clue.

2. Other cryptic clues are solved by piecing together the answer from clues in the sentence. Below are some keywords that tell you how to solve the clue.

	Keywords	Word/letter/part of answer
A	without/outside/about	A word or letters is/are around another
B	without/not	Certain letters have been dropped/deleted from a word
C	within/inside	A word or letter(s) is (are) inside another
D	numbers/many/five/ten/fifty/hundred/thousand	(i) A number is part of the answer (ii) A Roman numeral is part of the answer for example V, X, L, C, D, M
E	some/part/inside/the contents of	The word is hidden in the clue sentence
F	back/going back/backwards	The word or letters is/are written backwards in the answer
G	a quarter/point/direction	Letters from the compass points are in the answer, for example N, S, E, W
H	pole	Magnetic poles – that is, N and S
I	words where the initial letter is often used in the answer: cold hot shirt model religious instruction physical exercise training	 C H T (as in T-shirt) T (after an early car, the Model T Ford) RE/RI PE/PT
J	article	'a', 'an', 'the'
K	one	'A' or 'I'
L	head/first	The first letter of a word in the clue is part of the answer
M	tail/last	The last letter of a word in the clue is part of the answer
N	duck/love/round/hole/nothing	'O'
O	rock/ice	Diamond
P	hesitation	'er', 'um'
Q	oriental	'E' for eastern
R	newspaper man/journalist/press	'ed' (for editor)
S	If a number is written as a number – for example, 2 – it may refer to Clue 2 rather than the number two.	

3. Some clues have 'sounds like' in the cryptic part. This means that the cryptic hint will give you a word that sounds like the real answer but is spelled differently.

4. A different type of clue, not with a definition and cryptic hints, involves looking at the whole clue and thinking laterally. It is sometimes indicated by an exclamation mark or question mark.

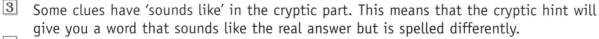

Teaching Notes

This is a treasure hunt with a difference for the object is to complete a blank crossword by finding clues and solving them. The exercise could be done without moving from a desk or table by just issuing the clues on a sheet, as they would be in a newspaper. However, spreading clue sheets (with additional pictures and objects) about, and requiring movement, is much more exciting.

Key Elements

- ❖ wordplay
- ❖ word humour
- ❖ application

- ❖ analysis
- ❖ vocabulary extension
- ❖ synthesis.

Contexts

'Two Across, Four Down' has been set up here as a treasure hunt during an enrichment session. In a written-only format, it could be used in lessons or for homework.

Organization

The individual clues, on the separate sheet, need to be written on coloured paper – yellow for across clues, blue for down clues and green for both across and down clues. Even in a treasure hunt format, that is all the information that children need to solve the clues and fill in the crossword. However, it makes it much more interesting and colourful for the participants if pictures and objects are added. Some suggestions have been made but substitutions and alterations can be made.

Before the commencement of the treasure hunt, at least half an hour needs to be spent on explaining how cryptic crossword clues work. The second pupil sheet can be used plus as much more detail as is thought to be required.

Across	Colour	Suggested object or picture	Down	Colour	Suggested object or picture
1	Yellow	Bird	1 and16a	Green	Silhouette of some children with question marks
5	See 28d		2	Blue	Large and small nail with arrow pointing at small nail
9	Yellow	Picture of tomato on a rug	3	Blue	House
10	Yellow	Paper aeroplane	4	Blue	Mount Fuji
11	Yellow	Boy and father	6	Blue	Poetry book
13	Yellow	Stonehenge	7	Blue	Child in very warm multi-layered clothing
14	Yellow	Ostrich	8	Blue	Running shoes
16	See 1d		12 and 29a	Green	Clock
18	Yellow	Rock	15	Blue	Bag of chips
21	Yellow	Teddy bear with bandage	17	Blue	Toy gun
23	Yellow	Image of sun or starburst with many rays	19	Blue	Piece of needlework
26	Yellow	Desert island with question mark over the beach	20	Blue	Fish with knife and fork
27	Yellow	Chick emerging from an egg	22	Blue	Peaches
29	See 12d		23	Blue	Atlas and dancing figures
30	Yellow	Seedhead	24	Blue	Basket of fruit
31	Yellow	Signpost	25	Blue	Television
32	Yellow	Sleeping cat	28 and 5a	Green	Wizard hat and wand
33	Yellow	Silhouette of woman holding flowers	29	Blue	Shirt

The crossword is demanding. Children may not solve all the clues. It is most important to advise them that this is not an 'all-or-nothing' situation. The treasure hunt winners may not have anything like a completed grid.

Solution

The grid (solution):

F	E	A	T	H	E	R	S		P	O	T	T	E	R
A		T		O		E			R		O			A
M	A	T		M	O	T	H		H	A	P	P	E	N
O		A		E		R		E	N		T			
U	N	C	E	R	T	A	I	N		G	H	O	S	T
S		K		C		I		E		T				I
			F	I	V	E		D	I	A	M	O	N	D
I		B		N				D		E				E
T	R	E	A	T	E	D		M	E	E	T			
C		T		H		A		A			B			S
H	O	R	S	E		H	A	T	C	H	B	A	C	K
		A		F		L		I		A	N			I
B	L	Y	T	O	N		B	L	U	R		A	I	M
U		E		O			D		R		A	N		P
S	E	D	A	T	E		M	A	R	Y	M	A	R	Y

THE CLUES

ACROSS

1 Bird covering is afraid of the inside. (8)

5 See 28 down.
9 The rug has some tomato on it. (3)

10 A night-time flier is a parent without hesitation. (4)
11 We are not with pa and nephew, unfortunately, to make it take place. (6)
13 Enact ruin poorly when you are not sure. (9)
14 Inside a tough ostrich is a spook. (5)
16 See 1 down.
18 A card that is a rock. (7)
21 Sounds like a wooden bear was made better. (7)
23 Come together with a thousand-points (4) model.
26 This animal could be on the shore. (5)
27 Chicks are born not at the front of this type of car. (9)
29 See 12 down.
30 Pop group put fifty into the prickly seed. (4)
31 Some claim this is where they are going. (3)
32 The directions to the fruit were calm and make you go to sleep. (6)
33 Repeatedly, she was contrary in the nursery rhyme. (4, 4)

DOWN

1 and 16 across. 12 29s well-known number of characters. (6, 4)
2 Sounds like a small nail is hit. (6)
3 This cartoon character likes to return to the family house. (5)
4 Go over the route again to the unusual oriental crater. (7)
6 The poem is about a group of mountains and an article, not apple juice! (9)
7 Completely dressed up using three shirts, three holes and physical exercise. (3, 2, 3)
8 Some grandmothers entered the 100 m race. (3)
12 and 29 across. The author could be told by nine. (4, 6)
15 Bad diet could make this ebb and flow. (4)
17 You will be hopping mad if you shoot yourself here! (2, 3, 4)
19 Some needlework stitches will make you want to scratch. (4)
20 The gambling newspaper chief ate fish and was disloyal. (8)
22 This writer is a backward boy eating the last peach. (4)
23 22s character waltzes in Australia! (7)
24 Prohibit two articles to get this fruit. (6)
25 The naughty creature was in a TV channel in clothes that were too small. (6)
28 and 5 across. Wizard! Not yet! (5, 6)
29 'It's strange ... true'. Exchange a shirt for a direction to catch this vehicle. (3)

Village Gossip

You may have seen the television programme *Call My Bluff*. This is a local version called 'Village Gossip', although there are significant changes in the way that it is played.

At the start, you will be introduced to three local inhabitants:

PC Denis Dodds   Lady Lettice Lostock   Farmer Fred Finch

Please make them very welcome.

Your Task

- ❦ For each round you will be told an unusual word. Write that word onto your answer sheet, below.
- ❦ Listen carefully to three definitions of that word. One of them is the correct definition. PC Denis Dodds will give you definition A, Lady Lettice Lostock will give you definition B and Farmer Fred Finch will give you definition C.
- ❦ After hearing the three possibilities, make a decision in your team as to the correct one. Enter the letter for that definition (A, B or C) in the First Choice column on the answer sheet.
- ❦ Decide what you think is the second most likely answer and put the letter into the Second Choice column.

Remember to look for clues in the construction of the words.

Scoring

If your **First Choice** is the correct one your team will score five points. If your **Second Choice** is the correct definition, your team will score two points.

NO.	WORD	ANSWER	
		FIRST CHOICE	**SECOND CHOICE**
1			
2			
3			
4			
5			
6			

Teaching Notes

Although this activity causes great amusement, children should be reminded that their chance of success will be increased if they look for clues within the words. That amusement is heightened if the village celebrities are portrayed effectively. One method that works extremely well is to have one person, whom the children know well, to play all three parts. Three appropriate hats – a plastic police helmet, a lady's flowery hat and a trilby, for instance, are worn in turn as the panel of one moves along the 'celebrity table'. Children have been very enthusiastic about this approach, especially if the person puts on accents to match the three local people. An obvious alternative is to have three different people play the parts. Whichever method is chosen, the 'locals' need to work out a patter to expand and elaborate the short definitions, below, that they will deliver.

The Words and Definitions

Definition A is described by PC Denis Dodds, definition B by Lady Lettice Lostock and definition C by Farmer Fred Finch. The correct definitions are highlighted in the table below.

	Word	Person	Definition
1	Tridentate	A	An area in the central region of Brazil, occupied by the Pooloo Indians.
		B	An object which has three prongs, teeth or points.
		C	A nerve situated on the inner side of the arm, close to the surface of the skin near the wrist.
2	Lanceolate	A	Something which is rare or unusual, especially something not normally seen during the day.
		B	A type of hoop worn under a skirt, especially in Tudor times, to shape and spread it.
		C	An object which is narrow and tapering to a point at each end.
3	Gomuti	A	An East Indian feather palm tree, whose sweet sap is a source of sugar.
		B	A special mix of spices, including cinnamon, nutmeg and mace, pounded into a paste with goat's cheese to make a dish for the feast of Korama.
		C	A type of writing discovered in North Africa when the city of Carthage was uncovered by archaeologists in 1924.
4	Biocycle	A	Any of the major regions of the biosphere, such as the land or the sea, which is capable of supporting life.
		B	A pesticide which only kills insects harmful to wheat crops.
		C	A motorized two-wheel vehicle, invented in 1994, which is fuelled by grass.
5	Zamindar	A	A musical instrument with five strings of different lengths, used in Latvia until the second half of the nineteenth century.
		B	The owner of a large agricultural estate in India.
		C	A semi-precious stone much used in bridal rings by the Victorians.
6	Postlude	A	The top bar of a farm gate nearest the hinge.
		B	A final or concluding piece or movement in music.
		C	A method of painting with oil and coloured powders.

1   The number of rounds can be extended if a longer event is required.
2   It is sensible to have a tie-break question, of some sort, available in case teams have the same number of points.

Tournament: A Word to the Wise

The Clue Cat

Identify ten well-known expressions from the pictures below.

Remember: If the Clue Cat appears, look carefully at its position

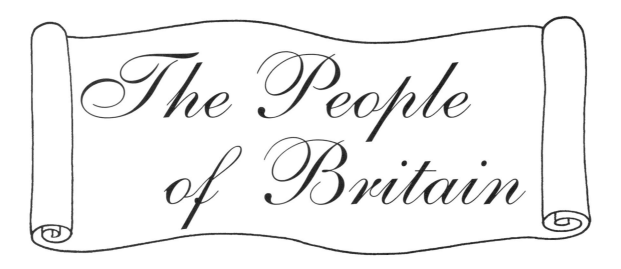

The People of Britain

What you Have to Do

Consider places that you know, but also study appropriate maps or atlases.

Draw up a list of people who live in appropriate places in Great Britain.

Use your imagination and sense of humour to create suitable pairings in this piece of geographical word play.

Your answers can be of two types:

1   The _____ people of _____

    for example: The relaxed people of Ambleside, The spotless people of Bath

2   The _____ of _____

    for example: The horseriders of Canterbury, The gravediggers of Bury

Success Criteria

Your list will be judged not just in terms of length but also the quality and originality of the responses.

Teaching Notes

There are five rounds that collectively provide a varied and exciting tournament. The order suggested means that the children are faced with a change of styles. The rounds can be used individually as separate activities for other situations. They can also be mixed and matched with other activities and resources both in this theme and in the Reading theme.

Tournaments such as these have been a very popular part of courses over a number of occasions. The rounds together add up to a very exciting 'whole'.

Round One: Synonyms

There is no pupil sheet. A word is read out, together with a number. The children, in teams, discuss and write down a synonym (a word that means the same or nearly the same) that has the correct number of letters to match the number given.

An example to use is:

camouflage (8), with the answer being 'disguise'.

	Word	Number of letters	Synonym
1	close by	4	near
2	pail	6	bucket
3	untruth	3	lie
4	secret	6	hidden/untold
5	follow	6	pursue
6	prepared	5	ready
7	gift	7	present
8	hurt	6	injure
9	orator	7	speaker
10	naughty	11	mischievous/disobedient

Credit should be given for alternative answers that fit.

Round Two: 'The Clue Cat'
ANSWERS

1. Flying colours
2. Under the weather/head in the clouds
3. Somewhere over the rainbow
4. Beside yourself/beside myself/copycat?
5. Above suspicion
6. Trunk road
7. At sixes and sevens
8. Next in line/first in line/jumping the queue
9. Crocodile tears
10. On top of the world

Some alternative answers have already been given. Others should be credited if they are appropriate. However, alternative answers must always take account of the cat's position, apart from numbers 1, 6 and 9.

Round Three: Cluewords

There is no pupil sheet.

To be read out

Your task is to identify ten words. For each word you will hear four 'cluewords' that become progressively more helpful. The first 'clueword' could lead in a number of directions, but the target word becomes clearer as the other three 'cluewords' are added.

An example could be:

1 columns   **2** pages   **3** print   **4** daily

leading to the target word 'newspaper'.

Divide your paper into four columns with the numbers 1, 2, 3 and 4 at the top of each column. After each clue is read out, write down what you think the target word is to which it refers. You must write in column one after clue one, in column two after clue two and so on. If you have no idea, put a line in the appropriate column. You can change your mind by writing a different target word in a later column. This is very likely to occur as you get more 'cluewords'. The scoring system is as follows. For the column in which you get the correct target word for the first time, you score four points for column one, three points for column two, two points for column three and one point for column four. This system reflects the fact that it is less difficult to identify the target word as you receive more information.

Target word no.	Column one	Column two	Column three	Column four
1	pattern	click	needles	wool
2	deck	cut	shuffle	playing
3	root	false	bite	dentist
4	communication	tone	line	directory
5	strap	hands	time	wrist
6	snack	round	filling	bread
7	shutter	likeness	lens	film
8	sea	leisure	wipe-out	board
9	trap	rodent	whiskers	computer
10	games	shake	numbers	cube

For scoring it is important that the columns are used correctly.

Answers

1   knitting   6   sandwich (perhaps 'burger' can be scored)
2   cards   7   camera
3   teeth   8   surfing
4   telephone   9   mouse
5   watch   10   dice

Round Four: The People of Britain

It is helpful if teams are provided with atlases or maps of Britain. Discretion is needed in terms of which answers to credit. Children tend to produce long lists containing excellent suggestions. This is a very popular activity. It could be used as an open-access competition in school.

Some classic answers have been:

'The bad cooks of Blackburn'

'The librarians of Reading'

'The auditors of Stockport'

'The meat-eaters of Liverpool'

'The candlemakers of Wick'

'The messy people of Staines'

'The decorators of Paignton'

'The murderous people of Kilkenny'

'The auctioneers of Biddington'

and hundreds of others!

Round Five: Antonyms

There is no pupil sheet. A word is read out, together with a number. The children, in teams, discuss and write down an antonym (a word that means the opposite) that has the correct number of letters to match the number given.

An example to use is:

careful (8), with the answer being 'reckless'.

No.	First word	Number of letters	Antonym
1	full	5	empty
2	open	6	closed
3	timid	4	bold
4	failure	7	success
5	brave	8	cowardly
6	proud	6	humble
7	innocent	6	guilty
8	rigid	8	flexible
9	early	5	tardy
10	common	10	remarkable

For both Rounds One and Five, 'Synonyms' and 'Antonyms', the difficulty of the words used could be altered to fit different ages of children.

PASSING SENTENCE

There are 30 words to find, six for each of five groups:

1	Nouns are on green cards
2	Verbs are on blue cards
3	Adjectives are on yellow cards
4	Adverbs are on white cards
5	Prepositions are on pink cards

The colour of the card denotes the part of speech. On the card is the number of letters in the word to be named. There are one or more clues on the card and either a picture clue or an object clue, or both. The colour of the card explains the type of word you must find, but the clues could also refer to other linked parts of speech, for example secretly is an adverb, and would therefore be indicated by a white card. However, the clues might involve secret as an adjective (secret society) or secret as a noun (keeping a secret).

The clues are very varied. Some are cryptic – their meaning is hidden. Some involve detailed photographs in which only one item is important. Some give a definition of the word and others involve well-known phrases and sayings involving the word or a closely-associated word. Be ready for anything!

Your Tasks

Visit all 30 sites. Try to work out the word and write it down, together with its number. Add as much explanation as you can on the meaning of the clues – this is as important, if not more important, than naming the word, and will certainly count in your total score!

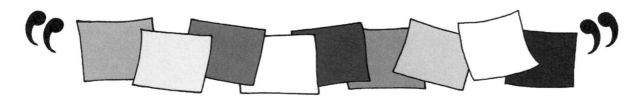

Teaching Notes

Treasure hunts are most enjoyable but they can also be very instructive. There is a strong content base in 'Passing Sentence' and the use of cryptic clues leads to the use of higher-order thinking skills.

Key Elements

- ❖ parts of speech
- ❖ deduction and inference
- ❖ observation
- ❖ team collaboration
- ❖ following instructions
- ❖ analysis.

Contexts

'Passing Sentence', in this format, is very much designed for a long enrichment session. Reducing the number of words and locations allows a shorter time allocation.

Organization

Thirty locations are needed. Some cards and objects can be placed around corners and out of direct sight, but it is not particularly helpful to have them truly hidden, the object is to solve the clues rather than just finding the cards. The hunt is less predictable if the different coloured cards are randomly placed rather than grouping the same colours together.

The written clues that follow have to be transferred onto correctly coloured cards. Pictures and, especially, objects, make the treasure hunt more interesting and exciting. Most are easy to find. Where there is difficulty, substitutes can be employed. Children are encouraged to explain how each of the clues leads to the identification of the word. In this way, in scoring the answers, credit can be given for correct thinking even if the final word is not totally correct.

An Introductory Example

Before children set out on the treasure hunt, it is helpful to go through an example that does not feature in the 30 locations.

---

31 White card (adverb) (6)
a 'To treat in a reasonable manner'
b 'An honest way of dealing with things that involves a four-sided figure of equal sides'
c A picture of a rollercoaster or funfair – separately.

The word is 'fairly':

a the definition
b 'fair and square'
c fairground.

The importance of the coloured card (white) is shown because it is an adverb, not a noun. The pupil sheet explains that other parts of speech may be used in the clues, aside from the targeted part of speech.

The Cards

NOTE:

The number of each card is written on it (1–30) as are the number of letters in the word and many of the clues. 'Separately' indicates an additional picture or object. The part of speech has to be worked out from the colour of the card.

1   Green card (noun) (4)
a)   'A long hollow cylinder'
b)   'Sometimes follows a test in the science laboratory'
c)   Map of the London underground – object – separately

The word is **TUBE** – a) the definition, b) test tube, c) the nickname

2   Pink card (preposition) (4)
a)   'Going on strike is doing this with the equipment'
b)   Picture of a bird with arrow pointing from caption 'the underplumage' – separately
c)   Picture of leaves falling from a tree – separately

The word is **DOWN** – a) the expression 'down tools', b) area of feathers on a bird, c) falling down

3   Yellow card (adjective) (5)
a)   'Can be comical but also strange and perplexing'
b)   'A knock on this part of the elbow is definitely not amusing'
c)   A model/picture of a clown - separately

The word is **FUNNY** – a) three definitions, b) the funny bone, c) a clown is supposed to be funny

4   White card (adverb) (7)
a)   'With no regard for her own safety, Jacqueline raced back into the burning house to rescue the trapped children. She was commended for the way she had behaved'
b)   Picture of a male native American Indian – separately

The word is **BRAVELY** – a) description of Jacqueline's behaviour, b) an Indian brave

5   Blue card (verb) (4)
a)   Object/picture of walking boots or shoes – separately
b)   'This could involve pirates and a particular piece of wood'
c)   Brochure for a forest trail – separately

The word is **WALK** – a) what you do in the footwear, b) 'walk the plank', c) another word for trail

6   Blue card (verb) (3)
a)   Picture of a badger – separately
b)   'To do this with part of your body is to be obstinate'
c)   A trowel – object – separately

The word is **DIG** – a) what badgers do well, b) the expression 'dig your toes in', c) what you do with a trowel

7   Pink card (preposition) (2)
a)   'The leg side in cricket, and avoid committing an offence in football'
b)   Picture of a bee on a flower – separately
c)   Picture of an object on top of music coming from a person's mouth – separately

The word is **ON** – a) on side in cricket and onside in football, b) the position of the bee, c) the expression 'on song'

8   Green card (noun) (4)
a)   Picture of a tap with a drop of water just about to fall – separately
b)   'An abrupt fall over a cliff, for instance'
c)   A hat – separately

The word is **DROP** – a) a drop of water, b) the expression 'a sheer drop', c) the expression 'at the drop of a hat'

9   White card (adverb) (7)
a)   'Turning rapidly to the left around a bend in the road'
b)   'Frost sometimes comes this way'
c)   A pair of scissors – object – separately

The word is **SHARPLY** – a) move sharply, b) the expression 'a sharp frost', c) scissors are sharp

10   Yellow card (adjective) (5)
a)   Picture/model of a lighthouse – separately
b)   'If you make this of a situation, you treat it as unimportant'
c)   Booklet about electricity – separately

The word is **LIGHT** – a) lighthouse, b) the expression 'to make light of', c) electric light

11   Pink card (preposition) (2)
a)   'To give in, in this situation, is to stop trying'
b)   A cup with small pink card saying 'Take away the water' – object – separately
c)   Picture of people holding objects over their heads – separately

The word is **UP** – a) the expression 'to give up', b) 'sea' sounds like 'C', cup minus C is up, c) holding things up

12   White card (adverb) (10)
a)   A set of film negatives – object – separately
b)   Sheet with a number of 'No's' on it
c)   'Taking a pessimistic view of things'

The word is **NEGATIVELY** – a) film negatives, b) respond negatively, c) the definition

13   Blue card (verb) (4)
a)   A frog – picture/object – separately
b)   '1968   1980   1988'
c)   Picture of dolphins leaping out of the water – separately

The word is **LEAP** – a) leapfrog, b) leap years, c) what the dolphins are doing

14   Green card (noun) (4)
a)   Picture of a meal with a fork on the plate – separately
b)   'A divergence of the road or river'
c)   A chessboard set up with pieces where a knight is threatening two opposing pieces at the same time – separately

The word is **FORK** – a) in the picture, b) a fork as a choice of routes, c) the technical name in chess when a piece threatens two pieces at the same time

15   Pink card (preposition) (9)
a)   Picture of map of the areas of Devon with label saying 'Position of mid-Devon to East Devon' – separately
b)   'One boat to another, or to a pier'
c)   'One way to describe (i)

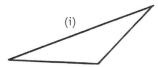

(i)

The word is **ALONGSIDE** – a) relative positions, b) the expression 'coming alongside', c) a long side of a triangle

16   White card (adverb) (10)
a)   Picture of someone in glasses – separately
b)   Picture of a wristwatch – separately
c)   'Showing care and vigilance'

The word is **WATCHFULLY** – a) a person watching, b) noun 'watch', c) the definition

17 White card (adverb) (7)
a) 'Done in a serious manner'
b) 'A movement by a dead person when shocked at the thought of a certain situation or event'
c) Picture of a gravestone – separately

The word is **GRAVELY** – a) definition, b) the expression 'turn in one's grave', c) a grave

18 Yellow card (adjective) (6)
a) 'Shining or clever'
b) 'Taking an optimistic view'
c) A button – object/picture – separately

The word is **BRIGHT** – a) definition, b) the expression 'looking on the bright side', c) the simile 'as bright as a button'

19 Blue card (verb) (7)
a) Picture of someone looking through a microscope – separately
b) 'Checking the health of a patient by a doctor, or testing a candidate's ability'
c) A magnifying glass – object/picture – separately

The word is **EXAMINE** – a) you examine objects with a microscope, b) an examination, c) a magnifying glass is used to examine objects

20 Yellow card (adjective) (5)
a) 'If too much, becomes haughty or arrogant'
b) 'Slightly projecting from a surface'
c) A peacock – object/picture – separately

The word is **PROUD** – a) excessive pride, b) definition, c) the simile 'as proud as a peacock'

21 Pink card (preposition) (5)
a) Picture of a cricketer bowling with a cross over the arm and a caption 'Not this type of bowling' – separately
b) 'A canine competitor thought to have little chance of winning'
c) 'Australia'

The word is **UNDER** – a) not overarm bowling, b) the expression 'underdog', c) 'down under'

22. Yellow card (adjective) (10)
a) Picture of winning sports player with cup/medal
b) 'Didn't they do well!'
c) A trophy – object/ picture – separately

The word is **SUCCESSFUL** or **VICTORIOUS** – a) what the player is, b) a colloquial definition, c) a prize for being this

23 Green card (noun) (4)
a) 'A mark, symbol or device used to represent something'
b) 'To write or acknowledge a document or agreement'
c) A physical sign of any sort – object – separately

The word is **SIGN** – a) one definition, b) to sign something, c) a physical sign

24 Blue card (verb) (7)
a) Picture of a celebrity involved in a charity event – separately
b) 'Helping your favourite team'
c) 'This is what a cane is to a plant'

The word is **SUPPORT** – a) supporting a cause, b) support a team, c) a plant support

25 Green card (noun) (5)
a) Picture of an office (including a chair) – separately
b) 'The person chosen to preside over a meeting'
c) 'A greeting often given to a visitor at the start of a meeting so that he or she will be more comfortable'

The word is **CHAIR** – a) one of the pieces of office furniture, b) chairperson, c) the expression 'take a chair'

26 Yellow card (adjective) (5)
a) 'Alfred, Peter and Catherine'
b) 'Considerably above the normal'
c) Picture of fire grates – separately

The word is **GREAT** – a) how these rulers were known (e.g. Alfred the Great), b) definition, c) homophone

27 White card (adverb) (8)
a) 'To tread in a cautious manner'
b) 'This is a spicy way to do things'
c) Picture of a ginger cat – separately

The word is **GINGERLY** – a) moving gingerly, b) ginger is a spice, c) ginger cat

28 Green card (noun) (4)
a) 'At sea this would disturb the situation'
b) 'A group of modern musicians'
c) Picture of seaside, including a rock pool – separately

The word is **ROCK** – a) the expression 'don't rock the boat', b) rock band, c) rock pool

29 Pink card (preposition) (7)
a) Sheet with numbers 3, 4, 5, 6, 7, 8 and underneath them the caption 'Their link with numbers 2 and 9' – separately
b) 'Ourselves, keeping something confidential'
c) Two bookends spaced, with an object between them – separately

The word is **BETWEEN** – a) numbers 3–8 are between 2 and 9, b) the expression 'Keep it between ourselves', c) where the object is in relation to the bookends

30 Blue card (verb) (4)
a) Picture of children playing – separately
b) 'Perform music without the score'
c) A play script – separately

The word is **PLAY** – a) what the children are doing, b) the expression 'play by ear', c) a play

Reading/Thinking Skills Courses, Activities and Resources

Introduction

Reading is not only an extremely pleasurable pastime it is also the key to so much learning and thinking. Analysis, inference, deduction, evaluation and synthesis are just some of the thinking skills involved in this section. Reading is not a passive activity. Children need to engage with the text and to respond imaginatively to the plots, characters, ideas and vocabulary.

The courses set out to not only share a love of reading and discover new authors and texts, but also to employ a range of thinking skills and a variety of outcomes. Enjoyment is a key issue.

Booktrust

One extremely useful source of information about children's literature is Booktrust.

Address:	Book House
	45 East Hill
	LONDON
	SW18 2QZ
Tel:	020 8516 2981
	020 8516 2977
Websites:	www.booktrusted.com
	www.booktrust.org.uk

Booktrusted News
The quarterly magazine features news and views on various aspects of the children's book world. Each issue concentrates on a particular theme and contains a related pull-out booklist. Also included are author and illustrator profiles, information about book prizes, reviews of new titles – from baby books to teenage reads – and a variety of articles about children's books and reading.

Best Book Guide
Best Book Guide is the new name for *100 Best Books* (back issues are still available) which has been expanded to include even more reviews. This guide is Booktrust's independent annual pick of the best in children's paperback fiction published in the previous calendar year. It is designed to help parents, teachers, librarians, booksellers and anyone interested in children's reading to select books for children from babies to teenagers. Printed in full colour, each book featured has a short review, easy colour coding to indicate reading age and interest level, plus some bibliographical information for easy ordering at bookshops and libraries.

Other Booktrust services and publications

1   **Children's Literature Collection** – holds the vast majority of children's books published over each two-year period in the United Kingdom. There is also a permanent collection.

2   **The Beatrix Potter Study Room** – houses a small collection of original literature, drawings and paintings by Beatrix Potter.

3   *Celebrate a Book: A DIY Guide to Planning a Book Event* – includes advice about planning a book event, obtaining funding, organizing author visits and some suggested activities for a range of age groups.

4   **Children's Book Week Resources** – National Book Week is an annual event held during the first full week in October. Booktrust has a range of posters, bookmarks and stickers to help promote and support this event.

5   *Looking for an Author?* – a directory of authors, illustrators and poets. This is an essential reference for anyone looking for an author or illustrator to attend a book event. The directory is now available free of charge to visitors of the National Centre for Language and Literacy (www.ralic.rdg.ac.uk) and Booktrust websites.

6   **Parents' Pack** – each pack contains general advice on obtaining and selecting books, together with specific guidance on the relevant age range and age-targeted booklists. They are free of charge.

7   *Pop Ups! A Guide to Novelty Books* – this is Booktrust's response to many enquiries on the subject of novelty books. The publication acts as a starting point for further investigation and discussion.

8   **Posters, Stickers and Bookmarks** – a good selection is available.

Possible Titles for Courses

'Reading Between the Lines'
'Matilda, Toad, the Famous Five,
Pearce, Pullman, Pratchett, Books Alive'
'That's my Reading of it'
'Read On – with – Harry Potter, Johnny Maxwell, Tracy Beaker and Fantastic Mr Fox'
'Read you Like a Book'
'Reading your Mind'
'Take it as Read'

Excitement and joy should always be integral to reading activities and, therefore, each of the above titles could be followed by the subtitle 'A Reading Party'.

The activities described in the following pages are linked particularly to reading. They could be transferred, very profitably and sensibly, to more general English courses and lessons.

Creating an Atmosphere

This is particularly important for reading courses/activities. Attention is given to this on page 20 in Section 1 of this book.

Part One: Starters, Icebreakers

'Reading Party Questionnaire'

One starting point is to learn more about the children as readers (page 88).

This gives information which provides a background for later activities in the course.

A relatively short time is needed for children to focus on this activity. Ten to 15 minutes is sufficient.

+	3	4	5	6	7	8	9	+	

'Sharing Favourite Passages'

In advance of the session, participants are asked to select favourite passages from books that they have really enjoyed. Children are very keen to do this, and you will have no problem getting volunteers to read out their favourite passage and explain why the passage particularly appeals to them! It is also recommended that the tutor selects one or two of their own favourite passages from children's literature to include in this activity.

Sharing books with others who love literature is an enormous pleasure. The more enjoyment we can generate in education the better!

1   The selections that children make can be informative as to their reading, and may also extend the reading of others in the group by introducing new authors and titles. The information gathered can help to make good provision for them.
2   Sharing passages is a beneficial activity early in a course, but it works equally well at other times. Revisiting this activity during the course is very popular.

As an introductory activity, 15–20 minutes gives an opportunity for several passages to be read (with the promise of further chances to read at other times).

+	3	4	5	6	7	8	9	+	

'A Good Read'

Discussion items 'break the ice' and allow children to get to know each other better.

A guidance sheet is included (page 89).

One hour to one hour 15 minutes, depending upon how long is spent on groups explaining their choices to others. It is possible to reduce this allocation.

		4	5	6	7	8			

'Tempting Titles'
MERATC

'Tempting Titles' (page 33) gives the synopsis for each of ten different novels. Children are asked to make up a tempting title for each, which is appropriate for the story and entices the reader or book-buyer.

Twenty to 30 minutes allows sufficient time to consider titles and to share ideas.

This activity can be done singly, in pairs or in groups. If this is the first activity in a course, then group-work might be preferable.

This can lead to a follow-up:

'Revealing Titles'
This piece reverses the process above (page 91).

Perhaps seven–ten minutes per title, if real thought is given. Total time depends upon the number of books dealt with.

Part Two: A Logical Connection

One might not immediately think of reading and logic together, but, if reading is recognized as an active process, deduction and inference are key skills in engagement with text. Predicting and hypothesizing about what might happen in a story are higher-order thinking skills and they depend upon analysing what has gone before.

'According to the Book'
ERATC
'According to the Book' (page 155) is a long, logical thought problem involving much synthesis of data. The basic task is to work out which novel the 20 members of the school Book Club ordered. There is a great deal of information – some facts about the children, a paragraph describing each of the 20 books and a series of clues. To add to the reading theme, the children are named after features connected with books that also form part of the clues.

Children have found this exercise absolutely fascinating.

One hour 30 minutes, including a detailed feedback.

When 'According to the Book' is undertaken, it is desirable to have the 20 books actually on display. This is a subtle way of recommending titles, as all the books have been included for their quality.

'Paragraph by Paragraph'
The tutor reads out a short story, organized into four paragraphs (page 93). After paragraphs one, two and three, the pupils try to predict the conclusion in paragraph four.

Five to ten minutes for each example used.

Part Three: What if?

'Mole, Rat, Badger, Toad and … Who?'
ERATC

The whole piece (page 77) looks at a variety of 'what if?' situations – adding a character, changing the period involved in a time switch, characters exchanging roles, geographical switches, removing a key character, changing the period of a detective novel, writing a politically correct Enid Blyton story, prequels and sequels. A large number of fascinating possibilities are opened up.

On a course, children are given the choice of tackling one of the nine themes. This work could equally well be tackled in normal lessons or for homework.

Time depends upon the depth to which a child goes. Thirty minutes would allow some of the themes to be tackled. One hour or longer could usefully be employed. Within the whole piece of work there is material for in excess of ten hours.

		4	5	6	7	8	9		

Part Four: Written Outcomes

The Mysteries of Harris Burdick

This wonderful material, written by Chris Van Allsburg, is available in both book form (Andersen Press: London, 1984) and in poster form (Houghton Mifflin Company, 1996). A mystery surrounds Harris Burdick who has put together the basic ideas for 14 stories (the poster having 15). He leaves the information with a publisher but never returns. That information consists of a fascinating and zany black-and-white drawing, the title and a one-line caption for each of the stories. Now the only way to see the finished product is for the pupils to use their own imagination.

There is also a website to visit: www.hmco.com/vanallsburg

How can you put a time on creativity? One hour can get a good response.

		4	5	6	7	8	9	+	

You will stimulate the most incredible creative writing with these materials.

Both the book and the set of posters are very highly recommended. If you want to add extra titles, make your own. Find an intriguing picture from a newspaper or other source and mount it on card. Think up a suitable title and add a mysterious one-liner.

The author has a picture of a greylag goose waiting for its luggage alongside other airline passengers. The title which it has been given is 'Flight of Fancy' and the caption reads: 'Some of the passengers still did not know the truth behind their journey.' What magic awaits!

Closed materials do not allow space for creativity and imagination. Totally open-ended resources have possibilities but sometimes even able children get lost in the wide open spaces. A sensational combination is to have a few, limited starters with many, many possible routes that can then be explored.

Part Five: For Fun, Among Other Things

'Fictional Farewells'
CRATC

This fun piece (page 49) speculates upon the inscriptions that might be written on the tombstones or monuments of 30 characters from traditional tales, classic children's books and modern stories. Wordplay is a key element. 'Fictional Farewells' fits the peculiar sense of humour possessed by many able children.

This piece of work can be used in a course but it is equally at home in total, or broken into sections, in the classroom or for homework.

Thirty minutes.

			5	6	7	8			

'As Mad as a Hatter'
Similes are the vehicle for this particular excursion into children's literature. It is a short, and rather zany, item (page 96).

As little as 15–20 minutes can be very productive.

			5	6	7	8	9		

Part Six: Longer Activities

'Puzzle Book' – A Tournament
There are three rounds to give variety – one is oral and involves discussion, the second is performing and the third is written.

The rounds can be used as separate activities for different time-spans.

Round One: 'Tangled Tales'
ERATC

Passage Two of this piece (page 84) is read out twice. Children individually write down as many of the 20 hidden children's book titles that they can spot. Some are obvious but others are disguised. Members of the team then confer to put together a composite list. Credit is given for exact titles with half-credits for suggestions that are close. For instance, 'Otherwise Known as Sheila the Great' is required for the full point. 'Sheila the Great' gets half a point.

Knowledge of children's books is at a premium but intuitive thinkers among the participants also make intelligent guesses.

Twenty-five minutes including going through the titles with comments.

			5	6	7	8	9		

1   When writing such a passage as 'Tangled Tales' some titles occur unintentionally. 'Boy' and 'Storm' both fit this category. Are there any more?
2   There are two passages in the book, and if children have met one previously there is the possibility of using the other.

Round Two: 'Charades'

'Charades' is a well-known activity for parties and family gatherings (page 98). This version of the game concentrates upon children's books.

Twenty-five minutes for two rounds. The time allocation can be changed.

		4	5	6	7	8	9		

Round Three: 'Puzzle Book'

This is the written round that gives the title to the whole tournament (page 99).

One hour, including going over the answers, causes teams to work with urgency. A longer period can be given. If used as separate items, the time scale is totally different.

			5	6	7	8	9		

Activities are interchangeable. Sections within tournaments can be taken out and used in very different circumstances, such as normal lessons and homework.

'Follow the Yellow Brick Road' – A Treasure Hunt

This is an active event which gets children 'on the move'. It gives an effective contrast to paper-based exercises (page 104).

Most of the physical objects used are easy to acquire or make. The odd section could be removed or replaced if the item cannot be reproduced. Pictures are not as interesting as objects but they will suffice.

Two hours in total including the formation of teams, initial instructions, the treasure hunt itself and going over the answers.

		4	5	6	7	8			

The two hours will be split in the sense that the tutor needs time to check the answer sheets.

'The Bare Bones' – A Presentation

ERATC

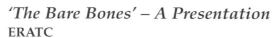

In this piece of work (page 81) children plan the 'bare bones' of a story, with a mixture of open-endedness and set parameters. Each team is given one map page, two artefacts and five photographs, mixed in terms of subject. The outcome is a team presentation to a panel of 'book publishers'.

One hour 45 minutes, including the introduction, preparation time, presentations and feedback.

		4	5	6	7	8	9	+	

The outcome can also be a written account or an individual presentation on behalf of the team. This allows 'The Bare Bones' to be tackled in other contexts.

The time scale will vary if the outcome alters. If presentations do not follow preparation time, the time allocation can be reduced by 30 minutes or more.

'Bookworm' – A Tournament

Round One: 'To Begin at the Beginning'
Using the first lines of a book is an interesting exercise (page 109). There is a very large number of variations possible.

Round Two: 'Almost Anonymous Authors'
This piece involves identifying authors through cryptic clues (page 110). The main task is used in the tournament. There is also an extension task for use elsewhere.

Round Three: 'Contents Page'
The children do not have a sheet to work from as the tutor reads out clues to identify the books (page 111).

Round Four: 'Reading Age'
The task is to place a series of books in chronological order of their publication (page 112).

Round Five: 'Camouflaged Characters'
Twenty famous characters have been hidden within a passage (page 113). Alternative outcomes are also outlined for this activity.

Two hours, or just under, is needed for the whole tournament, but time allocation will be different if rounds are used separately.

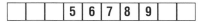

			5	6	7	8	9		

The teaching notes and answers have been collected together under the Tournament title 'Bookworm' (page 114) after the sheets that operate the five rounds.

'Drama at your Fingertips' – A Performance
Teams of children are required to create a puppet storyline, using designated puppet characters (including a 'rogue'), and to perform it in a puppet theatre (page 119).

At least two hours 30 minutes, including the performances themselves.

	4	5	6	7	8	9		

Reading Party Questionnaire

NAME: AGE:

How much reading do you do in the average week?

Who are your favourite authors?

Name some of your favourite books:

What are you currently reading?

Is there a particular genre which you prefer?

What in your opinion makes a 'good read'?

Which passages would you like to share with others?

Which books have you brought with you?

A Good Read

To what extent do lovers of books agree as to what makes 'a good read'?

Your Tasks

1 Study the list below of factors that may be most important in making a book 'a good read'.
2 Discuss these factors and any others that you wish to add.
3 Decide which eight points are of most importance for your group.
4 Write them out on slips of paper and then stick them, in order of importance, in the shape of a ladder, with the most significant at the top. If you wish, some can be rated of equal importance and would, therefore, occupy the same rung on the ladder.

The Points to Consider

- An opening that makes you want to read on.
- Strong characterization so that you can believe in the people.
- A subject matter that has appeal for you personally.
- A geographical, historical or cultural setting that interests you personally.
- Witty observation and comment that makes the characters and episodes meaningful.
- An excellent use and juxtaposition of a rich vocabulary.
- A strong plot that makes you want to keep turning the pages over.
- A powerful imagination that results in an extraordinary but engaging setting.
- Space for the reader to play a part.
- The opportunity to experience a fantasy world.
- A book that allows an emotional response – sad, happy, funny, frightening, mysterious.
- A book that gives the opportunity to reflect on serious/philosophical issues or gives a new insight into important questions.
- Interesting factual information or biographies.
- A good ending, a real surprise, or one that leaves room for a possible sequel or future developments.

Optional Extension Task

Look at three or four of your favourite books and write down the factors, in order of importance, that make them 'a good read'.

To what extent do these individual examples support the ladder you have constructed?

1
2
3
4
5
6
7
8

A Good Read

Teaching Notes

Fourteen factors have been listed on the pupil sheet. They give wide coverage of the likely views but, even so, other suggestions might be made. Working from an existing list fires off discussion quickly. As children are making decisions in groups, joint 'ladders' are produced which necessitates compromise and negotiation. In what seems to be a simple activity there are some important higher-order thinking skills.

Key Elements

- ❖ discussion
- ❖ negotiation and compromise
- ❖ prioritization
- ❖ supporting a viewpoint
- ❖ evaluation – making a judgement
- ❖ analysis – understanding how parts relate to a whole
- ❖ synthesis – reforming individual parts to make a new whole.

Contexts

'A Good Read' can be used in the following ways:

- ❖ as an early part of an enrichment course (as in this book)
- ❖ in a normal lesson, either singly, in pairs or in groups
- ❖ for homework
- ❖ as an activity for the English Club or Society, or Readers' Club.

Alternative Method

Teachers may prefer not to 'lead' children by supplying them with 'Points to Consider' but rather to work from a blank sheet and let pupils suggest their own points before they prioritize them.

Outcomes

A ladder does not have to be used but it does present a useful, and visual, vehicle. Groups can make a short presentation to explain the ladder and justify the order of importance. The ladders can then be exhibited for the rest of the course or in the normal classroom.

Extension Task

Teachers can get children to explore the relationship between the specific and the general. This is an important process. The ladder of eight points is set against particular books that individual children love. They write down the factors that contribute to 'a good read' in those individual books and see what correlation there is with the general list. If there are discrepancies thoughts are given as to why this should be and whether the general list is still valid or needs amendment.

Revealing Titles

When you choose a book to read, one of the deciding factors may well be the title. It should, along with the back cover, give you a feeling for the story.

Given the title of a book, how well can you provide the back cover 'blurb'?

Your Task

Consider each of the 16 following book titles, and then, for each, write a paragraph of information which sums up the plot of the story.

Look for clues in the titles including the likely genre to be involved.

How Much can you Make the Bare Title Reveal?

1 The Girl who Knew too Much

2 Daisies and Dandelions

3 Blue, Green and Gold

4 Gadzag the Great

5 Good Boy Bouncer

6 Oops

7 Winning Post

8 The Emperor's Ear

9 Lancashire Tails

10 Cool or Not?

11 Domino Danny

12 X Marks the Spot

13 PC Magic

14 See you in Court

15 Roman Remains

16 Crystal Creek

Extension Task

Make up some titles of your own that you believe are revealing.

Write your own supporting paragraphs.

Give the titles to a friend and get him or her to write supporting paragraphs.

Compare your paragraphs.

What are the similarities?

What are the differences?

Teaching Notes

'Revealing Titles' can be used as one, or a series, of short pieces or, if a number of titles are to be described, as a longer exercise. The 16 examples have been chosen with a mixture of open-endedness and stronger indicators, and they are likely to cover a variety of genres. The degree of lateral thinking and creativity exhibited will add to information about the children themselves. As the writing on each is limited to a paragraph, careful consideration has to be given to content.

Key Elements

- ❖ lateral thinking
- ❖ logical thinking
- ❖ deduction and inference
- ❖ genre
- ❖ short examples of creative writing
- ❖ careful selection of material.

Contexts

'Revealing Titles' can be used in the following ways:

- ❖ individually to start lessons
- ❖ collectively as an exercise in the normal classroom where differentiation by outcome will come into play
- ❖ as a normal/differentiated homework
- ❖ as an enrichment activity for those ahead on standard tasks
- ❖ as an activity within an enrichment session, weekend, summer school or cluster day
- ❖ as an activity for the English Club or Society, or Reading Club
- ❖ as an open-access competition.

Some Thoughts on Answers

Many of the titles have homographs or homophones within them. This is a deliberate ploy as it opens up a variety of interpretations. Some are reasonably indicative of a likely response, others are very vague. Some answers might cover:

1   *The Girl who Knew too Much* – an adventure or spy story might be indicated. A fantasy tale is another possibility.
2   *Daisies and Dandelions* – a horticultural theme is one route; or do the two flowers perhaps represent two rival groups of children?
3   *Blue, Green and Gold* – very open-ended indeed, although the flag of a country is possible, as is a story with a nature theme.
4   *Gadzag the Great* – might well lead to a fantasy story.
5   *Good Boy Bouncer* – is Bouncer a dog? A picture book for younger readers is a distinct possibility.
6   *Oops* – another very open-ended title, although a mistake or clumsiness is likely to feature, and a humorous tale is also possible.
7   *Winning Post* – literal interpretation may well lead to a sporting story but there is also a figurative meaning.
8   *The Emperor's Ear* – are we bound for China, Rome or Europe before the First World War? The ear stated could be literal and a picture book might result, or the ear might stand for being in the confidence of the emperor.
9   *Lancashire Tails* – the homophone is likely to point to animals.
10   *Cool or Not?* – there are a number of possibilities, one is bullying.
11   *Domino Danny* – it may feature the game. 'Domino' could be a nickname.
12   *X Marks the Spot* – a hunt for treasure or a murder enquiry are two of the more obvious outcomes.
13   *PC Magic* – PC for Police Constable would take the writer in a very different direction to PC meaning personal computer or politically correct.
14   *See you in Court* – the court could be legal, regal or tennis.
15   *Roman Remains* – an archaeological theme is a possibility, as is a detective story.
16   *Crystal Creek* – is this a person or a place? 'Crystal' conjures up all sort of mystical routes.

Paragraph by Paragraph

How good are you at predicting the route a story will take?

When you are watching a drama on television, do you say to yourself that you know what is going to happen?

When you are reading a book, are you pretty sure what is going to unfold in the next few pages?

Let us put your powers of prediction and hypothesizing to the test.

Your Task

A series of short stories will be read out, a paragraph at a time. After paragraphs one, two and three, discuss with other members of your group what you believe that the conclusion of the story will be in paragraph four. You may find yourself changing your mind as more information becomes available, or maybe you will stick to your original suggestion. It is possible that you will have several suggestions as to the outcome.

Extension Task

Try to create one or more 'Paragraph by Paragraph' stories of your own.

The beginning should be open-ended enough to allow various possibilities.

These possibilities will narrow as each paragraph is added.

Success Criteria for the Extension Task

▲ the suitability of the subject chosen for the story

▲ the appreciation of the particular genre

▲ the quality of the story itself

▲ how well the clues fit together

▲ the skill displayed in developing the story at an appropriate pace.

Teaching Notes

This piece of work is included in the reading section but it could be placed equally well in the general English section. As the endings must be concealed, the stories are printed here in the teaching notes, rather than on the children's sheet.

Key Elements

- deduction
- inference
- careful use of data
- prediction
- discussion
- appreciation of genre
- creative writing of a particular type.

Contexts

'Paragraph by Paragraph' can be used in many ways:

- as a piece of work in the classroom when differentiation by outcome will apply
- as an activity during an enrichment day, weekend, summer school or cluster day
- as an activity for the English Club or Society
- as group work through discussion, or as an individual task.

The Extension Task can be used additionally:

- as a normal homework task
- as an enrichment activity for those ahead on normal classwork
- as a differentiated homework
- as an open-access competition.

The Paragraph Stories

Story One

1. I sit on the ground, with my head buried in my hands. Soon it will be time. I await the dreaded summons.
2. It's time to move. My legs feel like lead and my head is in a whirl. What a way to end it.
3. I trudge from the centre. It seems to take an age to reach the spot. Why did it have to be at that end anyway?
4. I place the ball on the spot and retreat a couple of yards. The referee blows his whistle. I run up, hit the ball sweetly and it flies into the net. I've done it! I've scored the first goal in the penalty shootout!

Story Two

1. The middle-aged woman smiled and beckoned him over. 'Come on sir, why don't you have a try? What have you got to lose? Impress the young lady, why don't you?'
2. It would be good to impress Julie, his new girlfriend. Denis thought about the chances of success. How good was his eye?
3. Then again, maths had never been his strong point. Even so, surely he could deal with what effectively were the two and three times multiplication tables.
4. Denis plucked up his courage and handed over his 50 pence. 'The three darts must together score over 50 to win a prize,' said the stallholder at the fair. Denis aimed at the board and threw his first dart.

Enrichment Activities for Able and Talented Children © Barry Teare (Network Educational Press, 2004)

Story Three

1   My mother pats my shoulder and then ruffles my hair. 'Don't look like that. Stop worrying. It's just another day.' However, I know that she doesn't mean it.
2   When I arrive, my friends are huddled in a little group, as though they are sheep. 'Lambs to the slaughter, rather', I think. I look at their anxious faces. They don't like it any better than I do.
3   The bell sounds. We walk slowly, in single file, across the yard. We enter the building and go into the room. It is all set out ready.
4   The teacher clears her voice. 'Good morning everybody.' We sit down. 'Now you can turn the paper over. Good luck.' SATs day again, worse luck!

Story Four

1   The child wonders if the clock has stopped. The hands don't seem to be moving at all. The night drags on and on. Will it never be morning?
2   She drowses fitfully, tossing from side to side. Half-awake, she tries to gather her senses. Had she heard the rustle of paper and the clinking of something moving?
3   Now she's dreaming and the images are blurred and indistinct. There are dark shapes – cubes, rectangles and cylinders against the bedroom wall. The child snuggles down for comfort in the warm bed.
4   Slowly the little girl opens her eyes and then switches on the bedside lamp. Then she smiles, a big broad smile. Presents lie in a festive heap. It's morning, but not just any morning. It's Christmas Day.

Story Five

1   Four men sit expectantly around a table. One of them lifts a box onto it and then empties the bones onto the surface.
2   Time passes. Each man makes a contribution when he is able to do so. Occasionally there is the sound of knocking on wood.
3   Many of the bones have been used. A particular pattern has been created. A few are left. Will they fit?
4   'That's me finished,' says one of the men. His partner marks a score on the board. Their opponents will not have the opportunity to use their remaining bones. Dominoes is a fascinating game.

NOTE

The rectangular playing pieces in games of dominoes are often referred to as 'bones' because of the materials originally used. Today they are usually plastic.

As Mad as a Hatter

You will be familiar with similes.

They are used to add colour to writing by making comparisons.

Similes appear in two different formats.

One of them is illustrated in the well-known saying 'as green as grass'; the other features in a comparison such as 'running like the wind'.

If similes are applied to characters from children's books, there are entertaining results.

'As mad as a hatter' is an example of a simile found illustrated in the book *Alice's Adventures in Wonderland*.

Your Tasks

Task One

Complete each of the following with a suitable character or characters from children's literature. Explain your answers.

A   as poisonous as ...

B   as mean as ...

C   as wizard as ...

D   as wild as ...

E   grinning like ...

F   as fond of carrots as ...

G   steaming along like ...

H   as brave as ...

I   weaving a web like ...

J   as threatening to children as ...

K   as untruthful as ...

L   as unfortunate as ...

M   spouting like ...

N   as cold-hearted as ...

Task Two

Now have a go at creating some similes of your own, either in the format of 'as ... as ...' or 'like the ...' / 'like a ...'.

Make sure that you capture the essential quality of the characters chosen in the similes created.

> Let your imagination go!
> You can afford to be
> AS MAD AS A HATTER!

Teaching Notes

Similes are one of several interesting forms of speech. They brighten up writing and make reading more interesting. In 'As Mad as a Hatter' they are linked particularly to children's books.

Key Elements
- wordplay
- children's literature
- understanding essential characteristics
- use of the imagination
- word humour.

Contexts
'As Mad as a Hatter' can be used in a variety of ways:
- as part of a normal lesson when differentiation by outcome will apply
- for homework
- as an enrichment activity for those ahead on normal work
- as extension work during lessons on vocabulary
- as a differentiated homework
- as an activity during an enrichment session, day, weekend or summer school, especially concerning reading
- as an activity for the school Book Club or Society
- as an open-access competition.

Some Answers

Task One
There are a number of possibilities but ones that spring readily to mind are:

A Snape (potions master in the Harry Potter series)
B Scrooge
C Harry Potter
D The weasels (*Wind in the Willows*)
E The Cheshire Cat
F Peter Rabbit
G Thomas the Tank Engine
H Aslan (Narnia books – a play on 'as brave as a lion')
I Charlotte
J Miss Trunchbull (*Matilda*) OR The Demon Headmaster
K Pinocchio
L The Baudelaire orphans (Lemony Snicket books)
M Moby Dick
N The White Witch (Narnia)

Task Two
All sorts of examples might be written. The choice will reflect the children's favourite books and characters. The more successful examples will be those which illustrate a key characteristic.

Charades

Teaching Notes

There is no pupil sheet.

Rules

1   Each team takes it in turns to be given a book title which they have to guess. One member of the team is given the title and the other members of the team have to work out the title from the mime. The other teams watch but say nothing, as they will be given one guess at the title if the team fails to guess correctly, and they will gain a bonus mark.

2   The person miming must not speak or mouth the word; they can nod or point when a team member guesses correctly.

3   There will be a time limit of two minutes for each question.

Conventions

1   Number of words in the title – hold up correct number of fingers.

2   First word – hold up one finger (two fingers for second word and so on).

3   Syllables in a word – fingers with correct number resting on arm.

4   Sounds like – hold ear.

5   The whole word/title can be done at once if it is sensible to do so.

Titles

Team	First title	Second title
1	The Sword in the Stone	The Very Hungry Caterpillar
2	The Secret Garden	The Tale of Two Bad Mice
3	The Borrowers Afloat	The Worst Witch
4	The Scarecrows	The Rainbow Fish
5	The Demon Headmaster	Fantastic Mr Fox

Alternatives/Additional Titles

The Goalkeeper's Revenge
Goodnight, Mister Tom
The Lord of the Rings
Box of Delights
Charm School
Where the Wild Things Are

The Adventures Of Captain Underpants
The Toilet of Doom
The Illustrated Mum
The Silver Sword
Noughts and Crosses

Given above is one particular format. The rules and the titles can be changed as the teacher wishes; for example, the number of teams may vary.

Puzzle Book

One: Animal Characters

Who created:

a   Mr Toad

b   Timmy

c   The Cheshire Cat

d   Fiver

e   The Hodgeheg

f   Tarka the Otter

g   The Hundred and One Dalmatians

h   Blitzcat

i   Jemima Puddleduck

j   Esio Trot

Two: Take it as Red

a   Which famous character from a traditional fairy story might have 'wolfed down' her dinner (or vice versa)?

b   Which Cheshire-based author wrote *Red Shift* as well as *The Weirdstone of Brisingamen*?

c   Which coloured obstacle failed to prevent Brian Jacques from going on to write a successful series?

d   Which of Robin Hood's Merry Men liked this colour?

e   Which children prevented an accident by using their red flannel petticoats?

Three: Things that go Bump in the Night

a   Which long-running series is R. L. Stine responsible for (that fits closely with the title)?

b   Who was visited by the past, present and future at Christmas?

c   How is Jill Murphy's character Mildred Hubble better known?

d   Which Thomas was a 'Lively' ghost?

e   At the time when Cinderella was fleeing where was Philippa Pearce's Tom?

Four: Roald Dahl Wordsearch

Find all of the words associated with Roald Dahl books, for example titles or characters.

X	R	C	M	A	T	I	L	D	A	R	R	Q
O	E	H	E	S	H	D	E	I	H	P	O	S
F	V	A	D	T	E	Z	N	A	E	B	X	V
R	O	R	I	S	T	F	I	N	O	U	R	B
M	L	L	C	A	W	X	A	G	L	N	N	L
C	T	I	I	E	I	F	G	S	M	C	I	A
I	I	E	N	B	T	I	B	O	Y	E	T	K
T	N	Q	E	Y	S	Z	L	L	S	T	N	E
S	G	R	R	T	C	P	X	Y	L	L	E	P
A	R	E	G	R	O	E	G	N	V	W	U	E
T	H	E	M	I	N	P	I	N	S	A	Q	A
N	Y	G	H	D	G	H	J	A	M	E	S	C
A	M	T	H	E	B	F	G	D	F	R	N	H
F	E	P	R	O	L	O	S	G	N	I	O	G
Z	S	W	I	L	L	Y	W	O	N	K	A	Z

Five:

Transports of delight

a   What transport did Harry Potter and his friends use to play Quidditch?

b   Which 'airborne' transport accompanied E. Nesbit's Phoenix?

c   Which live transport rescued Bilbo, Gandalf and the Dwarves from the Wargs in *The Hobbit*?

d   Which transport did the Reverend W. Audrey especially get steamed up about?

e   How did Caspian, Reepicheep, Lucy, Edmund and Eustace get to the end of the world in C. S. Lewis' book?

Six: Where?

a   Where was Humpty Dumpty before his fall?

b   Where did Jim Hawkins and Long John Silver go to?

c   Where did Lucy meet Aslan?

d   Where did Charlie's Golden Ticket take him to?

e   Where did Richard Adams' rabbits flee to for safety?

Seven: Classics

a Who had a round table?

b Whose stories were 'Just So'?

c Where did Jules Verne's journey go to?

d Which Mary Shelley book turned out a monster?

e Who went through the looking glass?

Eight: Confused Characters

(Anagrams)

a HAT GLUE IS EXTRA (7, 3, 4: a French character)

b GRADE POT AND BIN (10, 4: an animal character)

c TROD TO COLD TILE (6, 8: an animal lover)

d LIVE PRAWN INK (3, 3, 6: a sleeping character)

e LENT BLUE CAR (5, 6: science is fun with him)

Nine: Cryptic Titles

a J. M. Barrie's boy is a cooking vessel falling away in volume (5, 3)

b Mary Norton's tiny people are always asking for a cup of sugar! (3, 9)

c Helen Cresswell rings up a satellite of the earth (8)

d Dick King-Smith's flock keep attached to their bacon (3, 5-3)

e Anna Sewell's dark and attractive quadruped (5, 6)

Ten: Cryptic Pictures

a A seagoing character (7, 7)

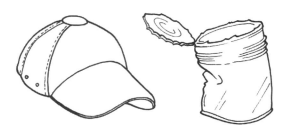  

b A fairy-tale character (3, 8, 6)

c A character who is also the title of a book (3, 7)

d A book title, the second of three (7)

e A character who is also the title of a book (3, 6, 9)

Enrichment Activities for Able and Talented Children © Barry Teare (Network Educational Press, 2004)

Teaching Notes

Answers

One
a Kenneth Grahame
b Enid Blyton
c Lewis Carroll
d Richard Adams
e Dick King-Smith
f Henry Williamson
g Dodie Smith
h Robert Westall
i Beatrix Potter
j Roald Dahl

Two
a Little Red Riding Hood
b Alan Garner
c Redwall
d Will Scarlett
e The Railway Children

Three
a Goosebumps
b Ebenezer Scrooge
c The Worst Witch
d Thomas Kempe
e Midnight Garden

Four
1 *Fantastic Mr Fox*
2 *Revolting Rhymes*
3 Charlie
4 Medicine
5 *Matilda*
6 *Dirty Beasts*
7 *The Twits*
8 Danny
9 Boggis
10 Bean
11 Bunce
12 Quentin
13 Blake
14 Peach
15 Sophie
16 Boy
17 Pelly
18 George
19 *The Minpins*
20 James
21 *The BFG*
22 *Going Solo*
23 Willy Wonka

Five
a Broomstick
b Carpet
c Eagles
d Thomas the Tank Engine
e The Dawn Treader

Six
a On the wall
b Treasure Island
c Narnia
d The Chocolate Factory
e Watership Down

Seven
a King Arthur
b Rudyard Kipling
c The centre of the Earth
d *Frankenstein*
e Alice

Eight
a Asterix The Gaul
b Paddington Bear
c Doctor Dolittle
d Rip Van Winkle
e Uncle Albert

Nine
a *Peter Pan*
b *The Borrowers*
c *Moondial*
d *The Sheep-Pig*
e *Black Beauty*

Ten
a Captain Pugwash
b The Sleeping Beauty
c The Snowman
d *Diggers*
e The Stinky Cheeseman

1 The activity can be shortened by cutting down the sections.
2 Content can be changed if the teacher wishes.
3 Individual items can be used separately in the classroom or for homework.

FOLLOW THE YELLOW BRICK ROAD

You are going on a long journey.

This journey will take you through many imaginary and far-off lands.

Along the way you will see objects that are important in children's literature.

You will meet some very interesting characters.

How well will you, and your travelling companions, deal with the challenges along the winding way?

Your Tasks

1 In small teams you will be sent off in different directions to discover 25 literary locations. Find all of the 25 places.

2 At each location look at the object that is placed there. Close to the object there is a card with a number of questions relating to the object and what it represents in children's literature. Try to work out the answers to the questions on the card.

3 Write your answers, with the correct number, on a piece of paper with your team name on it.

Practical Pieces of Advice

1 You can visit the places in any order as long as you write the correct number against the answer.

2 Work as a team and talk to each other, but remember other travellers might be nearby so don't give away valuable information by speaking too loudly!

3 If in doubt, have a go! You can't score points for unanswered questions.

4 Nobody is going to get all the answers. How many points can you and your travelling companions amass?

Teaching Notes

This is a fun activity that children really enjoy. It involves moving about, which gives a contrast to paper-and-pen exercises. The objects are scattered in a random order. It is sensible for them to be placed where nothing has to be moved or opened. However, they should not all be 'in open view'. The more space available the better, as this allows teams to operate away from each other, and gives a real impression of a treasure hunt. If good weather is guaranteed, an outdoor treasure hunt can be organized.

This activity needs to be set up, during the course and before the event. To make this possible, it is a good idea that a different area, not in view of the children, is used for the treasure hunt; it is more exciting if several areas can be used.

An event like this is aimed at children who have a reasonable knowledge of books. However 100 per cent is not the objective. Often individual members of a team will have differing likes and experiences, so all can contribute. As well as knowledge, three other factors contribute to success:

1   Teams who collaborate together and do not operate as individuals.
2   Keeping going – concentration and persistence are very important elements.
3   Piecing things together – points often result from intuitive thinking and intelligent speculation rather than always coming from exact knowledge.

Preparation Before the Event

The questions, with their number, need to be written on cards to be placed next to the relevant objects or pictures. The objects or pictures need to be assembled. Objects are more exciting and most are easy to acquire but, if hard to find, pictures can be used instead. Occasionally you may wish to replace one section with another.

THE TREASURE HUNT

For each of the 25 locations, the physical object is described; the questions to write on cards are listed, together with the answers.

	Object and Questions	Answers
1	**Black Spot (a small circle of paper, coloured black)**	
a	Who received this?	The old sea captain
b	Who delivered it?	The blind man, Pew
c	Where?	The Admiral Benbow Inn
d	What immediately happened to the receiver?	He collapsed and died
2	**Honey Pot (an ordinary jar of honey, or a 'grander' pot, as seen in the book)**	
a	Not Winnie-the-Pooh's but part of the cargo of a bird and an animal. Whose?	The Owl and the Pussycat
b	What was the colour of their conveyance?	Pea-green
c	What purchase did they make from a pig?	A ring
d	At what cost?	One shilling
3	**Noddy in his Car (this is a specific small toy. An alternative would be a picture stuck on card)**	
a	Where would you be if you saw this character in his car?	Toytown
b	Who is the driver?	Noddy
c	Who created him?	Enid Blyton
d	Who was the local policeman?	Mr Plod
e	What was the outstanding feature of his best friend?	Big ears

	Object and Questions	Answers
4	**Footprints (two footprints cut out of paper or card)**	
a	Why was Robinson Crusoe frightened when he saw these in the sand?	He had thought he was alone on the island and he did not know who had made them
b	Who was the author of the book?	Daniel Defoe
c	What day of the week is it, Man?	Friday
5	**Queen of Hearts (the Queen of hearts playing card)**	
a	Which famous character does this card represent?	The Queen of Hearts
b	What did she say should be the punishment for anyone who annoyed her?	'Off with their heads!'
c	Who did Alice follow to get to Wonderland?	The White Rabbit
d	Where was it difficult for Alice to get a cup of tea?	The Mad Hatter's Tea Party
6	**Peter Rabbit (a model, toy or a picture stuck on card)**	
a	Who is this character?	Peter Rabbit
b	Name three other characters created by the same author.	Tom Kitten, Mr Tod, Jeremy Fisher, and so on
c	Why was Mr McGregor feared by this character?	Mr McGregor killed Peter Rabbit's father and then chased him as he went into the garden
7	**Winnie-the-Pooh (the toy is best but a picture on card is an alternative)**	
a	Who is this?	Winnie-the-Pooh
b	Who did he belong to?	Christopher Robin
c	How did this character describe his intelligence?	'A Bear of No Brain at All', 'Silly Old Bear', 'A Bear of Very Little Brain'
d	Which of his friends had a detachable tail?	Eeyore
e	Who had too much bounce?	Tigger
8	**Pig (a small toy pig, painted black BUT leaving a pink/white patch around the buttocks)**	
a	This is a pig made famous by Dick King-Smith; he gets his name from where his pink patch is located. What is his name?	Saddlebottom
b	Why did this make his mother disown him?	She was ashamed. His mark was not in the correct place – it should have been on his back, to make him a Saddleback.
c	In which career did the pig become famous?	The Army
d	In which book for adults by George Orwell did the pigs become rulers?	*Animal Farm*
9	**Snowman (the toy is available as is a cake decoration)**	
a	Who wrote the picture book classic with this character as the title?	Raymond Briggs
b	The snowman takes a boy on a wondrous flight. Who do they visit (the title of another book by the same author)?	Father Christmas
c	What does *The Snowman* not have as a book?	Words
10	**Rabbit (any model rabbit, big or small. A picture is an alternative)**	
a	What would it be made of if it was in the story by Margery Williams?	Velveteen
b	What colour would it be, according to Judith Kerr, if it had been stolen by Hitler?	Pink
c	Who wrote *The Tale of Benjamin Bunny*?	Beatrix Potter

	Object and Questions	Answers
11	**Witch's Mask (commercial versions are available, especially around Hallowe'en, or make your own)**	
a	What would she be called if she was the creation of Valerie Thomas and Korky Paul, and she owned a long-suffering cat called Wilbur?	Winnie
b	In the story by Ursula Moray Williams, Gobbolino is the witch's …?	Cat
c	Whose witches could be identified because they always wore gloves?	Roald Dahl
12	**Donald Duck/Disney (any object that links in with Disney films)**	
a	Who wrote *The Jungle Book*?	Rudyard Kipling
b	Which boy was the main character?	Mowgli
c	Whose coils could hug prey to death?	Kaa, the snake
d	What was the name of the bear who befriended the boy?	Baloo
13	**Carol Book (a book containing carols. Most schools will have one)**	
a	Who wrote the story?	Charles Dickens
b	Who was the dead partner who returned as a ghost with a warning and a long chain?	Jacob Marley
c	Where was the story set?	London
d	Which small boy ends up by having an unexpectedly good Christmas?	Tiny Tim
14	**Wings (homemade – cut out of card or paper)**	
a	This is the third title of a trilogy by which famous author?	Terry Pratchett
b	What are the other two books in the trilogy?	*Truckers, Diggers*
c	Which winged resident of Hundred Acre Wood spelled his name as an anagram of the real word?	Owl, Wol
15	**Don't Panic (cover a book with paper and write DON'T PANIC in large letters on it)**	
a	Who would carry this according to Douglas Adams?	A hitchhiker
b	What 'car' is the hero's best friend?	Ford Prefect
c	What comes to an end at the beginning of the book?	The Earth
16	**Hook (a small hook, available in any hardware shop)**	
a	According to J. M. Barrie what rank does this object hold?	Captain
b	What sound terrifies him?	The ticking of an alarm clock
c	In which book does he appear?	*Peter Pan*
d	Why might the medical profession be interested in the leading character?	He never grows old, he can fly
17	**A trophy or cup labelled 'Champion of the World'**	
a	Who got this title?	Danny
b	Why was he awarded it?	Poaching the most pheasants at one time
c	Where was his home?	A caravan (behind a filling station)
18	**Dish and Spoon (a dish and spoon)**	
a	Which fairy-tale character tried three sizes of these objects before she could bear it no longer?	Goldilocks
b	In which nursery rhyme are these objects named?	'Hey, Diddle Diddle!'
c	In which other nursery rhyme might these objects have been abandoned due to a frightening arachnid?	'Little Miss Muffet'
19	**Silver Buckle and Comb (a comb and silver buckle – or cardboard replica covered in silver foil)**	
a	In a nursery rhyme, where was the buckle and what was the comb used for?	Buckle on his knee; comb for 'combing out his yellow hair'
b	Who used it?	Bobby Shaftoe
c	Where had he gone?	To sea

	Object and Questions	Answers
20	**Secret Seven Badge (a circular badge, paper stuck on, with the initials SS printed on it)**	
a	Whose is this badge?	A member of the Secret Seven
b	Where was the normal meeting place?	The shed
c	Name three of the members	Barbara, Colin, George, Jack, Janet, Pam, Peter
21	**Bean Seeds (runner bean seeds are ideal)**	
a	In which story was this the price of a cow?	'Jack and the Beanstalk'
b	Who came down to catch the main character?	The Giant
c	What did the main character steal?	The chicken that laid golden eggs
d	How did the main character know that he had been detected?	The Giant sang, 'Fee, Fie, Foe, Fum, I smell the blood of an Englishman'
22	**A Giant Object (for example, a very large pen; it needs to be well above real-life size)**	
a	Name any three characters or sets of characters in children's literature who would see this object at this scale.	Mike Teevee in *Charlie and The Chocolate Factory*, Alice when shrunken, The Borrowers, Jack in the Giant's castle, Sophie with the BFG, Lilliputians in *Gulliver's Travels* and so on
23	**Dancing Men Message (homemade on paper from Sir Arthur Conan Doyle's story 'The Dancing Men' in *The Return Of Sherlock Holmes* – an approximation will suffice)**	
a	Who is the detective?	Sherlock Holmes
b	Which medical friend recorded his cases?	Doctor Watson
c	Where did he live?	221B Baker Street
d	Who was his arch-enemy?	Moriarty
e	Where was he 'presumed dead'?	Reichenbach Falls
24	**Lion (a model, toy or a picture)**	
a	What object and person have to be added to make the title of a book by C. S. Lewis?	The Witch and The Wardrobe
b	What is this creature's name in that book?	Aslan
c	How did the children first reach the kingdom of this creature?	Through the back of the wardrobe
25	**Cat (any model or toy cat)**	
a	Which cat is named after a Cornish fishing village?	The Mousehole Cat
b	Which solitary cat was described by Rudyard Kipling?	'The Cat that Walked by Himself'
c	Which cat was the first title in Robin Jarvis' *Deptford Trilogy*?	*The Alchymist's Cat*

Enrichment Activities for Able and Talented Children © Barry Teare (Network Educational Press, 2004)

to Begin at the Beginning

'Are you sitting comfortably? Good! Then I'll begin. I am going to read you a story – or more accurately the start of several stories. So, to begin at the beginning ...

Your Task

1 Read the short extracts given below.

2 In your groups try to work out which books are started by the lines in the extracts and who the authors are.

the Beginnings

BOOK 1 'Alice was beginning to get very tired of sitting by her sister on the bank and of having nothing to do: once or twice she had peeped into the book her sister was reading, but it had no pictures or conversations in it, "and what is the use of a book", thought Alice, "without pictures or conversations?"'

BOOK 2 'It was Mrs May who first told me about them.'

BOOK 3 'The mole had been working very hard all the morning, spring-cleaning his little home.'

BOOK 4 'When a mouse is born he has to fight to survive.'

BOOK 5 'Mr and Mrs Dursley, of number four, Privet Drive, were proud to say that they were perfectly normal, thank you very much.'

BOOK 6 'If, standing alone on the back doorstep, Tom allowed himself to weep tears, they were tears of anger.'

BOOK 7 'Not long ago, there lived in London a young married couple of Dalmatian dogs named Pongo and Missis Pongo.'

BOOK 8 'Lyra and her daemon moved through the darkening Hall, taking care to keep to one side, out of sight of the kitchen.'

BOOK 9 'Until he was four years old, James Henry Trotter had a happy life.'

BOOK 10 'It was seven o' clock of a very warm evening in the Seeonee hills when Father Wolf woke up from his day's rest, scratched himself, yawned and spread out his paws one after the other to get rid of the sleepy feeling in their tips.'

Tournament: Bookworm

almost anonymous authors

How good is your knowledge of children's literature?

Can you identify the 15 authors below from the cryptic clues?

In all cases cryptic references are to the surnames (spellings may sometimes vary).

Your Task

Identify the 15 authors and explain in as much detail as you can what the clues mean.

1   A former Prime Minister and Jacqueline make a great 'double act'.

2   A religious symbol makes the wicked leader of the school angry.

3   Looking in the mirror shows how singing this at Christmas creates wonder in the land.

4   Exercise on the river and a fish or heather produces a young wizard with clay.

5   A kidnap demand leads to birds that herald the summer and jungles in Brazil.

6   Robert's compass point followed by everything could lead to the scarecrows.

7   The maker of barrels stops work because she cannot see as the dark is rising.

8   An important participant in a cricket match sees a river boy in the shadows.

9   A chain of hotels is linked to Whitby, Deptford and Hagwood.

10   An author whose name is made up from a green component of salad and a supply of water wrote a saga about a family where one child, Jack, was anything but ordinary.

11   Everything will be OK so long as you don't write really badly.

12   She makes a hole in the paper and penetrates the dark as the clock strikes 12 in the garden.

13   An old-fashioned railway carriage reverses 'to push a woman' under northern lights.

14   This hyphenated author, whose name is a mixture of royal and common, is an ace at creating mixed-up pigs and hedgehogs.

15   Cheating is an abomination.

Extension Task

Create some clues of your own to other 'almost anonymous authors' from children's literature.

contents page

Teaching Notes

There is no pupil sheet.

To be Read Out

"In a book, the contents page lists what is included. Here 'Contents Page' refers to four clues to help you identify the book. Divide your sheet of paper into four columns with the numbers one, two, three and four at the top of the columns.

After each clue is read out, write down what you think the book is to which it refers. You must write in column one after clue one, column two after clue two and so on. If you have no idea, put a cross in the appropriate column. You can change your mind by writing the name of a different book in a later column. This is very likely to happen as you get more information. Sometimes the first clue is vague and could lead you in many directions.

The scoring system is as follows. For the column in which you get the correct title for the first time, you score four points if it is in column one, three points if it is in column two, two points if it is in column three and one point if it is in column four. This reflects that it is less difficult to identify the book as you get more information."

the clues

Book	Column One	Column Two	Column Three	Column Four
1	The Admiral Benbow Inn	Dr Livesey	The Hispaniola	Long John Silver
2	Riddles	'There and Back Again'	The Lonely Mountain	Smaug the dragon
3	Fly	A 'Large White'	Farmer Hogget	'Good pig'
4	Meetings	Badges	Scamper	Their first case
5	Golden House	Stephen Tyler	Spot the dog	Meeting a magician
6	Grandpa Joe	The Oompa-Loompas	Golden Tickets	Willie Wonka
7	The open road	The washerwoman	Poop-poop	The Chief Weasel
8	Class 4C	The Science Fair	Parenting	Bags of flour
9	Meanness	Ghosts	Jacob Marley	Tiny Tim
10	A broken-down garage	27 and 53	Brown ale	Wings

Tournament: Bookworm

Reading age

Below there are 12 well-known children's books that were written over a considerable period of time.

They have been listed in alphabetical order of authors.

Your Task

Rewrite the list in chronological order of initial publication date, starting with the earliest and finishing with the most recent.

Do you know their 'reading age'?

---

the twelve books

Enid Blyton	*The Secret Seven*
Betsy Byars	*The Midnight Fox*
Roald Dahl	*Fantastic Mr Fox*
Anne Fine	*How to Write Really Badly*
Alan Garner	*The Weirdstone of Brisingamen*
Brian Jacques	*Redwall*
C. S. Lewis	*The Magician's Nephew*
A. A. Milne	*Winnie-the-Pooh*
E. Nesbit	*The Railway Children*
J. K. Rowling	*Harry Potter and the Goblet of Fire*
Robert Louis Stevenson	*Kidnapped*
E. B. White	*Charlotte's Web*

---

camouflaged characters

Hidden messages, double meanings and puzzling people bring mystery and intrigue to many books. The passage below, on the surface at least, describes in very ordinary terms the features of a family home. Beneath the surface lurk 20 'camouflaged characters' from children's literature.

Your Tasks
Remove the camouflage and identify the 20 characters. Write down who they are and the books in which they appear. Try to go a stage further by naming the authors.

Be a literary detective and unmask the camouflaged characters!

notes
1 The characters are normally only referred to by part of their name.
2 No character is named twice.
3 The spelling of the character's name may be different to that used in the passage but the sound will be the same.
4 More than one character from the same book may appear.
5 Some characters will be more obvious than others.

examples (not in the passage)
1 'You have done really well here. Fantastic, mister!' The full camouflaged character is Fantastic Mr Fox.
2 'The animal began to scamper around the cage.' Scamper is the dog in the Secret Seven stories.

the passage

We can learn a great deal about people from their homes. The Browns have a neat and tidy kitchen. There is a storage area for mugs and on each hook there is a beaker. It is unusual to see a pan left out on the top of the kitchen stove. Modern materials have been used to make cleaning easy and quick to do. The cooking area has a hood that directs steam and smells out of the kitchen and through a vent to the outside.

The bathroom has been designed to give space for toiletries and items regularly in use such as a bath sponge, soap and deodorants. The tiles on the walls are dominated by two colours – green and hazel. Diamond-shaped windows give a striking appearance to the outside wall.

There is one room that is unlike the others in that it looks more homely and lived-in. This is the study used by Uncle Albert and referred to fondly as 'the den'. He likes to potter here at weekends and gets rather ratty if the family do not leave him in peace, but instead badger him. On the table lies a reminder of one of the uses of the room – a playing card, the Queen of hearts. One of the children, Charlotte, enjoys painting and one of her better efforts is framed on the wall – a robin sitting on an overturned bucket. The family particularly likes 'the den' at night when the moon shines through a side window, putting an eerie light onto framed photographs including those of their previous homes in Paddington and Cheshire. Cat and dog photographs remind the family of much-loved pets now dead.

Extension Task
Construct a passage of your own that hides other 'camouflaged characters' from children's books.

Teaching Notes

Five rounds are used in this version of the tournament. They can be split up and used as separate activities for other situations. They can also be mixed and matched with other activities and resources both in this section and in the English section.

Tournaments certainly produce excitement and drama. Children have responded very positively to them. It is a case where 'the sum is greater than the parts'.

Round One: 'To Begin at the Beginning'

1   The pupil sheet assumes that teams will read the extracts. However, in a tournament another approach is taken. The extracts are read out twice, the teams confer (quietly, so that other teams cannot hear) and then record their answers.

2   Particular books have been used here but any number of different ones could be substituted. Some are more obvious than others. As well as knowledge, deduction and inference are important factors.

The Answers

Book   1   *Alice's Adventures in Wonderland,* Lewis Carroll
Book   2   *The Borrowers,* Mary Norton
Book   3   *The Wind in the Willows*, Kenneth Grahame
Book   4   *The Dark Portal,* Robin Jarvis (Book I of *The Deptford Trilogy*)
Book   5   *Harry Potter and the Philosopher's Stone,* J. K. Rowling
Book   6   *Tom's Midnight Garden*, Philippa Pearce
Book   7   *The Hundred and One Dalmatians*, Dodie Smith
Book   8   *Northern Lights*, Philip Pullman
Book   9   *James and the Giant Peach,* Roald Dahl
Book 10   *The Jungle Book*, Rudyard Kipling

Round Two: 'Almost Anonymous Authors'

'Almost Anonymous Authors' combines knowledge of children's literature with the interpretation of cryptic clues. It is likely to appeal particularly to children who love reading.

Key Elements

❖   wordplay

❖   children's literature

❖   interpretation of cryptic clues

❖   research (some authors are more difficult than others to identify)

❖   creativity and imagination (in the extension task).

Contexts

'Almost Anonymous Authors' can be used in a number of ways:

❖   as an open-access competition (the extension task would act as a discriminator, if required)

❖   as extension material to work on literature

❖   as an enrichment activity for those ahead on other tasks

❖   as an activity during an enrichment session, cluster day or summer school

❖   as differentiated homework

❖   as an activity for the English Club or Society, or Book Club

❖   as part of a tournament.

Answers

Credit should be given not only for identifying the author but also for the amount of detail which shows an understanding of the references included in the cryptic clues.

1 Jacqueline Wilson
- **a** Her first name is given.
- **b** Harold Wilson is the former Prime Minister.
- **c** *Double Act* is the name of one of her books.

2 Gillian Cross
- **a** A cross is a religious symbol.
- **b** The second part of the clue refers to one of her books, *The Demon Headmaster*.
- **c** Cross also means angry.

3 Lewis Carroll
- **a** One of his famous books is *Alice Through the Looking Glass*.
- **b** A carol would be sung at Christmas.
- **c** *Alice's Adventures in Wonderland* is his most famous work.

4 J. K. Rowling
- **a** 'Exercise on the river' is 'row' and a ling is a member of the cod family or another name for heather.
- **b** Harry Potter is the young wizard with clay.

5 Arthur Ransome
- **a** A kidnap demand asks for a ransom or sum of money.
- **b** Birds that herald the summer are swallows.
- **c** Jungles in Brazil could be Amazons.
- **d** Arthur Ransome wrote *Swallows and Amazons*.

6 Robert Westall
- **a** One of the compass points is 'west'.
- **b** 'Everything' can be expressed as 'all'.
- **c** The Robert described is therefore Westall.
- **d** *The Scarecrows* is one of Robert Westall's books.

7 Susan Cooper
- **a** The maker of barrels is known as a cooper.
- **b** *The Dark is Rising* is Susan Cooper's great series.

8 Tim Bowler
- **a** An important participant in a cricket match is the bowler.
- **b** *River Boy* and *Shadows* are among the books written by Tim Bowler.

9 Robin Jarvis
- **a** Jarvis run a chain of hotels.
- **b** Whitby refers to *The Whitby Witches*.
- **c** Deptford refers to the *Deptford Mice Trilogy*.
- **d** Hagwood refers to *Thorn Ogres of Hagwood*.

10 Helen Cresswell
- **a** A green component of salad is cress.
- **b** A well provides one source of water.
- **c** The saga is about the Bagthorpe family and the first book was named after one of the children, *Ordinary Jack*.

11 Anne Fine
- **a** OK could be interpreted as 'fine'.
- **b** One of Anne Fine's books is *How To Write Really Badly*.

12 Philippa Pearce
- **a** Making a hole in a piece of paper could be said to pierce it.
- **b** An alternative meaning of 'pierce' is to penetrate the dark.
- **c** 'As the clock strikes 12 in the garden' refers to one of Philippa Pearce's famous books, *Tom's Midnight Garden*.

13 Philip Pullman
- **a** An old-fashioned railway carriage is a 'Pullman'.
- **b** Reverses 'to push a woman' would lead to 'pull a man'.
- **c** *Northern Lights* is the first of Philip Pullman's trilogy *His Dark Materials*.

14 Dick King-Smith
- **a** King is royal but Smith is a common name.
- **b** *Ace* is one of Dick King-Smith's books.
- **c** Two other books are *The Sheep-Pig* (Babe) and *The Hodgeheg*.

15 Robert Swindells
- **a** To cheat is to swindle.
- **b** *Abomination* is a book written by Robert Swindells.

Extension Task

Pupils have the opportunity to describe authors of their own choice through cryptic clues. Their suggestions can be judged on the basis of:

1 The suitability of the choices that allow wordplay.
2 The quality of the wordplay employed in the cryptic clues.
3 Knowledge of the author's work used in the clues.

Round three: 'contents page'

It is really important that the answers are placed in the correct columns or that a cross is entered if no answer is forthcoming. Otherwise teams get more points than they are entitled to.

Answers

Book 1	*Treasure Island*, Robert Louis Stevenson
Book 2	*The Hobbit*, J. R. R. Tolkien
Book 3	*The Sheep-Pig* (Babe), Dick King-Smith
Book 4	*The Secret Seven*, Enid Blyton
Book 5	*The Steps up the Chimney* (The Magician's House I), William Corlett
Book 6	*Charlie and the Chocolate Factory*, Roald Dahl
Book 7	*The Wind in the Willows*, Kenneth Grahame
Book 8	*Flour Babies*, Ann Fine
Book 9	*A Christmas Carol*, Charles Dickens
Book 10	*Skellig*, David Almond

This is a good example of exemplar material. If the particular books don't fit your purpose use the same technique with different titles.

Round four: Reading age

Deduction, inference and chronology play a part in this exercise. Looking for the clues supplements knowledge.

Answers

1	1886	Robert Louis Stevenson	*Kidnapped*
2	1906	E. Nesbit	*The Railway Children*
3	1926	A. A. Milne	*Winnie-the-Pooh*
4	1949	Enid Blyton	*The Secret Seven*
5	1952	E. B. White	*Charlotte's Web*
6	1955	C. S. Lewis	*The Magician's Nephew*
7	1960	Alan Garner	*The Weirdstone of Brisingamen*
8	1968	Betsy Byars	*The Midnight Fox*
9	1970	Roald Dahl	*Fantastic Mr Fox*
10	1986	Brian Jacques	*Redwall*
11	1996	Anne Fine	*How to Write Really Badly*
12	2000	J. K. Rowling	*Harry Potter and the Goblet of Fire*

Round five: camouflaged characters

'Camouflaged Characters' provides an enjoyable piece of work, especially for those who love books. A number of thinking skills are involved.

Key Elements

- ❖ children's literature
- ❖ wordplay
- ❖ analysis of text
- ❖ deduction and inference
- ❖ word humour
- ❖ research, creativity, ingenuity and imagination (in the extension task).

Contexts

'Camouflaged Characters' can be used in the following ways:

- ❖ as differentiated homework
- ❖ as enrichment work for those who have completed other tasks
- ❖ as an extension to work on literature
- ❖ as an open-access competition (the extension task would provide a discriminator, if required)
- ❖ as an activity for the English Club or Society, or Book Club
- ❖ as part of a tournament in an enrichment session.

Methods of Working

1 Verbal delivery

The teacher reads out the passage once or twice. The children work individually, in pairs or in small teams. If the third option is used, the teams need a short time to discuss their views and produce a joint answer.

2 Reading delivery

In this method, the passages are given out in a written format. Again, the work can be done individually, in pairs or in small teams. This version is less difficult as the ability to reread the passage is a considerable advantage. The reading delivery could be used after pupils have listened to a preliminary hearing.

Extension Task

This optional activity opens up a new range of challenges. It is not easy to write such a passage. The success criteria for judging children's passages are likely to include:

- ❖ the number of characters included in a reasonable length
- ❖ the ingenuity displayed in hiding the characters
- ❖ the quality of the writing
- ❖ the overall flow and sense maintained in the passage.

Additional parameters can be added by the teacher:

- ❖ the subject of the passage could be named
- ❖ the characters must come from at least six different genres.

Answer

The 20 'intended' characters have been highlighted in the teachers' version of the passage. Children might identify other valid characters that were not deliberately included. In such cases, credit should be given if the children provide adequate proof.

The Passage

We can learn a great deal about people from their **homes** (1). The **Browns** (2) have a neat and tidy kitchen. There is a storage area for mugs and on each **hook** (3) there is a **beaker** (4). It is unusual to see a **pan** (5) left out on the top of the kitchen stove. Modern materials have been used to make cleaning easy and quick to do. The cooking area has a **hood** (6) that directs steam and smells out of the kitchen and through a vent to the outside.

The bathroom has been designed to give space for toiletries and items regularly in use such as a bath **sponge** (7), soap and deodorants. The tiles on the walls are dominated by two colours – green and **hazel** (8). **Diamond** (9)-shaped windows give a striking appearance to the outside wall.

There is one room that is unlike the others in that it looks more homely and lived-in. This is the study used by **Uncle Albert** (10) and referred to fondly as 'the den'. He likes to **potter** (11) here at weekends and gets rather **ratty** (12) if the family do not leave him in peace, but instead **badger** (13) him. On the table lies a reminder of one of the uses of the room – a playing card, the **Queen of hearts** (14). One of the children, **Charlotte** (15), enjoys painting and one of her better efforts is framed on the wall – a **robin** (16) sitting on an overturned **bucket** (17). The family particularly likes 'the den' at night when the **moon** (18) shines through a side window, putting an eerie light onto framed photographs including those of their previous homes in **Paddington** (19) and **Cheshire**. **Cat** (20) and dog photographs remind the family of much-loved pets now dead.

The Full Details

1 This is a homophone. Sir Arthur Conan Doyle's Sherlock Holmes is the character and various books can be quoted, including *The Hound of the Baskervilles*.

2 The Browns are the long-suffering family of *Just William*, the brainchild of Richmal Crompton.

3 Captain Hook appears in J. M. Barrie's *Peter Pan*.

4 Tracy Beaker is one of Jacqueline Wilson's most famous creations. She is the main character of *The Story Of Tracy Beaker* and *The Dare Game*.

5 Here is the title figure of the book referred to in answer 3, *Peter Pan*.

6 Robin Hood is a legendary figure who has entered children's literature through the work of several authors, including Roger Lancelyn Green.

7 Sponge is one of the two beastly aunts who make James' life a misery in Roald Dahl's *James and the Giant Peach*.

8 Hazel is one of the rabbits in *Watership Down* written by Richard Adams.

9 Tim Diamond is 'the worst detective in the world' in Anthony Horowitz's hilarious books *The Falcon's Malteser, South by South East* and *Public Enemy Number Two*.

10 Uncle Albert features in a series of science books. The author is Russell Stannard.

11 Harry Potter stars in the series bearing his name and written by J. K. Rowling.

12 Ratty is one of the wonderful animal characters in Kenneth Grahame's classic *The Wind in the Willows*.

13 Badger can be placed in the book immediately above (answer 12), or there are alternatives such as Susan Varley's *Badger's Parting Gifts* or *Badger on the Barge* by Janni Howker.

14 The Queen of Hearts is one of the many eccentric characters in Lewis Carroll's *Alice's Adventures in Wonderland*.

15 Charlotte could be the central character of *Charlotte Sometimes* by Penelope Farmer or of *Charlotte's Web* by E. B. White.

16 Christopher Robin is the famous and much-loved boy in A. A. Milne's *Winnie-the-Pooh* series.

17 Charlie Bucket is the delightful hero of *Charlie and the Chocolate Factory* by Roald Dahl.

18 *Here Comes Charlie Moon* is written by Shirley Hughes.

19 Paddington Bear delights in a number of books by Michael Bond.

20 The Cheshire Cat grinned his way through Lewis Carroll's *Alice's Adventures in Wonderland*.

Drama at your Fingertips

Teaching Notes

There is no pupil sheet for this activity.

The children are divided into groups of three or four. They are given five finger puppets per group. One of these puppets is a 'rogue' figure – it does not fit easily with the other four. The groups make up a storyline that must include all the puppets, including the 'rogue'. A rough script is then prepared. A puppet theatre is provided by the teacher, but the groups design and make their own props and scenery. Each group rehearses their puppet play and then performs it for the other groups. A jury gives a feedback to the groups, based upon success criteria which the groups know at the start of the activity.

What you Will Need

1   A puppet theatre. These are inexpensive to buy from toyshops and they give a 'professional' framework in which to operate. The danger is that without a puppet theatre being available the groups will spend all their time creating one.

2   A number of finger puppets. Sets on a theme, or a story, are available or they can be purchased separately. If sets are used, a 'rogue' puppet has to be added from elsewhere to ensure that an original storyline is developed and not just a retelling of the traditional story.

Examples of the characters are:

	Standard characters	The 'rogue'
A	Goldilocks, The Three Bears	A sunflower
B	Hansel, Gretel, The Witch, The Woodman	A duck
C	King, Queen, Princess, Prince	A crocodile
D	Monkey, Hippopotamus, Lion, Giraffe	A farmyard pig
E	Ladybird, three Flying Insects	A spotty dog
F	Red Riding Hood, Granny, The Wolf, The Wolf dressed as Granny	A black 'Scottie' dog

3   Paper, scissors, card, pens, coloured pencils, paints, sticky tape, paperclips and so on!

The Success Criteria

1   How well the members of the team work together.
2   The extent to which the five puppets, including the 'rogue', are included in the plot.
3   The quality of the storyline.
4   To what degree the 'script' uses wordplay and word humour.
5   The appropriateness of the props and scenery designed and made for the puppet play.
6   The quality of the performance itself.

Many able children have an 'oddball' sense of humour. This activity opens up all sorts of fun possibilities. The 'rogue' puppet is a very important ingredient. In the author's experience, this activity has produced fantastic results: fun, joy, excitement and enormous creativity, flair and imagination!

Mathematics Courses, Activities and Resources

Introduction

Mathematics is the subject that, perhaps above all others, evokes a strong reaction in people. Presented 'properly', mathematics is challenging, exciting, entertaining and hugely enjoyable. It is blessed with an enormous wealth of enrichment materials. Running enrichment courses is, therefore, a good deal easier than in some curriculum areas.

Many parents live in awe of mathematics and see it as a vital ingredient of their child's success. Enrichment courses tend to be oversubscribed. Demand runs at a high level. However, there is often a rather narrow view of mathematics with over-concentration upon computational skills. Mathematics is really more than one subject and children can be very able in some aspects but not in others. The courses, activities and resources presented here try to reflect the width of the subject. They also try to present material through a range of outcomes and avenues, some of them quite unusual.

Possible Titles for Courses
'Mathematics Makes the World Go Round'
'The Sum of the Parts'
'Snakes and Races, Squares and Quotients'
'The Magical Mystery Tour of Maths'
'Marvellous Mathematical Medicine'
'Mathematical Medley'

Part One: Starters, Icebreakers

'The Cornish Pool Piskey'
This novel, light piece (page 129) is an amusing introduction to a course or, of course, it can be used separately.

Fifteen minutes should produce interesting results.

		4	5	6	7	8	9		

Starting a course with such a novel item settles nervous children and persuades them that they are not going to be doing reams of sums.

'One Number, Many Ways'
In a course, this piece (page 131) is best done as a discussion item. It allows everybody to join in and it promotes the notion of alternative, and numerous, answers.

Twenty minutes have been set for the actual task, but allow an extra five minutes introduction and perhaps five minutes per group to present their findings at the end.

| | 3 | 4 | 5 | 6 | 7 | 8 | 9 | + | |

It is helpful, early on, to use an exercise that plays to mental agility and that departs from the notion that there is only one way to reach an answer.

'Mathematical Medley'

A different approach as a starter is to set a series of small, contrasting problems and then allow the pupils to choose the order in which they answer. This forms the basis of 'Mathematical Medley' (page 133).

Collectively the time required is perhaps one hour 15 minutes to one hour 30 minutes, but individually the parts can be used in short time slots.

| | | | 5 | 6 | 7 | 8 | | | |

'The Island of Stool'
CRATC

This piece (page 60) takes up the familiar 'socks and burglars' scenario but applies it to three-legged, four-legged and five-legged people on some fantasy islands.

Some ten minutes is all that is needed for those who understand what is required.

| | | 4 | 5 | 6 | 7 | 8 | | | |

'An Open and Shut Case'
CRATC

This is a quick puzzle (page 56) based upon combinations. The case involved is, indeed, a document case.

Fifteen minutes is sufficient for those who understand the nature of the puzzle.

| | | | 5 | 6 | 7 | 8 | | | |

'In the Balance'
ERATC

The arithmetic involved is easy, but there is a key problem-solving element to be appreciated first. 'In the Balance' (page 118) works well as a group exercise.

The time allowed is variable, given that additional solutions can be sought. Forty minutes, at least, are needed but the work can proceed profitably for some time after that.

| | | 4 | 5 | 6 | 7 | 8 | | | |

Part Two: Logical Thinking

'Is Pythagoras at Home?'

Logical thinking is key to much mathematics. Solving problems through the matrix method adds a subject-based tool. This unusual item (page 138) draws upon the lives of eight famous mathematicians and employs different types of numbers and subject-specific vocabulary. Its fantasy setting will appeal to the particular sense of humour possessed by many able children.

Twenty to 30 minutes might suffice for those who possess the background knowledge, but if research is involved more time would be needed.

				6	7	8	9		

For full explanation of teaching the matrix method, see page 247 in the Detective Section.

'Life is a Lottery for Mathematicians'
CRATC

This is a problem that links logical thinking with mathematical language and simple calculation (page 195). Numbers used in the National Lottery form the core.

Twenty to 30 minutes is the right time for those who work quickly.

			5	6	7	8			

The matrix method can be employed generally, as it is in the Detective Section, or it can involve specific mathematical content. Teaching the matrix method is fully explained on page 247.

'Tsunami Puzzles'

These puzzles originated in Japan. They are extremely suitable for mathematics because they demand clear, logical thinking and are set out in the form of a grid or matrix. Sets of numbers vertically and horizontally are cross-referenced to indicate which squares can be blocked in and, eventually, a picture emerges. Careful and precise working habits are required, but children find them very enjoyable, and they can become addictive!

Books of Tsunami Puzzles can be purchased from W H Smith on a monthly basis or they can be received on subscription from:

British European Associated Publisher Ltd
Stonecroft
69 Station Road
Redhill
Surrey
RH1 1EY

Regular-sized and giant versions are now available. The *Sunday Telegraph* also publishes a large puzzle weekly, under the title 'Griddlers', collections of which are published in book form.

Without previous experience, 20–30 minutes are needed for the small puzzles but the giant versions require closer to two hours.

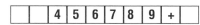

Children writing their own 'Tsunami Puzzles' is an extension activity that really challenges.

Mathematical thinking can be promoted by very unusual materials.

'Riley's Revision Ruse'
CRATC

Codes of all sorts can be considered mathematical, in that something stands for something else which is the basis of algebra. 'Riley's Revision Ruse' (page 72) is a number code based upon a large number of mathematical terms.

Over one hour is needed as there is much data to sort out.

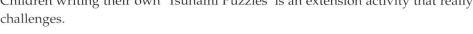

'Mrs Pascal's Proposition'
MERATC

This is a number code based upon simple equations and sets (page 232).

Perhaps 30–40 minutes is about right for this piece.

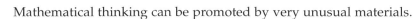

'Can You Spot Them?'

This code is based upon dominoes, mathematical terms and simple calculations (page 160).

Forty-five minutes to one hour is about right but, as with all codes, seeing the correct interpretation is critical.

Part Three: Problem Solving

Problem-solving activities can be practical or in a written format or the subject of discussions.

'Donkey-Work'

This is a variation of a famous Arab mathematicial problem (page 143). It can be tackled individually or as a group discussion.

Fifteen to 20 minutes.

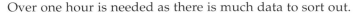

'Lucky Programme'
ERATC

This is another problem-solving activity that can be used for written work or as a discussion: based upon a school fair (page 122).

Ten minutes, specifically, to match the time that the fair organizers had to solve the problem. Allow additional feedback time if the piece has been tackled as a discussion item.

		4	5	6	7	8	9		

'Christmas Draw'

Having left a meeting temporarily, you find yourself in charge of the Christmas Draw. This is a general problem-solving activity that occurs very much in the real world (page 145).

About one hour.

			5	6	7	8	9		

'Watch Carefully'
MERATC

This piece of work involves the months of the year, leap years and simple calculations all within a problem-solving format (page 58).

About one hour.

		4	5	6	7	8			

'Make a Date'
MERATC

Number and spatial awareness are both involved in this piece (page 77) which also produces some practical work where three cubes are formed. A design element is also involved. 'Make a Date' has at its centre a desk calendar.

Thirty-five minutes allows the problem to be solved and the cubes made, but only once the 'trick' has been discovered.

		4	5	6	7	8			

The more that mathematics can be incorporated within non-routine tasks, the better.

Part Four: Vocabulary and Terminology

The 'Cockcroft Report', curriculum guidelines and the numeracy framework all recommend plenty of use of subject-specific language.

'Snakes and Races, Squares and Quotients'
MERATC

This unusual item plays to mathematical vocabulary and a large number of varied operations (page 263). The format is a competition, but on courses it can also be used as a 'running exercise'. A communal board is established and, at various points during the course, 15 or 20 minutes are spent by adding in the entries for a few more spaces. Children really enjoy devising interesting entries for the board.

Completing all 100 spaces requires two hours or more, but this time can be split into shorter periods for group participation. For younger children, or to take up less time, the board can be reduced to 50 spaces or even fewer.

| 3 | 4 | 5 | 6 | 7 | 8 | 9 | + | |

'Five'

Not only mathematics but English and general knowledge are involved in this piece (page 147) that asks how the number five is associated with various words and phrases.

It is worthwhile to link mathematics into a cross-curricular context to prevent its isolation as, in some people's view, a 'dry subject about sums'.

Twenty minutes allows a reasonable attempt, but research into unknown areas adds significantly to this time.

| | | | | 6 | 7 | 8 | 9 | + | |

'A Calculated Risk'
ERATC

This piece (page 108) has been amazingly successful with children on courses, to the point that some have refused a break in an effort to defeat Professor Prism and secure the services of the devious Doctor Decagon. Essentially there are 12 contrasting problems to solve, but the 'carried forward' number and the fantasy background have transformed children's perception. Twenty-five different terms and operations are included in one overall task.

One hour 15 minutes, depending upon age, plus time to go over the exercise.

| | | | | 6 | 7 | 8 | 9 | | |

With mixed-age courses some children have not met some of the particular terms. The background of these is taught within the exercise for those who need it.

Presentation is very important indeed. The highly enthusiastic response to 12 problems is explained by the fun context.

'If This Is ...'

This exercise relies upon mathematical terms and symbols (page 149).

Thirty minutes should allow a reasonable attempt to be made.

| | | | | 6 | 7 | 8 | 9 | | |

'Math Talk'

Theoni Pappas has written 25 poems for two voices in *Math Talk* (Wide World Publishing, 4th printing 1999). The poems contain mathematical ideas and subjects, such as zero, the möbius strip and proper fractions.

As little as five minutes allows one poem to be used.

		4	5	6	7	8	9		

The more varied the inputs and outcomes the better is the delivery of the subject. Performing mathematics is a brilliant idea.

Having been introduced to the idea, children can write their own poems about mathematics. Why not include the best in an anthology? Want a title? *Why not From any Angle?*

Part Five: Games and Novelties

'Fox, Rabbit, Rat'
MERATC

This amusing verbal game (page 45) involves a number of important educational skills. It is a perfect contrast to written work and complicated problems, and it is wonderful to hear the children laughing while working at the activity!

Twenty minutes gives a reasonable introduction to the game but more time than that is desirable.

		4	5	6	7	8	9	+	

'Animal Mathematics'

This is a novel way of looking at bases (page 152). Co-ordinates, synthesis and handling data carefully also feature in this piece.

How long is a piece of string? An able child, who recognizes the mathematics behind the problem, might finish it in 10–15 minutes. It could occupy other children for some time.

			5	6	7	8			

'The Number Devil'

This wonderfully entertaining book by Hans Magnus Enzensberger (Granta Publications, 2000) was a bestseller in Germany before a successful introduction to Britain. It tells the story of 12-year-old Robert who hates his boring mathematics lessons at school. Then, in his dreams, Robert meets the Number Devil who takes him on a series of adventures to Pascal's Triangle, the Fibonacci Sequence and factorials, among other things. The book is beautifully illustrated and is also very funny both because of the mischievous sense of humour of Robert's visitor and, also, because of the Number Devil's habit of using his own words for mathematical terms. The index at the back explains all the exchanges. This is also a book to recommend to children who love mathematics to read for pleasure.

To read the book completely would take some time, but chapters can be used in lesson-sized chunks.

| | | 5 | 6 | 7 | 8 | | |

Putting humour into the teaching of mathematics is a highly desirable course of action.

'Spots Before Your Eyes'
CRATC

This detailed piece (page 65) is based upon the fascinating domino game of 'Fives and Threes'. Multiplication of those two numbers, strategy and clear thinking are key features. It finishes with a logic problem to identify 'Harry's Hand'.

One hour 20 minutes.

| | | 5 | 6 | 7 | 8 | | | |

There is much mathematical content included in the 'Games Courses, Activities and Resources' section in this book.

'The Book of Permutations'

The basic material for this work on permutations can be found on page 21 of Carol Vordeman's *How Maths Works* (Dorling Kindersley, 1998). For able children the fun exercise of making up the animal booklets needs to be extended. One way is to give the number of different animals that can be created in other booklets and ask children to work out how these booklets were put together.

Examples: 216 animals   (is 6 × 6 × 6, therefore 6 animals in 3 sections)
2,401 animals   (is 7 × 7 × 7 × 7, therefore 7 animals in 4 sections)
3,125 animals   (is 5 × 5 × 5 × 5 × 5, therefore 5 animals in 5 sections)

Giving the made-up, mixed-up animals names is also great fun.

Twenty to thirty minutes.

| | | 4 | 5 | 6 | 7 | | | |

'Do You Know Your Birthday?'

There is a formula involving simple equations and calculations that works out the day of the week that a particular person was born on. It provides a short, amusing interlude that entertains children. Various versions are available. It can certainly be found on page 29 of Brian Bolt's *The Mathematical Funfair* (Cambridge University Press, 1989).

Twenty minutes to demonstrate and to record the method. Working out their own birthdays depends on the speed and accuracy of calculation.

| | | 5 | 6 | 7 | 8 | | |

Part Six: Longer Activities

'The Curse is Upon You!' – An Adventure

This gives a very different outcome: that of an extended piece of writing (page 154). On some courses, participants have become totally absorbed, and the tutor's presence has become superfluous at the writing stage!

Two hours covers the reading of the stimulus, the gathering of data and the written account itself.

		5	6	7	8	9	+	

'The Mathematics Detectives' – A Treasure Hunt

There are ten general mathematical items to be located and then 35 sheets refer to 'Numbers', 'A Game of Two Halves', 'Have you Met your Match?', 'Directions', 'Terminology', 'Sequences' and 'Shapes and Figures' (page 156).

Twenty minutes introduction is followed by one hour 30 minutes on the treasure hunt itself. Feedback is detailed and requires some 45 minutes.

		5	6	7	8			

'Mathematics Pentathlon' – A Tournament

The teams move around the stations that pose varying mathematical challenges (page 162). There is a limited time at each station.

One hour 15 minutes to one hour 30 minutes for the introduction and tournament. Feedback and scoring requires another 30 minutes.

The treasure hunt and, especially, the tournament can be reduced in time terms by having fewer locations, or each station can be tackled as a separate unit.

Longer activities help to build up the span of concentration; this is an important asset for able children.

THE CORNISH POOL PISKEY

Pool is played on a table like the one shown in the diagram below. There are seven coloured balls, seven striped balls, a black ball and a white cue ball (used to strike the coloured balls to move them). To win, a player pots the seven balls he or she is playing (either coloured or striped) into the pockets, and then, and only then, the black ball.

Steve learned to play the game while on holiday in Cornwall last summer. What interested him was that each time a striped or coloured ball, or indeed the black ball, was potted it ran down and finished in a chute (A) set into one side of the table where it remained until the end of the game. These balls could only be retrieved by placing two 20p coins in the slot for a new game. However, when the white ball went into a pocket in error, it ran down and then out into a well (B) set in the side of one end of the table so that the game could continue. Steve realized that the white had to return to play during the game whereas the other balls could stay down. He asked a friend how this worked. His friend told him, with a grin, that inside the table was a Cornish Piskey who sorted out the balls correctly! Steve did not believe in supernatural pool tables, but he was puzzled.

Your Task

Can you help Steve and explain how the white ball behaves in a different way from the other balls – that is, without recourse to magic, aliens and Cornish Piskeys! Explain your answer in enough detail to show that it works.

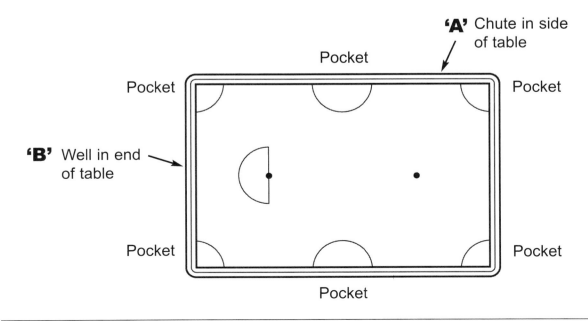

'A' Chute in side of table

Pocket

Pocket

Pocket

'B' Well in end of table

Pocket

Pocket

Pocket

Teaching Notes

This is a light-hearted piece but it does get children to think, especially if they have not seen the inside of a pool table. It also has the advantage of being concerned with a real-life situation that they may well have met.

Key Elements

- ❖ handling data
- ❖ design
- ❖ spatial awareness
- ❖ clarity of explanation
- ❖ logical and lateral thinking
- ❖ problem solving.

Contexts

'The Cornish Pool Piskey' can be used in a number of ways:

- ❖ as a starter or short item during an enrichment day, weekend, summer school or cluster day
- ❖ as a discussion item
- ❖ as a written item
- ❖ as a novel item within a mathematics or thinking skills lesson
- ❖ as differentiated homework
- ❖ as an activity for the Mathematics Club.

Solution

Children may come up with alternative solutions to the actual one. Credit for their thinking should be given if they can justify their solution.

The critical point is that the white ball is slightly smaller than the rest. Holes are not used to discriminate between the balls, however, as they would be blocked by one of the other balls lodging there.

Each pocket has a channel of cupped wire which feeds into a central channel (all, of course, on a downwards slope). All the balls, including the white, travel towards point 'B' at the end of the table. Then there is a forced right-hand turn which takes the black ball, the coloured balls and the striped balls along the wires into the chute in the side of the table at 'A'. The smaller white ball does not run along the final channel leading to the chute but, instead, drops through it and onto a slope facing the other way and proceeds from there into the well at point 'B'.

Mind you, in Cornwall they believe that this is a ridiculously complicated system and that a piskey (a Cornish pixie) is much more suitable!

One Number, Many Ways

Some people have a rather narrow view of maths.

They think mainly of pages of 'sums' each with one, and only one, correct answer.

They might be nicknamed 'straight-line' people.

Good mathematicians are much more flexible and they see many possibilities.

Let us see just how flexible you can be.

Your Tasks

You and the other members of your team will be given the choice of a small number of envelopes. Inside the envelope that you choose will be a card with a number written upon it.

1 Brainstorm as many different ways as you can to reach the number through a variety of routes and operations.
2 Make sure that your answers involve genuinely different operations. You cannot, for instance, give ten answers all of which involve simple addition and nothing else.
3 Get one member of the group to record your answers so that they can be presented to other groups.

You have 20 minutes to find 'One Number, Many Ways'.

Teaching Notes

This simple-looking exercise can, in fact, become as complex as the participants wish it to be, for it is very open-ended indeed.

Key Elements

- ❖ brainstorming
- ❖ open-endedness
- ❖ alternative answers
- ❖ mental agility
- ❖ many operations and terms covered in a single piece.

Contexts

'One Number, Many Ways' can be used in the following ways:

- ❖ as normal classwork where differentiation by outcome will occur
- ❖ as a team discussion and presentation
- ❖ as a written exercise
- ❖ as an activity during an enrichment day, weekend, summer school or cluster day
- ❖ as differentiated homework
- ❖ as enrichment work for those who have completed other work
- ❖ as an activity for the Mathematics Club
- ❖ as a written open-access competition for individuals or teams.

Organization

1 Appropriate numbers need to be chosen and written on cards which are placed in envelopes; numbers like 12, 20, 42, 36 and 105 open up a number of possibilities.

2 Each team chooses an envelope and then they all start brainstorming at the same time.

3 The teacher needs to stress the fact that operations used to get the number must not be simple repetitions.

4 Twenty minutes has been given as a nominal time, but this can be altered by the teacher.

5 The style of presentation could involve a competitive element in that the winning team is the one that produces the greatest number of ways that are deemed to be different, as judged by the teacher and the other groups.

Mathematical Medley

Try your hand at each of the following in this mathematical medley.
Remember to read the data carefully – you do not want to get 'out of tune'!

On the Cards

Left  1  2  3  4  5 **Right**

There are five cards face-down on the table.
Can you identify them in their correct positions from the information below?

Picture cards are defined as Kings, Queens and Jacks. For this puzzle they each have a value of 11. Aces count as 1. All other cards are counted at their face value.

a All four suits are represented. There are three black cards.

b All five cards have a different value and each value is an odd number.

c The card of the lowest value is in the centre, with the card of next lowest value to its immediate left as the viewer sees the table. (All positions are referred to as the viewer sees them.)

d The Queen is on the extreme right and the three cards to the left of the Queen add up to the same value as the Queen.

e The only club has the second highest value and it is positioned on the extreme left.

f The two cards of the same suit add up to a value exactly double that of the diamond.

Waiter

Three businesswomen went out to a restaurant for a meal. The waiter at first asked for £36 and the three women each paid him £12. The waiter then discovered that the bill should have been £31 and he took five one-pound coins back to the table. Rather than having to use change to divide the coins, he gave £1 back to each of the three women and kept £2 for himself.

Now, each woman had paid £11 – a total of £33 – and the waiter had £2 in his pocket, – that is £35 altogether. What had happened to the other pound from the original £36?

Ready to Order?

The coach containing 27 passengers pulled up at the roadside restaurant for breakfast. The passengers were asked whether they wanted egg, bacon or sausage, or a combination of these items. The waiter went through into the kitchen and said that four people did not want a cooked breakfast, 15 wanted egg, 17 wanted bacon and 10 wanted sausage. He was able to tell the chef that three passengers wanted all three items and that of those who wanted egg nine of them wanted bacon but no sausage and two of them wanted sausage but no bacon.

The chef said that the information was incomplete as he needed to know how many people wanted just sausage and how many just bacon and also how many people wanted bacon and sausage but no egg.

Can you help him?

Time to Think

(with acknowledgement to Lewis Carroll)

The clock on Greta's mantelpiece was broken – it had not run for some time. Her friend, Kevin, told her that keeping the clock was pointless.

Greta responded by saying that her broken clock actually told the time accurately on more occasions than the clock in Kevin's living room which lost an hour a day.

Was she right?

Soft Soap

The Superior Soap Company produces a range of luxurious, scented soaps. These soaps are manufactured in the shape of cakes or circular cheeses and they weigh 1kg each. Most customers want much smaller pieces than that. The sales manager, appropriately named Larry Lather, tries to keep staff 'on their toes' by a number of challenges. He set the staff a little problem. How many pieces should shops cut the soaps into to satisfy the preferred size of most customers? Larry Lather also asked what the minimum number of cuts to achieve that division was, and how many different ways could they be made. He supplied one vital piece of information in a puzzle format.

The number of grams in the preferred size for the majority of customers can be worked out in the following way:

'Take the perfect number that lies between 5 × 5 and 6 × 5. Multiply that perfect number by the square root of 25. Now take away from the number that you have reached as a result of the first two operations, the eighth positive odd number.'

Larry Lather told his staff that the answers are not too difficult to work out. Is this just 'soft soap' or can you prove him right?

Teaching Notes

The five items that make up 'Mathematical Medley' can be used as separate items or collectively as a longer piece. They are quite mixed in terms of content.

Key Elements

- ❖ following instructions
- ❖ using data carefully
- ❖ logical thinking
- ❖ lateral thinking
- ❖ mental agility
- ❖ spatial awareness
- ❖ subject-specific language.

Contexts

'Mathematical Medley' can be used in a variety of ways:

- ❖ as individual items in short time slots
- ❖ collectively as a longer piece
- ❖ as enrichment work for those who have completed other work
- ❖ as differentiated homework
- ❖ as an activity during as enrichment day, weekend, summer school or cluster day
- ❖ as an activity for the Mathematics Club.

Solutions

On the Cards

Clue a   There is one diamond and one heart, and then either two spades and one club or two clubs and one spade.

Clue b   Odd values are 1 (Ace), 3, 5, 7, 9, and 11 (picture card). Five of the six values are used.

Clue c   Card 3 is an Ace or a 3 and 1 or 3 must be used, if not both; therefore Card 2 is either a 3 or a 5 as:
(i)   if there is no Ace, Card 3 is a 3 and Card 2 a 5
(ii)   if there is no 3, Card 3 is an Ace and Card 2 a 5
(iii)   if there is no 5, Card 3 is an Ace and Card 2 a 3.

Clue d   The Queen is Card 5 with a value of 11. Cards 2, 3 and 4 therefore add up to 11. The only combination that allows this is 1 + 3 + 7 and therefore card 3 is an Ace, Card 2 is a 3 and Card 4 is a 7.

Clue e   Card 1 is a club. It must be a 9 to have the second highest value. There are two spades among the other cards.

Clue f   The two spades and the diamond come from the values 1, 3, 7 and 11. The only solution is 3 + 11 = 7 x 2. Therefore Card 2 is the 3 of spades and Card 5 is the Queen of spades which in value are double Card 4 which is the 7 of diamonds. Card 3, which we know already is an Ace, must be a heart.

Left   1    2    3    4    5   **Right**

Waiter

This is a variation of an 'old chestnut'. Any confusion is caused by the wording of the question. The £2 in the waiter's pocket comes out of the £33 paid by the businesswomen and should be SUBTRACTED from that amount leaving the £31 paid for the meal. There is, therefore, no missing pound.

Ready to Order?

This can be set out as a Venn diagram. The four passengers who do not want a cooked breakfast are outside the circles. The 15 who ordered egg can be placed as one egg only, nine egg and bacon, two egg and sausage and three egg, bacon and sausage.

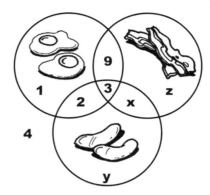

We need to find x (those who want bacon and sausage but no egg), y (those who want just sausages) and z (those who want just bacon).

$23 = 15 + x + y + z$ (1)

$5 = x + z$ (2)

$5 = x + y$ and $\therefore y = 5 - x$ (3)

Substitute (3) into (1)

$23 = 15 + x + 5 - x + z$

$\therefore z = 3$

$\therefore x = 2$ and $y = 3$

Thus, two passengers want bacon and sausage but no egg, three want just sausage and three want just bacon.

An alternative method of solution is to say that 23 people ordered 42 items of food (15 + 17 + 10). Of the 19 'extra' items, six of them can be accounted for by the three passengers who had all three items of food, nine in all. This leaves 13 still to consider. We know about 11 of these – nine who ordered egg and bacon and two who ordered egg and sausage. Thus the two 'extra' items can only be passengers who wanted bacon and sausage but no egg. From the total figures for sausages and bacon it is a simple matter to calculate that three passengers want just bacon and three passengers want just sausage.

A different method uses a chart.

Total passengers: 27

No cooked food: 4 $\therefore$ 23 cooked food orders

Egg: 15 (total) – 3 (all items) → 12 – 9 (with bacon) → 3 – 2 (with sausage) → 1 (just egg)

Bacon: 17 (total) – 3 (all items) → 14 – 9 (with egg) → 5

Sausage: 10 (total) – 3 (all items) → 7 – 2 (with egg) → 5

Egg	Bacon	Sausage	People	Cumulative Total
3	3	3	3	3
9	9		9	12
2		2	2	14
1			1	15

Eight remaining passenger orders

	Bacon	Sausage		
	5 remain	5 remain		
	x	x		
	x			
		x		

Only combinations that work

	Bacon	Sausage	People	Cumulative Total
	2	2	2	17
		3	3	20
	3		3	23

Total	15	17	10	

Time to Think

This is based upon one of hundreds of puzzles, conundrums and riddles created by Lewis Carroll. Greta was correct in that her broken clock was accurate twice each day whereas Kevin's clock, that was losing an hour each day, was only correct once every 12 days.

Soft Soap

The first point to settle is the number of grams favoured by most customers. A perfect number is where the sum of the factors, other than the number itself, equals the number. Between 25 and 30 the perfect number is 28 because $1 + 2 + 4 + 7 + 14 = 28$. The square root of 25 is 5, and $5 \times 28 = 140$. The eighth positive odd number is 15. Subtract that from 140, you have 125 grams.

If the soaps are manufactured as 1kg cakes, then they should be divided into eight pieces of 125 grams. The minimum number of cuts to get eight pieces is three. This can be achieved in two obvious ways plus a third more 'bizarre' method.

1 One cut horizontally through the centre of the soap, followed by two vertical cuts at right angles to each other, going through both halves.
2 Divide the soap in half with one vertical cut, then place the two halves one on top of each other. Cut in half again (bisecting the angle) going through both layers, and place all four pieces on top of each other. A third and final vertical cut bisecting the angle will give eight 125 grams pieces.
3 A more bizarre approach would be to make two vertical cuts at right angles to each other so that the soap is in quarters. A third cut is made: a circular concentric cut with a radius such that it would give eight equally weighted, but rather strange shaped, pieces. In mathematical and practical terms, this is a much more difficult method.

'Soft Soap' combines vocabulary, following instructions, using data accurately and spatial awareness.

Is Pythagoras at Home?

In Sumland, somewhere lived a number of mathematicians.

They were:

Pythagoras	Fibonacci	Descartes	Venn
Napier	Pascal	Euler	Möbius

Their fantasy addresses were:

169 The Triangle	27 Bridges Street	15 Theorem Road	29 The Strip
404 Cartesian Way	10 Diagram Close	81 Sequence Street	14 Bones Lane

However, none of the mathematicians lived at the address that would be most closely associated with their names.

Your Task

From the information in the introduction and the clues below, work out the correct fantasy address for the eight mathematicians. Then you can call and be in a position to ask the question 'Is Pythagoras at home?'

The Clues

1 A palindromic number is part of the address of a British mathematician.
2 The mathematician who lived longest ago has an address involving a square number.
3 The man, whose real name is Leonardo of Pisa, time-travels to the address linked by words with his nickname, to visit the Swiss mathematician whose topological insight sorted out the route for a grand parade back and forward over the Pregel River in Konigsberg.
4 The mathematician who invented logarithms joked that he lived at a 'prime address'.
5 A French mathematician lives at a cube number address.
6 The mathematician who spent so much time exploring and writing about the 'arithmetic triangle' lives appropriately at the address that contains the higher of the two triangular numbers used here.
7 The address involving a physical system to help multiply quickly is home to the man whose 'group of musicians' has only one surface and likewise one edge.

Teaching Notes

Mathematical terms, numbers and key information about a number of famous mathematicians form this logical thinking problem, given a fantasy, fun setting. Research books need to be available to help pupils in their solution.

Key Elements

- ❖ the lives of famous mathematicians
- ❖ subject-specific vocabulary
- ❖ types of numbers
- ❖ logical thinking
- ❖ careful use of data
- ❖ research.

Contexts

'Is Pythagoras at Home?' can be used in a number of ways:

- ❖ as enrichment material for those who have completed other work
- ❖ as differentiated homework
- ❖ as an activity during an enrichment day, weekend, summer school or cluster day
- ❖ as an activity for the Mathematics Club.

Solution

This logical problem can be solved by a written method, by a matrix or by physically moving around slips of paper. Children should choose the method that suits them best personally.

Introduction: when the mathematicians are linked to a term associated with their work, the following pairings occur – Pythagoras' Theorem, Fibonacci Sequence, Descartes and Cartesian (geometry), Venn Diagram, Napier's Bones, Pascal's Triangle, Euler's Bridges and Möbius Strip. These combinations are eliminated from the solution.

Clue 1   404 Cartesian Way is the home of either Venn or Napier. Other mathematicians are eliminated for that address.

Clue 2   This is Pythagoras, who must live at either 169 The Triangle or 81 Sequence Street. Other addresses are eliminated for him.

Clue 3   Leonardo of Pisa's nickname was Fibonacci who therefore time-travelled to see Euler (the Swiss mathematician who sorted out the 'Bridges of Konigsberg' problem) at 81 Sequence Street. This also means that Pythagoras must live at 169 The Triangle.

Clue 4   This is Napier who must live at 29 The Strip as 29 is the only address involving a prime number. By process of elimination, Venn must live at 404 Cartesian Way.

Clue 5   Either Descartes or Pascal live at 27 Bridges Street as $3^3 = 27$. Fibonacci (Italian) and Möbius (German) are ruled out for that particular address.

Clue 6   Pascal is the mathematician. 10 and 15 are both triangular numbers but 15 is the greater; therefore Pascal lives at 15 Theorem Road and, as a result, Descartes must live at 27 Bridges Street.

Clue 7   The multiplication aid is Napier's Bones or Rods and, therefore, 14 Bones Lane is the address under consideration. A 'group of musicians' is a band, always associated with Möbius, the properties of which are described in the clue. Therefore, Möbius lives at 14 Bones Lane with the result that Fibonacci lives at 10 Diagram Close.

	Pythagoras	Fibonacci	Descartes	Venn	Napier	Pascal	Euler	Möbius
169 The Triangle	✓	X	X	X	X	X	X	X
27 Bridges Street	X	X	✓	X	X	X	X	X
15 Theorem Road	X	X	X	X	X	✓	X	X
404 Cartesian Way	X	X	X	✓	X	X	X	X
29 The Strip	X	X	X	X	✓	X	X	X
10 Diagram Close	X	✓	X	X	X	X	X	X
81 Sequence Street	X	X	X	X	X	X	✓	X
14 Bones Lane	X	X	X	X	X	X	X	✓

CAN YOU SPOT THEM?

Captain Code sets a number of challenges for her new recruits into the Secret Service. This is only of moderate difficulty and her charges did well with it.

Can you be as successful?

Your Tasks

Look carefully at the cryptic clues and work out what exactly they mean. Apply your knowledge to decode the secret message, showing the details of your working at all stages.

THE CRYPTIC CLUES

1   It is just a game to sort out MOD NOISE. (The title of this piece is an indicator also.)
2   There are two-and-one-third dozen pieces initially to be considered.
3   Alphabetically that makes a surplus of two and therefore you need to eliminate the lowest-value piece and the highest-value piece.
4   Create a table in order of ascending value: lowest value at the top of table
5   In 5^3 the three normally indicates 'to the power of'. Here, the three gives the order in the table of pieces of the same value. The value of the pieces is made up of two components as befits the game involved. For the table order, think of the lower of the two components first.
6   Apply the table alphabetically but think 'srettel'.

THE SECRET MESSAGE

$$4^2 - 8^1 - 9^1 \quad 9^2 - 6^1 - 6^3 - 7^3 - 6^2 - 6^1$$

$$9^1 - 8^3 - 8^3 - 9^1 - 10^1 - 4^2 \quad 11^1 - 4^2$$

$$3^1 - 6^1 - 5^1 - 7^1$$

Extension Task

Write messages of your own using this particular code.

Teaching Notes

'Can You Spot Them?' is a number code involving a number of thinking skills.

Key Elements

❖ abstract

❖ simple calculation

❖ wordplay

❖ careful handling of data

❖ synthesis.

Contexts

'Can You Spot Them?' can be used in the following ways:

❖ as differentiated homework

❖ as enrichment work for those ahead on other tasks

❖ as an activity during an enrichment day, weekend, summer school or cluster day

❖ as an exercise in a thinking skills course

❖ as an activity for the Mathematics Club.

Solution

All tricky codes allow interpretation of information in a variety of ways, but only one leads to the solution. Credit should be given for sensible creative ideas, even if they do not prove to be the correct method. Trial-and-error is a feature of decoding. The teacher needs to keep a balance between stepping in too quickly and watching frustration reach an unhelpful level.

THE CRYPTIC CLUES

1   This is an anagram. MOD NOISE makes DOMINOES. The word 'spot' in the title also helps.

2   Two-and-one-third dozen is 24 + 4, in other words 28. There are 28 dominoes in the normal set.

3   There are 26 letters in the alphabet and, therefore, two of the 28 pieces are not required. The two dominoes to ignore are blank : blank, the lowest value, and six : six, the highest value.

4 and 5   Forgetting the double blank and the double six, the dominoes need to be arranged on a table with the lowest value first, now the blank : one. 'Two components' refer to all dominoes being made up of two numbers, given that blank is a number of value zero. The domino, for example, two: three, is used in the table in that order, not as three : two. This helps to differentiate between dominoes of the same value.

6   Place the letters A to Z against the table, but 'SRETTEL' is 'LETTERS' backwards, therefore the placement is actually Z to A.

CAN YOU SPOT THEM?

THE TABLE

Domino	Value	Coded	Letter
Blank : One	1	1^1	Z
Blank : Two	2	2^1	Y
One : One	2	2^2	X
Blank : Three	3	3^1	W
One : Two	3	3^2	V
Blank : Four	4	4^1	U
One : Three	4	4^2	T
Two : Two	4	4^3	S
Blank : Five	5	5^1	R
One : Four	5	5^2	Q
Two : Three	5	5^3	P
Blank : Six	6	6^1	O
One : Five	6	6^2	N
Two : Four	6	6^3	M
Three : Three	6	6^4	L
One : Six	7	7^1	K
Two : Five	7	7^2	J
Three : Four	7	7^3	I
Two : Six	8	8^1	H
Three : Five	8	8^2	G
Four : Four	8	8^3	F
Three : Six	9	9^1	E
Four : Five	9	9^2	D
Four : Six	10	10^1	C
Five : Five	10	10^2	B
Five : Six	11	11^1	A

THE SECRET MESSAGE

$$4^2 - 8^1 - 9^1 \quad 9^2 - 6^1 - 6^3 - 7^3 - 6^2 - 6^1$$

T H E   D O M I N O

$$9^1 - 8^3 - 8^3 - 9^1 - 10^1 - 4^2 \quad 11^1 - 4^2$$

E F F E C T   A T

$$3^1 - 6^1 - 5^1 - 7^1$$

W O R K

Donkey-Work

Albert Ride joked that his family name meant that it was inevitable that he, and his brother Jim, should have become involved in owning donkeys for seaside rides. Albert had one child, a girl called Betty. He would have liked to leave the business to her but he had doubts about her ability. Jim had more confidence in his niece. He suggested to Albert that they set Betty a problem to solve about the donkeys to prove her suitability. Albert readily agreed to the suggestion. He was pleased when Betty succeeded in her 'Donkey-Work'.

Would you have been as successful?

Betty's Donkey-Work Problem

A man owned a number of valuable donkeys. When he died he gave very detailed instructions about them in his will. He requested that the donkeys be passed to his three daughters in a particular way. His eldest daughter was to receive ½, his middle daughter ⅓ and his youngest daughter ⅑. The dead man's brother, the uncle of the three girls, was left to administer the will. This uncle also owned a number of donkeys. He told the girls that their father had owned 17 donkeys in total.

Betty's Tasks

1 Explain the problem facing the three daughters as a result of their father's will.

2 Find a way of solving that problem.

3 Give the mathematical reasons for the problem.

4 Decide whether the solution fully answers the terms of the dead man's will.

5 Create a similar problem about donkeys but using different figures.

Donkey-Work

Teaching Notes

The basis of this piece of work is an Arab mathematical problem concerned with camels. Here the problem has been developed and involves donkeys.

Key Elements

- ❖ problem solving
- ❖ fractions
- ❖ using data appropriately
- ❖ application
- ❖ discussion.

Contexts

'Donkey-Work' can be used in a number of ways:

- ❖ as extension work to material on fractions
- ❖ as written work
- ❖ as a discussion item
- ❖ as enrichment work for those who have completed other work
- ❖ as differentiated homework
- ❖ as an activity during an enrichment day, weekend, summer school or cluster day
- ❖ as an activity for the Mathematics Club.

Some Answers

Task One

When you try to work out $\frac{1}{2}$, $\frac{1}{3}$ and $\frac{1}{9}$ of 17 you do not finish up with whole numbers. Bits of donkeys are not an attractive proposition!

Task Two

One way forward is to add a donkey to take the total to 18. A popular method is to ask the uncle for one of his donkeys. Now the eldest daughter receives nine donkeys ($\frac{1}{2}$ of 18), the middle daughter receives six donkeys ($\frac{1}{3}$ of 18) and the youngest daughter receives two donkeys ($\frac{1}{9}$ of 18): 9 + 6 + 2 = 17. The girls can then return the extra donkey to their uncle.
This solution has seen the problem being used as an assembly reading. The girls believe that their uncle will be surprised but he says instead 'Whatever in life you give in love will be returned to you'.

Task Three

The origin of the problem is that $\frac{1}{2}$, $\frac{1}{3}$ and $\frac{1}{9}$ do not add up to one.
$\frac{1}{2} + \frac{1}{3} + \frac{1}{9} = \frac{9}{18} + \frac{6}{18} + \frac{2}{18} = \frac{17}{18}$
Children might also say that the problem arises because 17 is a prime number.

Task Four

The solution is a neat one but it does not carry out the terms of the will exactly. Half of 17 is not nine. Because the original fractions do not add up to one, there cannot be a solution that fits exactly. However, the spirit of the will has certainly been observed.

Task Five

If the fractions are $\frac{1}{2}$, $\frac{1}{3}$ and $\frac{1}{8}$ and the total is 23, a similar problem results. Another route is $\frac{1}{2}$, $\frac{1}{4}$ and $\frac{1}{5}$ with a total number of donkeys of 19. How many more are there?

Christmas Draw

You are a member of the Parent–Teacher Association of the local comprehensive school. At a recent meeting you were called out of the room to take a telephone call. On your return you were told that the meeting had voted to ask you to take charge of the Christmas Draw.

The previous organizer, Mr Hill, has left a slip of paper with a few pieces of advice.

You need to deal with the following points:

- The cost of the prizes and how attractive they are to be
- The number of tickets to be printed
- The price at which the tickets are to be sold
- The method of ticket distribution
- The recovery of unsold tickets and ticket stubs to ensure that none are left unaccounted
- Plans to promote the draw to ensure that it is a success
- A financial statement showing expected income and expected expenditure and, therefore, a predicted profit.

Mr Hill's Slip of Paper

1. The numbers of pupils in the school are: Year 7–181, Year 8–168, Year 9–178, Year 10–182, Year 11–172.
2. Younger pupils tend to sell more tickets.
3. You need more tickets available than you will eventually sell because some will be returned unsold.
4. Printing costs are £6 per 1,000 tickets with a minimum of 3,000 to be printed.
5. Tickets are produced in books of five.
6. A profit of £500 or more is the target.
7. There are normally three main prizes with other minor prizes.

Your Task

Explain in detail your plans for the Christmas Draw.

Christmas Draw

Teaching Notes

This is a more general problem-solving activity with mathematical content.

Key Elements

- ❖ problem solving
- ❖ decision-making
- ❖ organizational skills
- ❖ engagement with data
- ❖ calculation.

Some Thoughts on the Solution

This piece of work concentrates on decision-making and organizational skills. There is no set 'answer' as such, but there are some key points to bear in mind.

A major decision concerns the prizes to be offered. Expensive and attractive prizes will increase expenditure but in the long run may produce a greater profit because more tickets will be sold. The money available for prizes could be decided first and from that it would be calculated how many tickets needed to be sold to produce the desired profit. The alternative approach is to estimate the total number of tickets that the school could reasonably expect to sell. This would give the anticipated revenue and from that could then be calculated the money available for prizes.

The exercise also asks for the drawing up of a promotion campaign. The whole area of advertising and sales is brought into question. It may be that incentives could be offered to the pupils who sell the most.

The distribution of tickets is important. They need to be in the hands of the pupils most likely to sell them. Because you do not want those who are selling well to wait for extra tickets to be issued to them, spare books need to be available. If you expect to sell, for example, 10,000 tickets you therefore need more than 10,000 tickets to be printed.

Another important aspect is security. People will be worried about buying unless they feel sure that all the tickets will go into the draw. This means that a strict system is required to ensure that all stubs, monies and unsold books are returned.

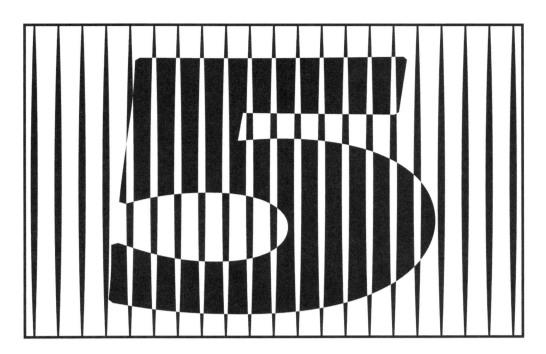

Explain in detail how each of the following involves the number five.

1 Pentagon

2 *Watership Down*

3 The letter V

4 Guy Fawkes

5 An English banknote

6 A square-based pyramid

7 Pentagram

8 Doubly so, according to Fibonacci

9 May

10 Pentateuch

11 Enid Blyton

12 Sight, touch and so on

13 Pentameter

14 Third of a series of particular numbers

15 Small denomination English coin

16 The probability of not getting a six with one throw of a dice

17 Gold rings

18 A musical symbol during the Second World War

19 Pythagoras, three and four

20 Pentasyllabic

21 The confession of faith; prayer; alms; fasting; the pilgrimage to Mecca

22 Representing the Olympic Games

23 ... and two small fishes

24 30–39km/h, a fresh breeze

25 Internal security service

Five

Teaching Notes

'Five' is a light piece using mathematical vocabulary but also terms from other areas. It is beneficial for children to see mathematics within a wider context. It can be used individually or within groups. The teacher has to make a decision as to whether a group works out what they can from joint knowledge and experience or whether reference facilities should be available.

Solution

1   A five-sided figure
2   The rabbit called 'Fiver'
3   The Roman five
4   November 5th
5   A £5 note
6   Five faces
7   A five-pointed star
8   Five is the fifth number in the Fibonacci sequence
9   The fifth month of the year
10   The first five books of the Old Testament
11   *The Famous Five*
12   The five senses
13   A verse of five feet
14   Five is the third prime number
15   5p
16   $\frac{5}{6}$, or five chances out of six
17   Five gold rings on the fifth day of Christmas
18   The opening bars from Beethoven's Fifth Symphony, where the rhythm is as 'V" in Morse code or is Roman for five
19   Five units is the hypotenuse in a right-angled triangle where the shorter sides are three and four units
20   Having five syllables
21   The Five Pillars of Islam
22   The five interlocking rings which is the symbol
23   Five loaves in the 'Feeding Of The Five Thousand'
24   Point 5 on the Beaufort Scale measuring wind speed
25   MI5

IF THIS IS ...

If a half is represented by two bananas, then a whole would clearly be represented by four bananas.

Simplicity itself, isn't it?

Below are some situations that need rather more thought.

They cover a variety of mathematical areas.

The key point is that you must

express the answers in the form given in the problems,

so look carefully at the methods used.

The Ten Teasers

1   If this, V, is a pentagon, what is a nonagon?

2   If this, n, is a century, what is a millennium?

3   If this ...

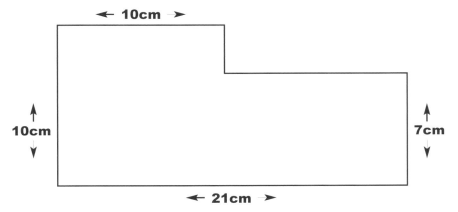

is sixty-two, what is ...

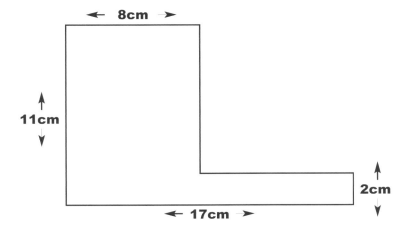

... ?

4   If this, 30, is BABY, what is HAND?

5   If this, 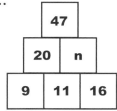, is the probability of picking a King from a pack of normal playing cards, minus the jokers, what is the probability of picking an even-numbered card (ignoring Jacks, Queens and Kings) from a similar pack?

6   If this, x!, is 24, what is 40,320?

7   If this, 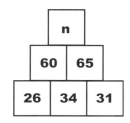, is 25% of 600, what is 90% of 500?

8   If this, 3^3, is n in ...

	47	
20	n	
9	11	16

what is n in ...

	n	
60	65	
26	34	31

... ?

9   If this, 15y, is E to NW clockwise, what is SW to W anticlockwise?

10 If this, ||||| ||, is related to 49, what is the representation of the same relation to 81?

Extension Task

Set some of your own 'If this is ...' by considering other areas of mathematics than those used here.

Use a variety of symbols.

Teaching Notes

Here is a novel way of looking at mathematical operations, vocabulary and symbols.

Key Elements

❖ following instructions

❖ precise interpretation of data

❖ subject-specific vocabulary

❖ symbols

❖ mental agility

❖ covering a variety of topics within one exercise

❖ calculation.

Contexts

'If this is ...' can be used in the following ways:

❖ as enrichment work for those ahead on other tasks

❖ as differentiated homework

❖ as an activity during an enrichment day, weekend, summer school or cluster day

❖ as an activity for the Mathematics Club

❖ as an open-access competition with the extension task acting as a decider, if it is needed.

Answers

Pupils need to be reminded that answers must be expressed in the exact format used in the questions.

1 IX – the Roman numeral nine for a nine-sided figure.

2 10n, or n^2, as a millennium is ten times as long as a century.

3 Fifty-six (in written form) for the perimeter of the shape.

4 27. This is the simplest number code of all; A is 1, B is 2, C is 3 and so on. BABY is 2 + 1 + 2 + 25 = 30; therefore, HAND is 8 + 1 + 14 + 4 = 27.

5 ●●●●● There are four chances in 52 of picking a King and 20 chances of choosing a two, a four, a six, an eight or a ten: five times as many.

6 2x! 4! or 4 factorial is 4 × 3 × 2 × 1 = 24.
    40,320 is 8! or 8 factorial, 8 × 7 × 6 × 5 × 4 × 3 × 2 × 1.

7 ■■■ 25% of 600 is 150, whereas 90% of 500 is 450: three times as many.

8 5^3. In the first number pyramid n equals 27 or 3^3. In the second number pyramid n equals 125 or 5^3.

9 21y. E to NW clockwise is 225 degrees or 15 × 15. SW to W anticlockwise is 315 degrees or 21 × 15.

10 ⦀⦀⦀⦀ ‖‖‖‖ . The relation of ⦀⦀⦀⦀ ‖ to 49 is that seven is the square root of 49. The square root of 81 is nine and this can be represented by ⦀⦀⦀⦀ ‖‖‖‖ , as a tally record, as used in statistics.

Animal Mathematics

Many people are aware of different number systems. The one we use today originated with the Hindus in the north of India some 2,000 years ago and was taken up by Arab traders. Something that looks rather different is the roman numeral system. How many people are aware, however, of the variations used by various animals? This exercise introduces you to the fascinating world of 'Animal Mathematics'.

Your Tasks

1. Study the information below that describes the layout of a particular classroom, the desks from which three exercise books came and the co-ordinates of the three animals' desks.
2. Examine the sums that have been marked correct by the teacher. They may not look right to you but they are correct within the variations employed by particular animals.
3. Work out the names of animals A, B and C and explain your reasons for saying so.

The Classroom

As the teacher looks at the room she sees five rows of five desks. Next to the desk (1,1) is a door set in the wall that is at right angles to the wall behind the teacher. Exercise Book One came from the desk furthest away from the door. Exercise Book Two came from the desk two directly in front of the one where Exercise Book One was. Exercise Book Three came from the desk on the same row as Exercise Book Two, but on the very opposite side of the room. Animal A sat at (5,3), Animal B sat at (5,5) and Animal C sat at (1,3).

The Exercise Books

Exercise Book One

23	+	313	+
3		222	
32	✓	1201	✓

Exercise Book Two

37	+	216	+
45		374	
104	✓	612	✓

Exercise Book Three

25	+	14	+
44		3	
113	✓	21	✓

Teaching Notes

This fun item causes amusement but it also makes children think carefully.

Key Elements

- ❖ bases
- ❖ handling data carefully
- ❖ following instructions
- ❖ co-ordinates
- ❖ synthesis
- ❖ mental agility.

Contexts

'Animal Mathematics' can be used in a number of ways:

- ❖ as extension work on bases
- ❖ as an enrichment activity for those ahead on other tasks
- ❖ as differentiated homework
- ❖ as an activity during an enrichment day, weekend, summer school or cluster day
- ❖ as an activity for the Mathematics Club.

Solution

The layout of the classroom can be set out as a diagram from the information given. Exercise Books One, Two and Three can then be indicated.

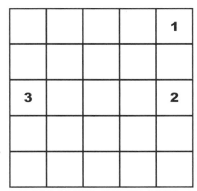

DOOR

TEACHER AT FRONT

Animal A sits at (5, 3) and therefore owns Exercise Book Two.
Animal B sits at (5, 5) and therefore owns Exercise Book One.
Animal C sits at (1, 3) and therefore owns Exercise Book Three.

The sums look wrong in all three exercise books but they have been marked correct by the teacher. This is because the sums have been calculated in bases other than the normal base ten. Exercise Book One uses base four, Exercise Book Two uses base eight and Exercise Book Three uses base six.

Animal A therefore uses base eight and might be an octopus or a spider (eight arms or legs).
Animal B uses base four and could be any four-legged animal such as a dog or horse.
Animal C uses base six and can be any insect, as they have six legs.

The Curse is Upon You!

Mathematics can be delivered in many different ways but nothing quite so strange, perhaps, as via a story, a walk and a piece of writing.

Pay attention because

The Curse is Upon You!

Step One
Are you sitting comfortably? Good! You are going to hear a story and then perhaps you will not be quite as comfortable. The story is *The Maths Curse*, a wonderful creation by Jon Scieszka and Lane Smith. In the story, told in the first person, a little boy believes that a maths curse has been put on him by his mathematics teacher, Mrs Fibonacci. The boy describes his day from the time he wakes up. The curse means that he sees everything that happens in the day as a mathematical problem.

Listen carefully to the story to understand the style and presentation and, also, to pick up the many jokes, for the story plays to a particular sense of humour.

Step Two
You will go out on a walk. This is a fact-finding mission. Mathematics is all around you – in nature, in sport, at the breakfast table, when you go to the shops. Make notes, on your mathematical journey, about angles, co-ordinates, and numbers in practical use – in fact, anything from any branch of mathematics. Put on your 'mathematical glasses'. At this stage, collect raw data and don't be worried about the finished product.

Step Three
Write a story in the style of *The Maths Curse*. Draw upon the information that you gathered on the walk and all other aspects of your life elsewhere. Take note of the success criteria that are detailed below. The only way that you can free yourself is by writing down all your thoughts. So, off you go, for the curse is upon you!

Success Criteria

Your story will be judged by the following criteria:

☠ the quality of the mathematics included
☠ the variety of the mathematics included
☠ the appreciation of Jon Scieszka and Lane Smith's style
☠ the sense of humour displayed
☠ the extent to which a genuine story is produced.

Enrichment Activities for Able and Talented Children © Barry Teare (Network Educational Press, 2004)

Teaching Notes

A long piece of prose is an unusual outcome for a mathematics assignment. The numeracy framework requires that pupils should solve 'story' problems but this piece of work extends the task dramatically and places children as the authors, not the solvers.

Key Elements

- ❖ mathematics in real life
- ❖ synthesis
- ❖ appreciation of genre
- ❖ application
- ❖ observation
- ❖ word humour
- ❖ sustained writing
- ❖ tackling many mathematical areas in the one piece
- ❖ sustained concentration.

Contexts

'The Curse is Upon You!' can be used in a number of ways:

- ❖ as timetabled work over a number of lessons where differentiation by outcome will apply
- ❖ as a series of differentiated homeworks
- ❖ as an extended activity for those ahead on other tasks
- ❖ as an activity during an enrichment day, weekend, summer school or cluster day
- ❖ as an activity for several meetings of the Mathematics Club
- ❖ as an open-access competition with a long time-span for entry.

Organization

The piece works best when it is all completed in one extended time period. However, it could be split up into different activities. A very important ingredient is the book *The Maths Curse* by Jon Scieszka and Lane Smith (Puffin Books, 1998). If there is time, the work can be supported by reference to mathematics at large, such as the application of the Fibonacci sequence in the natural world.

It adds greatly to the experience to undertake a walk to gather information, with children observing their surroundings with their 'mathematical glasses' on. These observations get them to focus on the mathematical possibilities of their world. What they find may contribute directly to their stories, or they may wish to write a story based on different thoughts. It is also a novel approach to undertake a mathematical tour. If this is not possible, then a wide selection of visual stimuli (books, magazines, physical objects, posters and so on) could be used.

The story is the main outcome, but children may wish to include mathematical diagrams or 'pictures'.

The Mathematics Detectives

As mathematical detectives you are searching for mathematical problems and puzzles to test your skills. There are many questions to answer, including some cryptic mindteasers.

First, you need to find examples of ten '**Mathematical Items**' (1–10), which can be found as you look for the 35 sheets of problems and puzzles. For each item explain where you found the item and what the item is.

1	A symmetrical object	6	A square with a diagonal line bisecting the shape into two equal parts
2	A set of numbers and their purpose		
3	A cube	7	An arc shape
4	A plus sign	8	A series of parallel lines
5	A right angle	9	Two concentric circles
		10	An ellipse

Second, there are 35 sheets of different colours to find and work out the answers.

Colour   Description

Orange '**Numbers**' – All these sheets have a number as the answer. There is one particular number that answers all the clues on that sheet. The clues are not necessarily straightforward! You need to explain how each clue gives you the one number you think is the answer to all the clues for that sheet.

Pink '**A Game of Two Halves**' – You will see pictures of different sports/games, and your task is to think of any sayings or concepts from that sport/game that have a mathematical meaning.

Lilac '**Have You Met Your Match?**' – Each lilac sheet has a number on it, and you must construct an equation or operation with that given number of matches. The numbers you use must be the same in size, for example ▯ or ▯ both stand for 1.

The matches must be whole (no half matches, please) and straight. To help you, matches are provided with the sheet. Please remember to draw your answer on your answer sheet.

Blue '**Directions**'

Yellow '**Terminology**' – These sheets are about mathematical terms.

Green '**Sequences**' – You have to work out the next number in the sequence and explain what the sequence is and how it works.

Red '**Shapes and Figures**'

Remember: the colour of the sheet tells you what type of problem, question or puzzle you are dealing with.

Teaching Notes

This is a treasure hunt with a difference because all of the items to be found are mathematical. Moving around the areas used and the varied coloured sheets add to the excitement. Many areas of mathematics are encountered within this single piece of work.

Key Elements

❖ observation
❖ following instructions
❖ team collaboration
❖ analysis
❖ calculation
❖ mathematical vocabulary
❖ equations
❖ directions
❖ sequences
❖ shapes.

Contexts

'The Mathematics Detectives' in this format is very much designed for a long enrichment session. Reducing the number of sheets and locations allows a shorter time allocation.

Organization

Thirty-five locations are needed. Some sheets can be placed around corners and out of direct sight, but it is not particularly helpful to have them truly hidden (the aim is to solve the questions, not just find them). It makes it less predictable if the 35 sheets are mixed up in terms of the seven types of question. The written information that follows needs to be transferred onto correctly–coloured paper. Appropriate pictures added to the sheets increase interest. Two objects are required – a tin of Heinz baked beans (with all reference to 57 blotted out) and a golf card/golf ball.

For items 1–10, check that they can be found in the area of the treasure hunt. If not, contrive these items along the route, or alter what has to be found.

Ensure that children answer all that they can on paper, emphasizing that many marks can be scored by explaining fully their answers and not just giving the correct solution.
Children are grouped into small teams (three–five) of mathematics detectives.

THE LOCATIONS, INFORMATION AND ANSWERS

Numbers 1–10 are not specific locations. The teams try to spot items, somewhere within the area used for the treasure hunt, that fit the general description. Some answers from typical locations follow.

1 Windows, chair, table, ball
2 A security panel, remote control, telephone
3 Dice, sugar cube, box
4 First Aid sign
5 Door, table, window, notice board

6 No Smoking sign
7 Sections of a lampshade, chair back
8 Radiators, wooden floor, window blinds
9 Smoke alarm, light fitting, lampshade
10 Spoon, door handle, gap in chair back

Locations

	Colour	Description on sheet
11	**Green**	1, 4, 9, 16, 25, ?
12	**Orange**	**a** Picture of the Prime Minister **b** A millennium divided by a century
		c If this is your birthday it is √9 years to being a teenager
13	**Blue**	(diagram below)
		a Why did Mr Burns complain to the taxi company?
		b Why was he satisfied by their explanation? (Give as many reasonable explanations as possible)

Mr Burns took a taxi from the railway station to visit a friend (house marked X).

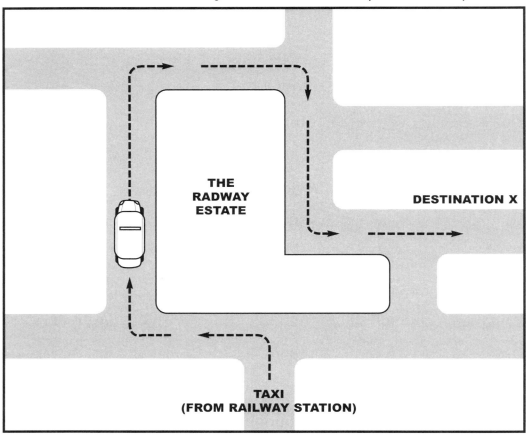

	Colour	Description on sheet
14	**Green**	1, 2, 4, 7, 11, 16, ?
15	**Red**	What do I have to multiply a cube by to get a dodecagon?
		(picture of cube on sheet adds interest)
16	**Orange**	**a** A tin of Heinz baked beans **b** Two consecutive odd numbers
		c To sum up they make a dozen!

	Answers		
11	**36:** Next square number	14	**22:** Add 1, 2, 3, 4, 5, 6 and so on
12	**10**	15	**2:** A cube has six faces and a dodecagon is a twelve-sided polygon
	a 10 Downing Street		
	b 1000 ÷ 100 = 10		
	c √9 = 3 10 + 3 = 13 (first teenage year)	16	**57**
			a Heinz 57 varieties
13	**a** The route went the long way round, as right, left and then right is shorter.		**b** 5 and 7 are two consecutive odd numbers
	b One-way system or roadworks or accident		**c** 5 + 7 = 12 (a dozen)

Colour	Description on sheet

17 Yellow   What do we call the side marked 'a'?

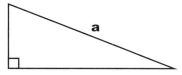

18 Lilac   Large number 11 with 11 matchsticks beside the sheet
19 Pink   Picture of motor racing
20 Red   What is this?

21 Yellow   Taking the numbers 3, 4 and 5 what is the difference between the sum and the product?
22 Blue   (diagram below)

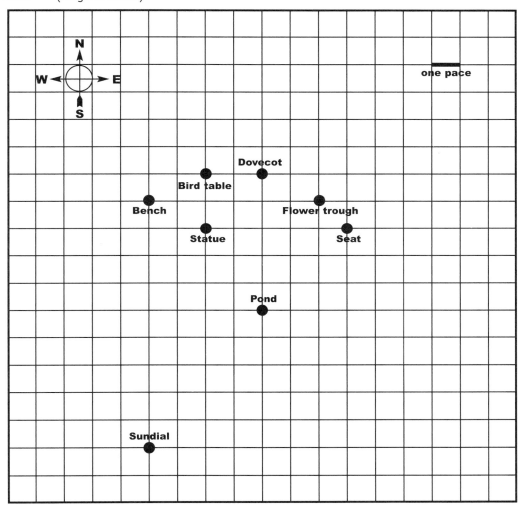

You start at the sundial – take two paces east, three paces north, one pace west, turn 90° right on the spot and take six paces north, again turn 90° right on the spot and take three paces east. Which garden feature is closest to you?

	Answers		
17	Hypotenuse	**19**	Average lap time, acceleration and so on
18	4 + 7 = 11 (there are others)	**20**	A regular hexagon
		21	**48:** The sum is 3 + 4 + 5 = 12 the product is 3 × 4 × 5 = 60 60 − 12 = 48
		22	The dovecot

Colour	Description on sheet
23 **Red**	Look at this net. What 3-dimensional object could be made?

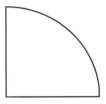

24 **Orange**	**a** Contains a 3 but 3 is not a factor
	b Of use in the bakery
	c Are you superstitious when sitting down to dinner?
	(picture of a pile of bread and cakes adds interest)
25 **Red**	If this is one

	a What do two make?
	b What do four make?
	c How many degrees does 1/3 contain?

26 **Blue**	(A large blue spot attached to a wall) Face the blue spot. Turn 90° in a clockwise direction. What do you see?
27 **Lilac**	Large number 15 with 15 matchsticks beside the sheet
28 **Green**	324, 108, 36, 12, ?
29 **Pink**	Picture of a snooker player
30 **Yellow**	Think about the number 6, the _____ are 1, 2, 3 and 6. What is the missing word?
31 **Orange**	**a** A golf ball or golf card with the comment 'Sounds like a term in the game' on the sheet
	b You really must be square to side with this number
	c Just out of the medals!
32 **Pink**	Picture of a cricketer
33 **Lilac**	Large number 13 and 13 matchsticks beside the sheet
34 **Green**	11, 22, 33, 44, 55, 66, 77, 88, 99, 101, ?
35 **Yellow**	If 310 is divided by 7, how is the number 2 involved and what do we call it?
36 **Red**	What consists of a circular base, a circular top of the same size and the curved surface formed by the vertical line segments joining them?
37 **Pink**	Picture of a dartboard

	Answers		
23	A triangular-based pyramid or tetrahedron	30	Factors
24	**13: a** 3 is in 13 but 3 is not a factor	31	**4: a** 'Fore' is a shouted warning about a golf ball that could hit someone
	b A baker's dozen is 13		**b** A square has four sides
	c 13 is regarded as an unlucky number to sit down to dinner		**c** Positions 1, 2 and 3 get medals
25	**a** Semi-circle	32	Run rate, batting average and so on
	b Circle	33	
	c 30° as a whole is 90°		
26	An object (teddy bear, vase of flowers or some other object placed correctly in relation to the blue spot)		(there are others)
27		34	**111:** ascending palindromic numbers
		35	310 ÷ 7 = 44 with 2 left over. 2 is called the remainder
	(there are others)	36	A cylinder
28	**4:** Divide by 3 each time	37	Treble, double and so on
29	Doubling in, an acute angle and so on		

Colour	Description on sheet
38 **Blue**	You are facing south. Where are you facing if you turn 270° in an anticlockwise direction?
39 **Orange**	**a** The square of a prime **b** Much in use in Germany **c** A single-digit number (Picture of, for example, German flag adds interest)
40 **Lilac**	Large number 19 and 19 matchsticks beside the sheet
41 **Yellow**	What name do we give to the line labelled 'b'?

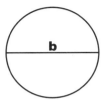

42 **Green**	$\dfrac{2}{3}, \ \dfrac{4}{6}, \ \dfrac{8}{12}, \ \dfrac{16}{24}, \ ?$
43 **Blue**	The two hands of the clock form an almost completely straight line. If the small hand is 150° past 12 o'clock **a** What is the closest number to which the large hand is pointing? **b** Explain why this is not quite a 'correct' time (A picture of a clock adds interest, but without hands as this may mislead)
44 **Pink**	Picture of a tennis player
45 **Lilac**	A large number 9 and 9 matchsticks beside the sheet

	Answers		
38	West	**43**	**a** 11
39	**9: a** 3 × 3 =9		**b** The hand would not quite be at five until the hour is reached.
	b 'nein' is 'no' in German and sounds like nine	**44**	Double fault, fifteen all and so on
	c 9 is a single-digit number	**45**	
40			
	(there are others)		(there are others)
41	Diameter		
42	$\dfrac{32}{48}$ – equivalent fractions		

Mathematics Pentathlon: Station One

what is your number?

For each of the following ten examples, find the number.

1 It is a two-digit odd number. It is less than two dozen. The sum of its digits forms an even number that is the cube of another even number.

2 It belongs in the six times table. It is a two-digit number. The sum of the digits is 12. The first digit is half the second digit.

3 It is a square number no more than a century. One digit is a square number, the other digit is a cube number.

4 It is an odd multiple of five. The product of its two digits is even. The sum of its digits makes a two-digit number consisting of two ascending odd numbers.

5 It is a two-digit prime number. It is less than three dozen. The product of the two digits makes a square number. The sum of the two digits is a prime number.

6 It is a two-digit number that is no more than the eighth Fibonacci number. It has six different factors. Three of these factors are odd and three are even.

7 It is a triangular number that is more than the seventh triangular number and less than the 14th triangular number. The two digits are different. The sum of the digits is even.

8 All three digits are odd, but each one is different. It is divisible by five. The first digit is the highest value. The sum of the digits is fifteen. The product of the digits is 105.

9 It is divisible by 11. It is less than 12 squared. The product of its digits is not a square. The sum of its digits is a square.

10 It is the cube of a single-digit number. The sum of the first two digits is equal to the third digit.

Mathematics Pentathlon: Station Two

symbolic

Create nine equations or 'inequalities' involving 'greater than' or 'less than' from exactly the following symbols and numbers.

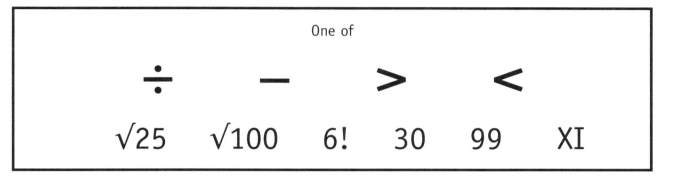

One of

$\div$ $-$ $>$ $<$

$\sqrt{25}$ $\sqrt{100}$ $6!$ 30 99 XI

Two of

The numbers 1, 2, 3, 4, 5, 6, 7, 8, 9, 10, 11

$+$

Six of

$\times$

Seven of

$=$

HINT

Look for the obvious answers first. This then reduces choice for using the other numbers and symbols.

Mathematics Pentathlon: Station Three

are you up to the mark?

Delroy liked to keep a record of his marks in mathematics.

During one particular period he scored the following:

$$\frac{5}{10} \qquad \frac{78}{100} \qquad \frac{54}{60} \qquad \frac{18}{40} \qquad \frac{100}{200}$$

$$\frac{7}{10} \qquad \frac{164}{200} \qquad \frac{21}{30} \qquad \frac{40}{80} \qquad \frac{17}{20}$$

$$\frac{49}{70} \qquad \frac{64}{80} \qquad \frac{105}{150} \qquad \frac{8}{10} \qquad \frac{26}{40}$$

Assuming that the pieces of work were of equal difficulty, work out the following:

1 What is the worst performance, given as the original mark?

2 What is the best performance, given as the original mark?

3 What is the mean, as a percentage mark?

4 What is the mode, as a percentage mark?

5 What is the median, as a percentage mark?

Mathematics Pentathlon: Station Four

mathematical eyes

1 **a** Which three-dimensional figure/object can be made from this net?

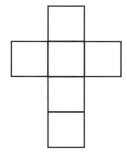

b Draw two other nets that would make the same three-dimensional object?

2 **a** What is the name for this four-sided figure?

b Draw its one line of symmetry.

3 On the planet Xanos there are two groups of inhabitants who are always fighting. These two peoples are the Circlons and the Squarons. Can you keep them apart by drawing three straight fences?

4 Here we see a map of the Isle of Approximation. If each of the squares represents 1km², work out the area of the island as accurately as you can by using your 'mathematical eyes'.

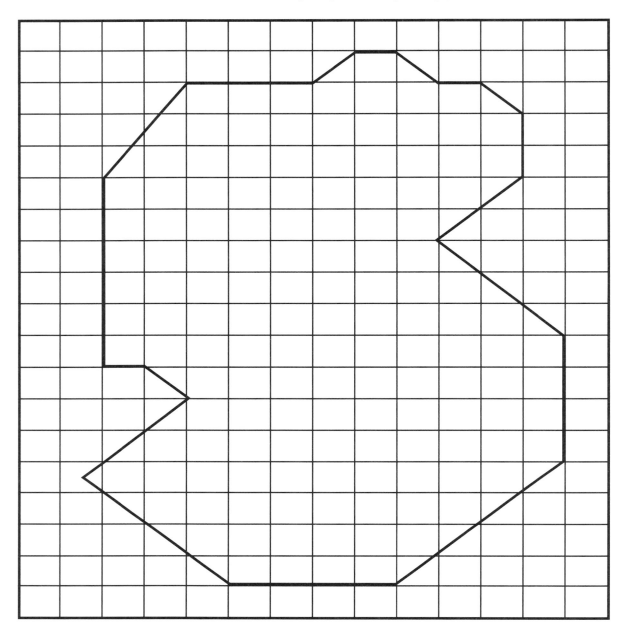

5 If each of the squares represents 1 cm², in the 5 × 5 grid:

   1 How many squares of 1cm side are there?

   2 How many squares of 2cm side are there?

   3 How many squares of 3cm side are there?

   4 How many squares of 4cm side are there?

   5 How many squares of 5cm side are there?

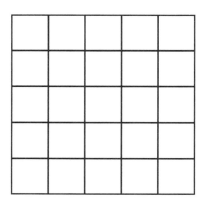

Mathematics Pentathlon: Station Five

puzzling

Work out the answers to the following. Keep your wits about you! Look for strategies.

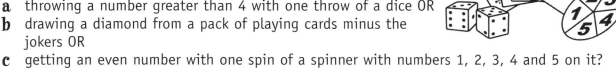

one
What is the most probable thing to happen from:
- **a** throwing a number greater than 4 with one throw of a dice OR
- **b** drawing a diamond from a pack of playing cards minus the jokers OR
- **c** getting an even number with one spin of a spinner with numbers 1, 2, 3, 4 and 5 on it?

two
Two cyclists set off, at the same time, to complete the same journey of 50 miles. Ben cycles at 15 miles per hour and has two stops, one of 20 minutes and one of ten minutes. Bill cycles at 12½ miles per hour and has one stop of 15 minutes. Who arrives first? How long elapses between the arrival of the first cyclist and the second cyclist?

three
Across a farmer's field there are 12 marker posts placed 40 metres apart. How far is it between the first post and the last?

four
Gill and Katy own 438 marbles between them. Katy has 46 more marbles than Gill. How many marbles has each child got?

five
Find two different ways to reach 36 by using each of the numbers 6, 4, 3, 6 once and once only.

six
Two men played Backgammon. They played nine games and each won the same number of games. None were drawn. How can this be?

seven
Following the exploits of Indiana Jones, we hear about the adventures of our own heroine, Virginia Smith. She was captured by the notorious Professor Hook who said that she had one chance to save her life. He gave her two bottles holding 5 and 7 litres respectively. There was a plentiful supply of water available and Virginia was given two minutes to find a way of measuring exactly 4 litres with the use of the two bottles only. Our heroine Virginia Smith solved the problem and escaped. How?

eight
Find four consecutive numbers that add up to 90.

Teaching Notes

When individual elements are put together to form a tournament, the resulting whole is greater than the sum of the parts. Moving from station to station allows a wide variety of material to be used and increases excitement and interest.

Key Elements

- teamwork
- working at speed
- handling data carefully
- problem solving
- mental agility
- subject-specific language
- symbols
- synthesis
- calculation
- percentages
- mean, median and mode
- wordplay
- spatial awareness
- approximation
- scale.

Contexts

'Mathematics Pentathlon' can be used in a number of ways:

- as individual items for enrichment work for those ahead on other tasks
- as individual items for differentiated homework
- as individual items for extension work on symbols and percentages
- as a tournament during an enrichment day, weekend, summer school or cluster day
- as individual items or complete special activity for the Mathematics Club.

Organization

For a tournament the children are divided into groups (3–5 is a good range in terms of size). The five stations are spaced out around the room. Each team moves around the stations in turn in a clockwise direction. They all meet the five sets of tasks but, obviously, in a different order. A set time is given, not too long, to inject some urgency into the work and promote concentration and focus. Something of the order of 12 to 15 minutes per station is suitable.

Answers

Station One: What Is Your Number?

1 17   Two-digit odd numbers under 24 are 11, 13, 15, 17, 19, 21 and 23. The addition of the digits make 8 or 2^3

2 48 $4 + 8 = 12$ 4 is ½ of 8

3 81   This is 9×9 8 is a cube number and 1 is a square number

4 85 $8 \times 5 = 40$ $8 + 5 = 13$

5 11 $1 \times 1 = 1$ (square) $1 + 1 = 2$ (prime)

6 18   The eighth Fibonacci number is 21. The six factors are 1, 2, 3, 6, 9 and 18, three being odd and three being even

7 91   The seventh triangular number is 28 and the 14th triangular number is 105. In between are 36, 45, 55, 66, 78 and 91

8 735 $7 + 3 + 5 = 15$ $7 \times 3 \times 5 = 105$

9 121   Twelve squared is 144 $1 \times 2 \times 1 = 2$, not a square $1 + 2 + 1 = 4$, a square

10 729   This is 9^3 $7 + 2 = 9$

NOTE:

These are believed to be unique answers, but if any alternative response fits the clues, it must be credited.

Station Two: Symbolic

In any order:

1 $6! = 6 \times 5 \times 4 \times 3 \times 2 \times 1$
2 $\sqrt{25} = 5$
3 $\sqrt{100} = 10$
4 $XI = 11$
5 $30 \div 10 = 3$
6 $9 \times 11 = 99$
7 $9 - 1 = 8$
8 $7 + 6 > 8$
9 $2 + 4 < 7$

This satisfies the conditions. Are there other solutions that take care of all numbers and symbols in just nine equations and 'inequalities'? The order used here works, with the most obvious items first.

Station Three: Are you up to the Mark?

The first task is to convert the marks into percentages:

$$\frac{5}{10} \rightarrow 50\% \qquad \frac{78}{100} \rightarrow 78\% \qquad \frac{54}{60} \rightarrow 90\% \qquad \frac{18}{40} \rightarrow 45\% \qquad \frac{100}{200} \rightarrow 50\%$$

$$\frac{7}{10} \rightarrow 70\% \qquad \frac{164}{200} \rightarrow 82\% \qquad \frac{21}{30} \rightarrow 70\% \qquad \frac{40}{80} \rightarrow 50\% \qquad \frac{17}{20} \rightarrow 85\%$$

$$\frac{49}{70} \rightarrow 70\% \qquad \frac{64}{80} \rightarrow 80\% \qquad \frac{105}{150} \rightarrow 70\% \qquad \frac{8}{10} \rightarrow 80\% \qquad \frac{26}{40} \rightarrow 65\%$$

Now place the fifteen percentages in order:

1	2	3	4	5	6	7	8	9	10	11	12	13	14	15
45	50	50	50	65	70	70	70	70	78	80	80	82	85	90

a The worst performance is $\dfrac{18}{40}$ (45%)

b The best performance is $\dfrac{54}{60}$ (90%)

c The mean is 69 ($1035 \div 15$)

d The mode is 70 (frequency 4)

e The median is also 70 (8th spot)

Station Four: Mathematical Eyes

1 **a** A cube
 b Any two from:

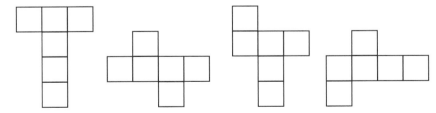

2 **a** Kite
 b

3

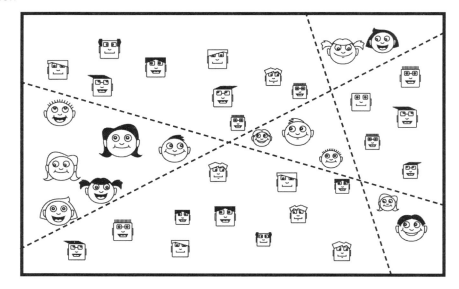

4   You count the full squares and then add up the 'bits' to get an approximate area of 136 + 11 = 147km².

5   **a** 25   **b** 16   **c** 9   **d** 4   **e** 1

Station Five: Puzzling

1   Answer is c.

   a $\dfrac{2}{6}$ = $\dfrac{1}{3}$ = $\dfrac{20}{60}$

   b $\dfrac{13}{52}$ = $\dfrac{1}{4}$ = $\dfrac{15}{60}$

   c $\dfrac{2}{5}$ = $\dfrac{24}{60}$

2   Ben cycles for three hours 20 minutes and has 30 minutes in stops, a total of three hours 50 minutes. Bill cycles for four hours and has a 15-minute break, a total of four hours 15 minutes; therefore, Ben arrived first, 25 minutes ahead of Bill.

3   440 metres. Many children will say 480 metres but there are only 11 spaces between the twelve marker posts.

4   Katy has 242 marbles and Gill 196. An easy method is to subtract 46 from 438 and halve the result for the lower number of marbles.

5   a   6 × 6 = 36   4 − 3 = 1   36 × 1 = 36
    b   6 × 3 = 18   6 − 4 = 2   18 × 2 = 36
    Are there any others?

6   This is a play on words. The two men were not playing each other and, therefore, could win the same number of games.

7   The 7-litre bottle is filled. From this, the 5-litre bottle is filled, leaving 2 litres in the larger bottle. The smaller bottle is then emptied and the 2 litres are transferred into it. The 7-litre bottle is filled again and water is poured into the smaller bottle until it is full. This takes 3 litres from the larger bottle, leaving exactly 4 litres of water.

8   The numbers are 21, 22, 23 and 24. An easy way in is to divide the total 90 by 4 and work from there.

Games/Thinking Skills Courses, Activities and Resources

Introduction

Many able children find games not only great fun but also very challenging and stimulating. Computer games are very popular and some can provide great intellectual stimulus. However, a danger of them is the isolation that, in some cases, they encourage. Games courses involve the really important element of social contact and interaction. There is also a tactile pleasure in physically handling the pieces of the games. It is, for instance, fascinating to watch children delighting in touching the tiles of Mah Jong, and the excitement when they 'twitter the sparrows' and then construct the Great Wall of China before play commences.

Mathematics plays a key role in many games. As well as calculation, logical thinking is important to success on many occasions. Searching out the strategies that increase the chances of success is part of a wider range of thinking skills that have been given new prominence by the Government and education advisers. There is encouragement to increase the proportion of higher-order thinking skills in the work of able pupils. In games courses participants exercise the mind in a pleasurable manner, thus combining enjoyment and intellectual development.

Learning should be hugely enjoyable!

```
+------------------------------------------------------------+
|                                                            |
|               Possible Titles for Courses                  |
|                        'Game On'                           |
|                  'It's All in the Game'                    |
|                      'Game Again'                          |
|                   'What's your Game?'                      |
|                     'Play the Game'                        |
|                  'Give the Game Away'                      |
|                   'Make a Game of it'                      |
|                                                            |
+------------------------------------------------------------+
```

Part One: Starters, Icebreakers

'Hilly Palm'
This is a word game with strong connections to noughts and crosses (page 177).

Forty-five minutes gives time to create, to play and to discuss. However, the extension task adds considerably to the time allocation.

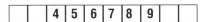

Strategy Games

Authors Reg Sheppard and John Wilkinson have put together a wonderful collection of 50 games and puzzles. *Strategy Games* is one of many splendid books from Tarquin Publications (1998). The 38 games and 12 puzzles can be photocopied for use within any educational establishment purchasing the book. At the start, there is a really useful section called 'Suggestions, Strategies and Solutions'. The contents are designed not only to cause enjoyment but also to promote mathematical thinking about patterns, relationships, number, space, tessellations, shapes, boundaries and networks. The authors also set out to help children to communicate ideas to each other and be drawn into new challenges by considering 'what if?' and 'why?' questions.

Times vary but many of the activities can be fitted into short time slots of 15–20 minutes, or so.

| 3 | 4 | 5 | 6 | 7 | 8 | | | |

These activities could be used in mathematics lessons or courses.

Brian Bolt

Brian Bolt has written brilliant collections of puzzles and games, published by Cambridge University Press, that many teachers use in mathematics. Among the very varied contents there are many items concerning chess, games involving pen-and-paper or easy-to-construct boards, and puzzles based upon dice and dominoes. Some titles to look out for include:

The Amazing Mathematical Amusement Arcade (1984)
Mathematical Funfair (1989)
Mathematical Cavalcade (1992)
A Mathematical Pandora's Box (1993)
A Mathematical Jamboree (1995).

There are activities to suit a great variety of timings.

| | | 5 | 6 | 7 | 8 | 9 | + |

David Silverman, Your Move

This book, published in 1973 by Kaye and Ward, is a treasure trove of games and puzzles that are ideal as 'starters'. However, you may have problems finding a copy as it is now out of print. 'Seven no Trump' (page 23), 'Woolworth' (page 25), 'The Racks' (page 39) and 'Bichrome' (page 91) have all been used to good effect.

Thirty to 35 minutes each.

| 3 | 4 | 5 | 6 | 7 | 8 | 9 | | |

Part Two: Mathematics And Logic

'What's your Game?'

This is a long, logical thought problem that involves games and also has a geographical content (page 179). Synthesis is a key element as there is a large amount of data to handle – a paragraph on each of the 20 games, details of teams competing in a games tournament and a number of clues.

About one hour is required for the work itself with another ten minutes, or so, required to go over the solution.

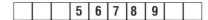

'Canny Crag'
MERATC

Based upon a dice game called 'Crag', this is an ideal exercise to include on a games course (page 73). However, as numbers figure prominently in 'Canny Crag' it is located in the Mathematics section, although can, obviously, be used in maths lessons or within maths courses.

One hour 15 minutes allows time to play 'Crag' as well as to complete the work and go over the 'answers'.

Raymond Smullyan

Chess problems are included in many publications and they are very popular. The normal format for chess problems is 'How do you checkmate in three or four moves?' Not so with Raymond Smullyan, who is a well-known mathematician and logician. He uses a technique called 'retrograde analysis', that looks to deducing certain facts about a game's past. In this way the reader becomes a Chess Detective!

The Chess Mysteries of Sherlock Holmes (Hutchinson, 1980) starts with a number of cases in which Holmes instructs Watson about what has happened in interrupted games, or games with a piece either knocked off the table or ambiguously placed between two squares. In the second half of the book, Holmes solves a mystery and a double murder and, as a bonus, there are ten problems set by Professor Moriarty.

The sequel is called *The Chess Mysteries of the Arabian Knights* (Hutchinson, 1981), the introduction of which explains how to tackle 'retrograde analysis' problems. Fifty new problems of chess detection are set out in six sections. A short appendix adds 12 conventional chess puzzles.

Part Three: Playing Games

There was a time when conscientious parents took time to play games with their children. As well as the family context element there was also great educational value, especially in basic mathematics. However, busier lifestyles led to a considerable decline in this although in recent years there has been a very welcome resurgence. A study carried out by Research Business International in 1997, and reported in the *Guardian*, showed a 7 per cent increase in board game sales in the previous year. Long may it continue!

There are major benefits in playing games at school, at home or in the family circle:

- ☞ social benefits from playing with others
- ☞ following instructions
- ☞ mathematical skills
- ☞ thinking strategies to enhance the chances of success
- ☞ word play and vocabulary development
- ☞ hand–eye co-ordination
- ☞ reading skills
- ☞ learning the boundaries of acceptable behaviour
- ☞ **enjoyment**!

A games course would not be a games course without some time actually playing games. Many could be considered but Mah Jong, Fives and Threes and Backgammon have been particularly successful.

Mah Jong

This is a total winner with children. They delight in the tactile aspects of handling the tiles and building the walls. They are entranced by the vocabulary of 'pung', 'chow', 'kong', and 'twittering the sparrows', and are intrigued by the names of the special hands such as 'Moon at the Bottom of the Well'.

After a course, especially in November or December, many children go away with a rewritten Christmas wish list!

Fives and Threes

A domino game, Fives and Threes is best played by four players, as two pairs. Simple mathematics is involved and strategy is very important, especially given that a player has to try and work with a partner's needs which have to be inferred as you are forbidden to talk about your 'hands'.

'Spots Before Your Eyes'
CRATC

This piece (page 65) explains the rules and sets a number of problems based upon play, finishing up with a logic problem to work out the dominoes in 'Harry's Hand' from a series of clues.

Backgammon

Luck plays a part in this game, as it does in Mah Jong and Fives and Threes but understanding strategy improves the chance of success considerably. Again, there is fascination with the specialist vocabulary – 'blot', 'the bar', 'inner table', 'outer table' and 'bear off'.

It is often said that games like those in this section take a few minutes to learn in terms of the rules but a lifetime to become an expert. Actual playings vary a little in time but 20 minutes is about right for one 'hand', perhaps a little less for Fives and Threes. However, in Mah Jong, Backgammon and Fives and Threes one 'hand' is part of a larger scoring game.

| | | 5 | 6 | 7 | 8 | 9 | + | |

Part Four: Longer Activities

'Making a Game of it' – A Presentation

Children are required to design a game that has a particular item, or items, as a key feature(s) (page 187). Groups make a presentation that is judged by particular success criteria.

One hour 45 minutes covers an introduction, work in teams, the presentations and the judging.

		4	5	6	7	8			

'The Games People Play' – A Tournament

There are two verbal rounds in this tournament, followed by one verbal or written round based upon particular games, and then a written round of 12 sections.

These activities can be used separately, to fit different time spans.

Round One: 'Monopoly Moves'

This is a visual memory round based upon the standard, original Monopoly board (page 193).

Round Two: 'Scrabbling for the Answer'

This round is word-based and features anagrams, or part anagrams, of the sort used in Scrabble and in other games (page 189).

Round Three: 'Darting Out'

Finishing in the darts tournament of '501' is the subject of Round Three (page 194).

Round Four: 'The Games People Play'

This final round provides the collective name for the tournament (page 190). Twelve sections cover a variety of approaches and include questions on a number of games.

Some of the games covered are more obscure than others. Members of the team add their experience and knowledge together. In any case, this is not a 20-out-of-20 mentality. 'How many points can be amassed?' is the correct approach, not 'Oh dear, I don't know that!'

Two hours are needed for the full tournament but the rounds can be used independently.

			5	6	7	8			

'The New Improved Version': A Presentation

Teams attempt to find ways of improving well-established games. The activity ends with a presentation to the respective game's manufacturer (page 198).

Two hours covers an initial introduction, the work of the teams, the presentations and the feedback.

		4	5	6	7	8	9		

'The Games Afoot' – A Tournament

This tournament comprises four rounds, two using materials in previous Barry Teare books and two included for the first time in this book.

Round One – 'Garbled Games'

This is a verbal round that encourages careful listening (page 200). The children have to discover 14 games hidden in passage one and 16 more in passage two.

Round Two – 'All in the Game'

In this written round the children create 20 pairs from a list of games and a second list of terms (page 201).

Round Three – 'Aerial Noughts and Crosses'
MERATC

Children construct a noughts-and-crosses board in their heads. They try to identify the placing of the winning line, having heard the filling of all nine spaces through the naming of co-ordinates (page 75).

When the teacher makes up the completed grids for use, it is sensible to have a good mixture of horizontal, vertical and diagonal winning lines. Examples where both noughts and crosses have a line of three but one will be the winner as it was completed first as well as examples where there was no winning line should be included.

Round Four – 'Games Teasers'
MERATC

Children try to solve 15 examples on the basis of numbers and initials (page 259). They are helped by introductory examples such as '52 C and 2 J in a P', which stands for '52 cards and 2 jokers in a pack of cards'.

One hour 45 minutes to two hours covers the introduction, the four rounds and the conclusion. However, the sections can be used separately in much shorter timeslots.

		5	6	7	8	9		

When and how you use these pieces is your decision. Collectively, they make an enjoyable and thought-provoking tournament. 'Garbled Games' could be regarded as English-based when the extension task is considered. 'Aerial Noughts and Crosses' is mathematical and can be used in maths lessons, maths courses or, indeed, thinking skills courses. 'Games Teasers' is included in the Competition Section of a previous book.

Hilly Palm

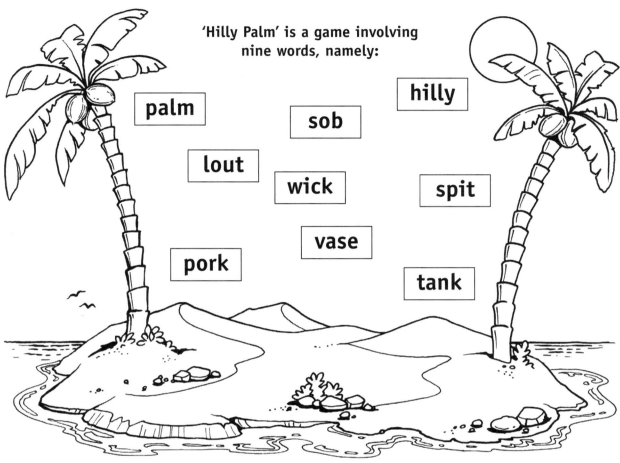

'Hilly Palm' is a game involving nine words, namely:

palm   sob   hilly   lout   wick   spit   vase   pork   tank

Your Tasks

1 Cut out nine slips of card and write out the words, one on each card. Lay them face up on a table.

2 Choose a partner to play the game with. Toss a coin to see who is to go first. Then, in turn, you and your opponent pick a card. The winner is the player who has possession of three cards that share a common letter.

3 Work out a strategy to maximize your chance of success.

4 'Hilly Palm' has links with another well-known game. What is that game? Explain your reasons for saying so.

Extension Task

Create your own game based upon the same principles but using nine totally different words. Give the game a suitable title, derived from the words.

Hilly Palm

Teaching Notes

This fascinating little game (there are many variations in existence) leads children to think logically about the words and to work out an appropriate strategy.

Key Elements

- ❖ analysis
- ❖ strategy
- ❖ deduction and inference
- ❖ transfer of ideas
- ❖ application (in the extension task).

Contexts

'Hilly Palm' can be used in a variety of ways:

- ❖ as part of a thinking skills lesson
- ❖ as enrichment work for those ahead on normal tasks
- ❖ as an activity during an enrichment day, weekend, summer school or cluster day
- ❖ as an activity for the English or Thinking Skills Club or Society
- ❖ as an open-access competition where the entry consists of responses to questions 3 and 4 and, especially, the extension task.

Some Answers

3   An obvious strategy is to work out the frequency of letters used in the nine words:

A	B	C	D	E	F	G	H	I	J	K	L	M
III	I	I		I			I	III		III	IIII	I

N	O	P	Q	R	S	T	U	V	W	X	Y	Z
I	III	III		I	III	III	I	I	I		I	

The most used are A, I, K, L, O, P, S and T, although it must be remembered that the L is slightly misleading as there is a double letter in 'hilly'. The word that contains four of the most-frequently used letters is SPIT. As a consequence, that is the key card to choose, followed by other words involving key letters, depending upon what is chosen by the opponent.

4   The fact that there are nine cards is a strong clue to the game of noughts and crosses. This becomes clearer when the cards are set out like a noughts and crosses board.

tank	wick	pork
vase	spit	sob
palm	hilly	lout

Three words will only have one letter in common when the board is looked at horizontally, vertically and diagonally. The horizontal letters are K, S and L, the vertical letters are A, I and O and the diagonal letters are T and P. In noughts and crosses the defence strategy is to go for the central space. The equivalent here is to choose 'SPIT' as soon as you are able. This opens up the maximum number of possibilities for future, useful cards.

Extension Task

This provides a real challenge. The key is to start with, what is essentially, the middle word and then work outwards. However, avoiding duplication of letters, other than those planned, is difficult.

    Enrichment Activities for Able and Talented Children © Barry Teare (Network Educational Press, 2004)

WHAT'S YOUR game?

With the growing popularity and revival of indoor games it is, perhaps, not surprising that more tournaments are being organized. Enthusiasts, linked by a magazine called *Games Galore*, were invited to compete in such a tournament run on the basis of teams.

The Events

Twenty very mixed games were selected for the tournament. They were chosen to range over many types – cards, dice, dominoes, board games, and so on. Another feature was to include games that had differing combinations of skill and luck involved.

These 20 games are described in the sheets headed 'A Galaxy of Games'.

The Teams

Teams of four were formed to represent various cities across Great Britain. The mix of men and women was left to the teams themselves. Unfortunately, at the last minute, a member of the Derby team was taken ill and they had to compete with just three players. Individuals, pairs or teams competed in each event on behalf of each of the cities. The teams are detailed on a sheet of that name.

"amazing!"

That was the newspaper headline after the tournament. Why? Normally some teams dominate but not this time. All 20 teams won one event each. Overall positions were determined by the team's placings in each game. The weakened Derby team finished tenth and won a single event like all the other teams!

Your Task

You are asked to work out which team won which event, including the game in which the weakened Derby team triumphed.

Piece information together from:

1 This title sheet
2 The catalogue of games – 'A Galaxy of Games'
3 Details of 'The Teams'
4 The clues

N.B. You may also find it useful to have a map of Great Britain available.

Further Points to Consider

1 How many of the 20 games do you know?
2 Which new ones might you like to try?

A GALAXY OF GAMES

MONOPOLY

This ever popular board game was invented in the mid-1930s. Players buy up sets of properties, railway stations and public utilities in London. Luck plays a part through the throw of the dice and Chance and Community Chest cards. The winner is the wealthiest player who bankrupts the other participants through charging them to 'land' on his or her properties.

FIVES AND THREES

This domino game uses the standard set-up to double six. Scoring along a pegging board is achieved by making the ends add up to multiples of five and three. The game is played by two pairs. One of the many skills is to 'read' your partner's hand. To win you have to score an exact number to reach the 61st hole.

BRIDGE

There are four participants, playing as two pairs. The first part of the game is where the pairs bid against each other as to the number of tricks they think they will win with clubs, diamonds, hearts or spades as trumps or with no suit as trumps, called, not surprisingly, no trumps. The play then follows with one player acting as 'dummy' – that is, laying down his or her cards face up on the table after the opening lead.

CLUEDO

This board game follows a detective theme. The players move into various rooms making suggestions about the murder of Dr Black. They have cards to help them towards the solution. The players try to eliminate possible answers through questioning the others. The object is to find out who was the murderer, what was the murder weapon and in which room the murder took place, before anyone else.

SNOOKER

This game is played on a table with six pockets and a set of balls – one each of white, yellow, green, brown, blue, pink and black, and 15 red. The two players use a cue to pot the balls into the pockets with the white ball and score points – one for a red and two to seven for the respective colours. There are rules on the order of potting and on what constitutes a foul.

POOL

Despite the similarity with snooker, there are some important differences. Each of the two players pots his or her own set before attempting to pot the one black ball. Winning is not by scoring as in snooker but by potting the black after your own set. The table is smaller than a snooker table.

CHESS

A very old game, first recorded from eighth century India. The 64-square board is coloured alternately black and white. Each player has 16 pieces – eight pawns plus a king and queen and two each of bishops, knights and rooks. The pieces make different moves. The two players try to capture the opponent's pieces to make it easier to win by trapping the king so that it cannot move out of 'check'.

DRAUGHTS

Played on a similar board to chess but here the two players use 12 identical pieces each – one having black and the other white. These pieces are positioned on the black squares and they can only move diagonally. A player attempts to capture all of his or her opponent's pieces by jumping over them, onto an empty square beyond. Any piece reaching the opposite side of the board is made into a king or crown, denoted by placing a second piece on top.

WHIST

This card game led to a number of others, such as Bridge. Two pairs play against each other although some variations like knock-out whist are for individual players. Tricks are won by laying the highest card of the four or by using a 'trump'. There is no bidding before the play, as in Bridge.

MAH JONG

This is best played by four players who play individually, although there are various versions for fewer players. One hundred and forty-four tiles are used, the majority in three suits – bamboo, circles and characters – but there are also winds, dragons, flowers and seasons. The tiles are arranged as a square with walls built using two rows of tiles to start the game. The winner is the first person to gain Mah Jong – 14 tiles in four sets of three and a pair. There are also a large number of special hands with strange titles.

BEETLE

Children are the normal players of this dice game. The numbers on the dice represent different parts of a beetle – body, head, legs, and so on. For obvious reasons the body has to come first. Play continues until one person has a complete beetle.

BACKGAMMON

Like chess, Backgammon is one of the classics. It is played on a board with 30 pieces: 15 of one colour and 15 of another. Moves are determined by dice. Backgammon is a race game for two players. The object is to be the first player to move his or her pieces round the board into the home or inner table and from there to remove them from the board, or to 'bear them off'.

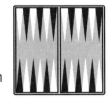

MANCALA

A game for two players, Mancala has often been called the national game of Africa. This is a generic name for hundreds of games in which seeds are moved from cup to cup around a board. The object is to win all your opponent's seeds.

SCRABBLE

This word game is one of the most popular games in the world. Letters of the alphabet on 104 tiles are worth differing points depending on the difficulty of using them. The players take turns to make words on a board in an interlocking fashion. Scores can be greatly enhanced by covering spaces that multiply the value of the letter or the whole word.

PIG

A game of pure luck, Pig can be played by any number of people. It is played with one dice. Scores are accumulated but the throwing of a one cancels all the scoring for a player in that particular round. Players, therefore, end their go before they are forced to by throwing a one. The normal winning total to be achieved is 101.

DARTS

There are a large number of games under this general heading. The players, who have three darts each, throw at a board on the wall from behind the 'oche'. The numbers 1 to 20 occupy a segment of the scoring circle with small areas designated as 'doubles' and 'trebles'. In the centre is an inner bull inside an outer bull. The object of the standard game, played by two individuals or two teams, is to score the exact number of 501, both starting and finishing by throwing a double, although variations are played.

YAHTZEE

This dice game, for any number of players, uses five dice. They are thrown together on the first go. The player retains which ones he or she wants to keep and throws the others on two more occasions. On each round the player secures a score according to various described categories. The player with the highest score wins.

RUMMY

A card game for two to six players, Rummy is very popular. Each player is dealt a number of cards depending upon the number of participants. He or she tries to be first to get rid of all the cards in his or her hand by forming three- or four-card groups of the same rank or runs of three or more cards of the same suit.

SHUT THE BOX

Boxes numbered one to nine are built into a purpose-designed tray. The players, any number, take turns to throw two dice. The total is used to close boxes that add up to that total. A player continues until he or she cannot close any new boxes with the latest throw. The numbers of the unclosed boxes are added up. The player with the lowest score wins.

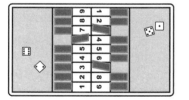

NINE MEN'S MORRIS

Some 3,000 years old, Nine Men's Morris is played by two people on a board consisting of three squares one inside the other. Four lines link the mid-points of the sides of the three squares. This forms 24 points of intersection or stars. Each player puts their nine counters on to these stars in turn. The players try to make a mill (complete line) of three pieces. This allows capture of an enemy piece. A player wins by getting his or her opponent down to two pieces.

NOTE

The description of a game in the clues refers to the essential components, for example:

1 'Dice games' involve dice as the main factor not just for throwing to make progress on a board as in, say, Cluedo.

2 'Card games' involve cards as the main factor not just as a contributory component as in, say, Monopoly.

the teams

Chester	Tom, Bernard, Richard, Sam
Leeds	Alison, Barbara, Simon, Colin
Nottingham	Michael, Janet, Julie, Peter
Swansea	Christine, David, Pamela, Susan
York	Graham, Roger, Paul, Alison
Cardiff	Anne, Maxine, Barbara, Rachel
Exeter	Marilyn, Tim, Susan, Andrew
Lancaster	Harry, Julian, John, Steven
Plymouth	Paul, Carol, Fiona, Liz
Cambridge	Terry, Philip, Ann, Hilary
Lincoln	Andrew, Brian, Barbara, Alice
Aberdeen	Cameron, Gordon, John, Kate
Belfast	John, Kathleen, Mary, Margaret
Edinburgh	Helen, Hazel, Alison, Ruth
Oxford	Bernard, Russell, Donna, Lionel
Derby	Deborah, Mark, Lucy
Durham	Catherine, Ruth, Sylvia, Beth
Southampton	Stephen, Len, Tony, Roger
Liverpool	Ben, Eric, Eve, Barbara
Gloucester	Graham, Gail, Grant, Gillian

THE CLUES

1 The southernmost and northernmost cities both won card games.

2 It was a team made up of members whose initials make palindromes that won the only domino game.

3 The card game aimed at individuals and never played as pairs brought success to a Welsh team of all women.

4 It was also an all-women's team which won a 'board game' but where the playing was not on the board but at the board.

5 Two all-male teams won the two games involving a table with pockets.

6 The city with the longest name won the game with the second shortest name.

7 One of the two English cities most famous for their universities found success 'on the streets of London'.

8 The most easterly of the 20 cities 'gathered in the seeds' very successfully indeed.

9 The two White Rose cities won the two games involving tiles.

10 Paul was the only man in his team but he proved to be a very successful dummy for his partner in his team's winning event.

11 It was very appropriate that Liverpool won a game that sounded like some of its most famous citizens even though the spelling is different.

12 The two games 'in a food chain' were won by the only city 'across the water' and a city made famous by Beatrix Potter's tailor and a nursery-rhyme doctor whose name rhymes with that city.

13 Hazel's calculating skills were not enough for her team to succeed in the game of 'finishing doubles'.

14 The four Gs won a game ending in that same letter.

15 It seemed appropriate for Tom's all-male team to succeed at the game stressing their gender.

16 The two games involving 32 white squares and 32 black squares were won by the two remaining teams with two men and two women.

17 Welsh and Scottish teams triumphed in dice games.

18 The team from a very old city with city walls thought it was amusing that their success should also involve walls.

19 It was the one man in the team who sealed the win with his successful run involving the throws of the two dice.

20 The city whose players could be seen on the MAST (initially) was successful in moving diagonally for the church, 1, 2 or 2, 1 when in armour and up and down and side to side when as a bird in 'an Englishman's home'.

Teaching Notes

'What's your Game' is a lengthy, logical thinking exercise that encourages analysis of data, synthesis and careful recording. There is a geographical element as some of the clues refer to the locations of cities. Use of this piece of work during enrichment courses has shown a remarkable lack of knowledge about Britain, even from able children. 'What's your Game?' has at its core the fascinating world of indoor games. The range of games included in the 'galaxy' provides not only enjoyment and social interaction but also a number of educational benefits. This piece of work takes some time to complete and it therefore encourages the development of a longer span of concentration – a very valuable asset for able children.

Key Elements

❖ logical thinking

❖ geographical content

❖ synthesis of data

❖ encouragement to explore the wonderful world of indoor games

❖ careful recording

❖ wordplay

❖ span of concentration

❖ information processing.

Contexts

'What's your Game?' can be used in the following ways:

❖ as part of a thinking skills course

❖ as enrichment work for those ahead on normal work

❖ as differentiated homework

❖ as an activity during an enrichment session, cluster day or summer school

❖ as an activity for the Games Club.

Solution

1 Plymouth and Aberdeen won two out of Bridge, Whist and Rummy, but we do not know which and which way round.
2 Lincoln (ABBA) or Liverpool (BEEB) won at Fives and Threes.
3 Rummy was won by Cardiff. This game is eliminated from **Clue 1**.
4 Either Edinburgh or Durham won at darts.
5 Two of Chester, Lancaster and Southampton won the snooker and pool events.
6 Southampton won at pool and from **Clue 5** it was Chester or Lancaster that won at snooker.
7 Either Oxford or Cambridge triumphed at Monopoly.
8 Cambridge won at Mancala and therefore, from **Clue 7**, it was Oxford who won at Monopoly.
9 Leeds and York succeeded at Mah Jong and Scrabble but which way round?
10 Plymouth took the Bridge event and therefore, from **Clues 1** and **3**, it was Aberdeen that won at Whist.
11 Beetle was taken by Liverpool (The Beatles) which means, from **Clue 2,** that Lincoln won Fives and Threes.
12 Backgammon and Pig are the games and Belfast and Gloucester (Dr Foster) are the cities, but which way round?
13 The only Hazel is in Edinburgh's team who did not win at darts and therefore, from **Clue 4**, Durham did.
14 The four Gs (Graham, Gail, Grant and Gillian) come from Gloucester and, therefore, with **Clue 12** this means that Gloucester won at Pig and Belfast at Backgammon.
15 Tom played for the all-male Chester team who succeeded at Nine Men's Morris and, with **Clues 5** and **6**, it was Lancaster that won the snooker.

16 The games are chess and draughts and the two teams with two men and two women not already allocated are Nottingham and Exeter.

17 Swansea and Edinburgh won at Yahtzee and Shut the Box, but which way round? This, therefore, means that the depleted Derby team won at Cluedo (the only game not yet mentioned).

18 With **Clue 9** we now know that York won Mah Jong and Leeds scored a success at Scrabble.

19 Swansea's team contains one man (Edinburgh are all women) and the game of two dice is Shut the Box. Edinburgh won at Yahtzee.

20 Exeter (Marilyn, Andrew, Susan, Tim) won the Chess (bishop, knight, rook/castle) and therefore, from **Clue 16**, Nottingham triumphed at draughts.

The Results

City	Game
Oxford	Monopoly
Lincoln	Fives and Threes
Plymouth	Bridge
Derby	Cluedo
Lancaster	Snooker
Southampton	Pool
Exeter	Chess
Nottingham	Draughts
Aberdeen	Whist
York	Mah Jong
Liverpool	Beetle
Belfast	Backgammon
Cambridge	Mancala
Leeds	Scrabble
Gloucester	Pig
Durham	Darts
Edinburgh	Yahtzee
Cardiff	Rummy
Swansea	Shut the Box
Chester	Nine Men's Morris

Making a Game of it

Imagine if you had invented a famous game like Monopoly or Scrabble.

Well, perhaps, that is just a little too much to expect but you could use your imagination to devise an intriguing game, working in collaboration with others.

Take up the challenge.

See if you can succeed in 'Making a Game of it'.

Your Tasks

1. Think carefully about the objects included in your box.
2. Devise a game in which those objects play a key role. You are entitled to use, in addition, the standard features of many games – a board, dice, cards, counters, play money and so on.
3. Make the game and write down the rules.
4. Prepare a short presentation to persuade the leading executives of a games company that your invention is the one that they should produce.
5. Keep in mind, at all times, the success criteria for judging, given below.

The Success Criteria

1. How well the team works together.
2. The extent to which the objects drawn play a key part in the game.
3. The clarity of the rules so that the method of play can be readily understood.
4. The quality of the game in terms of interest and entertainment.
5. The degree to which the presentation is likely to persuade company executives to produce your game.

Making a Game of it

Teaching Notes

This is an activity that able children take up enthusiastically and successfully. It has contrasting stages within it so that different skills and abilities are tested.

Key Elements

- ❖ following instruction carefully
- ❖ collaboration and teamwork
- ❖ creativity and imagination
- ❖ a mixture of some parameters but then open-endedness
- ❖ design
- ❖ a strong practical element
- ❖ presentational skills, including persuasion.

What You Will Need

- ❖ A series of objects to feature in the games. These objects should be unusual and capable of many uses. Each set of objects are boxed in a different coloured box. Examples of items used successfully include:
  - **a** The blue box – six wooden parrots, different colours as well as multi-coloured
  - **b** The green box – sets of plastic garden-plant labels, ten of each of ten colours
  - **c** The gold box – six giant plastic insects and two plastic frogs
  - **d** The purple box – three Christmas objects (miniatures – Christmas tree, snowman, garland), 17 holly leaves cut out from green card and 26 holly berries cut out from red card
  - **e** The orange box – wooden lighthouse, wooden ship(s) and two wooden sailor figures
  - **f** The red box – pack of 20 wooden ladybirds
- ❖ Strips of coloured card (or coloured counters) to match the boxes
- ❖ Standard games equipment, such as dice, shakers, spinners
- ❖ Card, paper, scissors, pens, coloured pencils, paints, sticky tape, paper clips and so on!

Organization

1 The children are sorted into teams of three, four or five.
2 The pupil sheet is handed out and the instructions for the event are explained.
3 Each team picks a piece of coloured card (or a coloured counter). This indicates which box the team will be working with.
4 The teams carry out their work.
5 The room is tidied and the furniture is rearranged to facilitate the presentations and to create a suitable atmosphere.
6 The pieces of coloured card (coloured counters) are chosen for a second time to determine the order of the presentations.
7 The presentations are given.
8 The panel of 'company executives' withdraw to make a decision. While this is going on the teacher could discuss with the children the skills involved in the activity.
9 The panel gives a feedback on each team, referring closely to the success criteria. The 'contract' is awarded to the team that best answered the success criteria.

If nobody is available to form a panel, the teacher carries out the assessment.

Enrichment Activities for Able and Talented Children © Barry Teare (Network Educational Press, 2004)

Tournament: The Games People Play

Can you look at the jumble of letters and rearrange them into a word.

This is the teasing world of anagrams.

Anagrams are the basis of many games, such as Scrabble, and they often figure prominently in crosswords.

You are presented with ten sets of letters, the vowels on one side, followed by the consonants. What is the longest word that you can make for each set of letters, A–J? The scoring of points depends upon the number of letters that you make into a correct word, one point per letter.

Seeing that all the letters make the word DELIGHTFUL scores ten points.

FLIGHT scores six

whereas FLIGHTED increases the points to eight.

	Vowels	Consonants
(a)	O A	Y H M N C R
(b)	E A I U	D T T L
(c)	O U A E	G N D S R
(d)	A I U	C T R S N
(e)	E E E	D C R P S T
(f)	I O U	H B L R R
(g)	U O A	B D P C R
(h)	O I E	S T R B M N
(i)	A A E	W T L R F L
(j)	E A E	H T P L N

THE GAMES PEOPLE PLAY

1 SNOOKER
a What is the maximum break?
b How is it made up?
c How is it possible that one player can score more than the maximum break in a frame of snooker?
d I pot the black but it cannot be replaced on its spot due to another ball being in the way – where is it placed?

2 MONOPOLY
a Which is the second most expensive set in total value?
b How many railway stations are there?
c Which is the first utility you meet after Go?
d As well as Chance what other feature gives good and bad luck cards?
e What inexpensive facility is available at the third corner of the board?

3 CRYPTIC PIECES
Work out the names of the pieces from the clues and number of letters:
a Of low value, manipulated by others (4)
b Sounds like a person who investigates (7)
c One small part of a floor or roof covering (4)
d A person who adds up (7)
e Comedian (5)
f Elegant head gear to move around this particular board (3, 3)

4 HOW MANY?
a Squares on a chess board?
b Tricks in a grand slam at Bridge?
c Dominoes of each number (that is, fours, fives and so on) in a set that goes up to double six?
d Suspects in the original 'Cluedo'?
e Tiles in a kong in the game of Mah Jong?

5 GAMES OF CONFUSION
(Anagrams)
Rearrange the letters to give the names of five games:
a MOCK BAG MAN (10)
b HARD GUST (8)
c ON MY POOL (8)
d GRACE BIB (8)
e DREADS LAND SNEAKS (6, 3, 7)

6 WINNING WAYS

What constitutes a win at:

- **a** Draughts
- **b** Monopoly
- **c** Chess
- **d** Mah Jong
- **e** Cluedo
- **f** Noughts and Crosses
- **g** Battleships
- **h** Bridge (one particular hand)
- **i** Pool
- **j** Hangman

7 COMING TO TERMS

What do the following mean?

- **a** Trumps
- **b** Stalemate
- **c** Trick
- **d** Twittering the sparrows or washing
- **e** Crown
- **f** To castle
- **g** Box or dead wall
- **h** Twist
- **i** Snap
- **j** Yahtzee
- **k** Run
- **l** Wedge

8 ON THE CARDS

- **a** Which number is the first played in Donkey?
- **b** What are Jacks, Queens and Kings often called?
- **c** In Bridge what can you bid in apart from spades, hearts, diamonds and clubs?
- **d** In Clock Patience which cards do you not want to see?
- **e** Which game's name is made up of an alcoholic drink and a possessive adjective?

9 COLOUR

What colour(s) are:

- **a** the three dragons in Mah Jong?
- **b** the four traditional colours for Ludo counters?
- **c** the first piece to move in a game of chess?
- **d** the Leicester Square, Coventry Street and Piccadilly set in Monopoly?
- **e** the 'holy' suspect in Cluedo?
- **f** the canine addition in Super Cluedo?
- **g** the four of diamonds?
- **h** the History/Yesterday questions in Trivial Pursuit?

10 PLACES

In which games do we find:

- **a** a castle for prisoners of war?
- **b** the wall?
- **c** 'Dead Hole'?
- **d** Vine Street?
- **e** Tudor Close?
- **f** the Carriage Depot?
- **g** the hexagonal hub?
- **h** the Bar?

11 CRYPTIC MOVES

Work out the correct moves from the clues and the number of letters.

a Close friend captures the king (4)
b A machine to grind on the river (4)
c Success when besieging a town or castle (7)
d Athletes go high or long (4)
e Left without ideas or money (8)

12 GAME WORDSEARCH

There are 30 games to be found horizontally, vertically, diagonally, forwards, backwards, up, down.

B	I	L	L	I	A	R	D	S	X	E	H	P	G	O
A	B	B	X	Z	P	H	D	O	X	S	A	I	G	L
C	L	U	E	D	O	A	O	L	B	E	P	G	Z	L
K	S	I	R	P	O	L	N	I	R	O	P	Y	C	E
G	G	P	Z	X	L	M	K	T	I	N	Y	M	X	H
A	I	G	O	H	S	A	E	A	D	I	F	M	N	T
M	O	N	O	P	O	L	Y	I	G	M	A	U	N	O
M	A	N	C	A	L	A	D	R	E	O	M	R	D	B
O	S	C	R	A	B	B	L	E	P	D	I	U	Z	R
N	O	C	I	X	E	L	Q	Z	X	P	L	C	C	A
T	I	C	T	A	C	T	O	E	D	F	I	Z	F	X
T	R	I	V	I	A	L	C	G	P	X	E	X	Z	F
P	U	R	S	U	I	T	B	B	A	S	S	E	H	C
D	U	N	G	E	O	N	S	A	N	D	X	Z	C	P
D	R	A	G	O	N	S	S	N	S	T	S	I	H	W

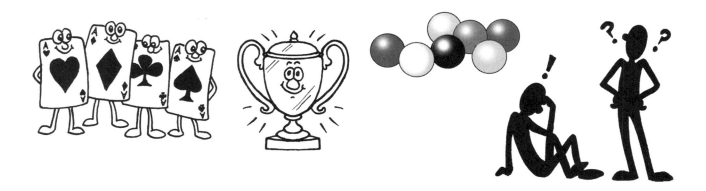

Teaching Notes

The complete tournament has four rounds. The first three rounds, detailed below, are found separately in this book.

Round One is a verbal round called '**Monopoly Moves**' (see below). There is no pupil sheet.

Round Two can be a verbal or written round (see page 189) called '**Scrabbling for the Answer**'.

Round Three is a verbal round called '**Darting Out**' (see page 194). There is no pupil sheet.

Round Four is a written round (see children's sheets page 190) called '**The Games People Play**'. It is a series of puzzles and unusual questions based upon a wide variety of games.

Round One: Monopoly Moves

The children are asked to study a standard monopoly board for some five minutes or so. They are advised to try and establish a visual representation in their heads. The board is then removed and a series of questions are asked about the layout of the board and movement around it. These questions can be of any type but, for convenience, a set is given below.

Questions

a   How many positions are there on the board in total?
b   I start at GO and throw a seven – why is my progress now doubtful?
c   Name any property worth £200.
d   What are the 'double possibilities' at the first corner after Go?
e   I am on King's Cross Station and I throw double 5, where do I get to?
f   I land on Community Chest on the side including Mayfair – the card sends me back three spaces – what do I have to do?
g   If I am on the Electric Company and I throw the maximum possible, where do I finish up?
h   On any of the three-part sets of properties, what can I throw and still be on the same set (without involving Chance and Community Chest)?
i   I am on Regent Street. Which number do I have to avoid throwing so that I will not have to pay Super Tax?
j   From Pentonville Road I look straight across the board. Which property is exactly opposite me?

These questions have been written to give a certain variety of operation. Any of them can be substituted. The number can be increased. If a board other than the standard, original, one is used, appropriate questions would need to be written. Other cities than London have been used in the Monopoly game and there are also specialist theme games in some versions.

Answers

a   40
b   Chance
c   Vine Street or a station or Go
d   In Jail /Just Visiting
e   Marylebone Station
f   Go to Jail
g   Trafalgar Square
h   1 and 1, or 1 and 2
i   7
j   Strand

Round Two: Scrabbling for the Answer

Word games are a useful contrast to mathematical or logical items. When used in a tournament, they increase variety and add to the number of strengths and abilities being challenged.

Contexts

The piece given here is a written version but the sets of letters can be given verbally.

As well as part of a tournament, 'Scrabbling for the Answer' can be used in a number of ways:

❖ as an extension to vocabulary work

❖ as differentiated homework

❖ as an enrichment task for those who have completed tasks early and well

❖ as a short activity during an enrichment session, weekend, summer school or cluster day.

Answers

a	monarchy (8 points)	f	horrible (8 points)
b	latitude (8 points)	g	cupboard (8 points)
c	dangerous (9 points)	h	brimstone (9 points)
d	curtains (8 points)	i	waterfall (9 points)
e	respected (9 points)	j	elephant (8 points)

NOTE: Shorter words score the appropriate points for the number of letters used correctly.

Round Three: Darting Out

Introduction for the Children

In the game of darts, this game is won by the player or team who first score 501 **exactly**, starting with 501 and working towards 0, both starting and finishing on a double. For each number on the dartboard, 1–20, there is a segment like a piece of pie. A dart landing in the main area of a number scores the number itself. On the outer edge of the number segment there is a small wired area known as the double. A dart landing in that area scores twice the number, for example a dart in double 19 scores 38. Midway between the centre of the dartboard and the double there is a narrow wired area known as the treble. A dart landing in that area scores three times the number, for example a dart in treble 11 scores 33. At the centre of the board are two concentric circles. The inner one is called the inner bull and a dart in there scores 50. The outer one is called the outer bull and scores 25.

A player throws three darts on each of his or her turns. So if Freddie Flight hit the single 20, the treble 18 and the inner bull with his three darts, he would score 124 (20 + 54 + 50). To reduce the score down from 501 as quickly as possible, the magic trio of darts is three treble twenties which scores the legendary **one hundred and eighty**!

To help those with little, or no, experience of the game, it is helpful to have a dartboard (or picture of a dartboard) to help explain the scoring.

Questions

How would you secure the following scores to 'go out' (finish) at the game of 501? Normally for these questions you have three darts to finish, unless otherwise stated. You must end with a double to finish successfully.

a   144

b   69

c   180

Enrichment Activities for Able and Talented Children © Barry Teare (Network Educational Press, 2004)

d 93
e 11 in two darts
f 65 (i) with two darts and no trebles
    (ii) with two darts and the lowest treble possible
    (iii) with three darts
g Peter Points, nicknamed the Sharp Cockney, likes to finish on double 16 if possible – it is his favourite. For the following say if this is possible and, if so, how:
    (i) 39 with two darts
    (ii) 152
    (iii) 160
    (iv) 82 with two darts

Clearly, any of the individual questions can be substituted to increase, or decrease, the level of difficulty.

Each team can write down appropriate answers in a short time scale (although the answer should be arrived at mentally, not on paper) or 'Darting Out' can be used as a speed round. In that case, the first team to answer correctly scores the points. An incorrect answer 'freezes out' other members of that team until the next question.

Some Answers to the Set Questions

In most cases there will be more than one way to solve the question. The following are merely examples. The teacher needs to give credit for alternative, correct responses.

a Treble 20, treble 20, double 12
b (i) With three: 1, treble 20, double 4
   (ii) With two: treble 19, double 6
c Cannot be done
d (i) With three: 3, treble 20, double 15
   (ii) With two: treble 19, double 18
e 1, double 5
f (i) With two and no trebles: outer bull, double 20
   (ii) With two and the lowest treble possible: treble 9, double 19
   (iii) With three: 1, treble 20, double 2
g (i) With two: yes, 7, double 16
   (ii) Yes, treble 20, treble 20, double 16
   (iii) No
   (iv) With two: yes, inner bull, double 16

Note
For **b** and **d** answers for two darts have been given in case the teacher would like to ask for solutions not involving three darts.

Round Four: The Games People Play

Answers

1 **Snooker**
   a   147
   b   Fifteen reds followed by a black each time plus the six colours.
   c   The other player gives away penalty points before or during breaks without ever scoring him/herself.
   d   The next highest valued colour spot that is available.

2 **Monopoly**
   a   Leicester Square, Coventry Street and Piccadilly
   b   Four
   c   Electric Company
   d   Community Chest
   e   Free Parking

3 **Cryptic Pieces**

a	Pawn		**d**	Counter
b	Checker or Chequer		**e**	Joker
c	Tile		**f**	Top hat

4 **How Many?**

a	64		**d**	6
b	13		**e**	4
c	7			

5 **Games of Confusion**

a	Backgammon		**d**	Cribbage
b	Draughts		**e**	Snakes and Ladders
c	Monopoly			

6 **Winning Ways**
   a   Taking all your opponent's pieces.
   b   Taking all your opponents' money and properties.
   c   Checkmating your opponent's king.
   d   Completing a Mah Jong – that is, four pungs/kongs and a pair, three pungs/kongs and a chow and a pair, or a special hand.
   e   Naming the murderer, weapon and room first.
   f   Completing a line of three noughts or crosses.
   g   Sinking all your opponent's ships first.
   h   Making your contract.
   i   Potting the black ball after all your particular colour.
   j   Hanging your opponent before he or she gets the word or vice versa.

7 Coming to Terms

   a A suit that will beat all others.
   b A drawn game at chess as one person cannot move without going into check.
   c A group of cards from one hand in a game.
   d Shuffling the tiles at the start of a game of Mah Jong.
   e Making a double at draughts by reaching your opponent's end of the board.
   f In chess by moving the positions of your king and one of the rooks or castles.
   g The 16 tiles not in the wall at Mah Jong. N.B. give credit for reference to 'Shut the Box'.
   h Taking another card in Pontoon.
   i Two cards the same following each other.
   j All five dice produce the same number over three throws.
   k Cards in sequence.
   l A piece (one of six) in Trivial Pursuit.

8 On the Cards

a	7	**d**	Kings
b	Picture cards N.B. credit 'Honours'	**e**	Rummy
c	No trumps		

9 Colours

a	(i) White (ii) Red (iii) Green	**e**	Green
b	(i) Red (ii) Blue (iii) Green (iv) Yellow	**f**	Black
c	White	**g**	Red
d	Yellow	**h**	Yellow

10 Places

a	Colditz	**e**	Cluedo
b	Mah Jong	**f**	221b Baker Street
c	Fives and Threes	**g**	Trivial Pursuit
d	Monopoly	**h**	Backgammon

11 Cryptic Moves

a	Mate	**d**	Jump
b	Mill	**e**	Bankrupt
c	Capture		

12 Game Wordsearch

1	Backgammon	**11**	Halma	**21**	Risk
2	Billiards	**12**	Happy Families	**22**	Rummy
3	Brax	**13**	Hex	**23**	Scrabble
4	Bridge	**14**	Lexicon	**24**	Shogi
5	Chess	**15**	Ludo	**25**	Snap
6	Cluedo	**16**	Mancala	**26**	Solitaire
7	Dominoes	**17**	Monopoly	**27**	Tic Tac Toe
8	Donkey	**18**	Othello	**28**	Trivial Pursuit
9	Dungeons and Dragons	**19**	Pig	**29**	UNO
10	Go	**20**	Pool	**30**	Whist

In this round it is not expected that the children will be able to answer all the questions; it is more a question of how much they can work out.

The New Improved Version

Often, when watching television, there are advertisements for the latest versions of particular products. In these advertisements, a line often used is 'the new improved version'.

Games manufacturers, similarly, produce new formats of a popular game. Cluedo is a really good example of this development. In Waddington's original Cluedo there were nine rooms, six suspects and six possible murder weapons. Cards were shuffled and handed out, face down, to the players, before play commenced but after one of each set had been placed in the Murder Envelope. Players moved around the board to ask questions once in a room. Cluedo: Super Sleuth moved on to 12 room tiles that were laid gradually to complete the plan of the house. Three incidental characters were introduced: Inspector Grey, Hogarth the butler and the Black Dog. Clue cards had to be gathered by moving around the tiles. Event cards instructed players to carry out certain actions and the newly introduced Item Cards gave assistance under particular circumstances. Cluedo Super Challenge: Passport To Murder returned to a prearranged board but now depicted nine areas at a railway station, some on the train and some on the platform. The six suspects remained but were joined by four station attendants and the number of murder weapons increased to nine. Thirty Case Clues were added to provide information to help solve the crime.

Waddington's have, therefore, produced a 'new improved version'. Can you emulate that company? Can you make an improved game, and convince a manufacturer that they would want to produce it?

Your Tasks
1. Your team will draw a card, from a number available, which refers to a well-known game.
2. Collect the correct game and remind yourself of its key features.
3. Plan a 'new improved version' of the game.
4. Design and make any additional items that you need.
5. Write down the changes in the rules.
6. Prepare a short presentation to explain to the manufacturers how their original game could be changed profitably.
7. Keep a close watch on the success criteria by which you will be judged.

The Success Criteria
★ How well the design team collaborates together.
★ The extent to which a new feature has, or features have, been added without losing the key elements of the original game.
★ The clarity of the amended rules so that the changes can be clearly understood.
★ The interest level involved in the new feature or features.
★ The quality of the visual aids, given the limited time available.
★ The degree to which the presentation is likely to convince the relevant manufacturer that a 'new improved version' is a good, and profitable, idea.

NOTE: All three versions of Cluedo are great fun to play. You would enjoy the contrasts by actually playing the games

Teaching Notes

'The New Improved Version' has a number of complementary features and can produce some stunning results. Listening to one group of very able children extolling the virtue of their invention 'Blackout Scrabble', is an experience that will live long in the memory.

Key Elements

- ❖ analysis of key features
- ❖ interpretation
- ❖ following instructions carefully
- ❖ discussion and co-operation in a team situation

- ❖ elaboration
- ❖ design
- ❖ creativity and imagination
- ❖ presentation skills.

What you will Need

- ❖ A selection of interesting and well-known games, such as Monopoly, Scrabble, Trivial Pursuit, Snakes and Ladders, and Ludo.
- ❖ Cards with the names of the games available written on them.
- ❖ Paper, scissors, pens, coloured pencils, paints, sticky tape, paper clips, card and so on.
- ❖ If possible, the three versions of Cluedo, so that the examples described can be illustrated and bring the activity to life.

Organization

1. The children form teams of three, four or five.
2. The pupil sheet is given out and the instructions are explained. If the teacher has copies of the three Cluedo versions they are used at this point.
3. Each team draws a card with the name of a game upon it.
4. The teams work upon the set task.
5. The room is rearranged for the presentations.
6. The game name cards are redrawn to establish the order of the presentations.
7. The presentations are made.
8. The panel of judges representing the games manufacturers withdraw to make their decision (the teacher can discuss the skills employed in the activity with the children while this is happening).
9. A representative of the panel gives a feedback on each team, noting the strengths and weaknesses according to the success criteria. The winning team is announced and claims a prize, if appropriate.

Depending upon the circumstances, other people may not be available to form a panel. In this case, the teacher acts as the sole judge.

Tournament: The Games Afoot

Garbled Games

You would hope to identify games by their titles, wouldn't you?

That does not seem too difficult, especially if you love playing games and are familiar with a wide range of them.

What, however, if those names were hidden within passages that had nothing to do with games?

Now, how well would you fare with 'Garbled Games'?

This is your chance to find out.

Your Task

1. Listen carefully to a passage called 'Rainforest Assignment'. It will be read to you twice.

2. Look out for the names of 14 games that are hidden in the passage.

3. Discuss ideas with the other members of your team and put together a composite list.

4. Now repeat the process with a second passage called 'Anticipating Christmas'. This time, there are 16 examples to be found. Although, more correctly, there are really only 15 to be found, as one game is named twice: once with its full title and then with a shortened name. Listen particularly for that 'double reference'.

NOTE

The games included in both passages constitute a real mixture. They cover card games, dominoes, board games and larger games.

Extension Task

Write a passage of your own including the hidden names of a number of 'Garbled Games'.

ALL IN THE GAME

- Many games have their own special language, covering components, strategies, calls and moves.
- They add greatly to the mystique and atmosphere.
- Below are 20 games.
- Opposite them are terms, one for each game.
- They are, however, out of order.
- See if you can match the games with their correct terms.

	Games		Terms
1	Mah Jong	a	Knock
2	Pool	b	Clickety-click
3	Dominoes	c	Mill
4	Chess	d	The murder bag
5	Bridge	e	Wellington
6	Whist	f	Fishing
7	Backgammon	g	Break
8	Bingo	h	Store
9	Nine Men's Morris	i	Wild draw four card
10	Draughts	j	En passant
11	Snooker	k	Body
12	Darts	l	Category
13	Mancala	m	Block
14	Monopoly	n	The colours
15	Scrabble	o	Oche
16	Napoleon	p	One club
17	Cluedo	q	Trumps
18	Trivial Pursuit	r	Huff
19	Beetle	s	Community Chest
20	UNO	t	Double-letter score

Teaching Notes

Round One: Garbled Games

This piece has been included here as a component part of a tournament. It could be used as an unusual classroom exercise or as a separate activity during an enrichment session of whatever length.

Key Elements

- ❖ listening skills
- ❖ word humour
- ❖ collaboration and teamwork
- ❖ intuitive thinking
- ❖ wordplay
- ❖ a challenging piece of writing (in the extension task).

Passage One: Rainforest Assignment

The pool above the waterfall was calm and quiet but below the river ran wildly. The foreman wanted to pull his men into a proper team. 'Don't brag about your previous assignments', he said. 'This is not about any individual going solo. We need to construct a pontoon bridge as quickly as possible but not in such a way as to hazard our safety. Use your common sense, work together and have patience. Nobody has a monopoly of good ideas so share your thoughts.'

The construction workers began to gather their equipment together. The terrain was rough and it would be easy to slip and fall. The more delicate pieces of surveying instruments were placed carefully in boxes. The men had been divided into three groups, with pre-assigned tasks and duties. Jack's group was to cut away the worst of the vegetation close to the right-hand bank. Movement in the dense rainforest would be awkward and the only reasonable method of carrying equipment was by donkey.

The men were a long way from home. The construction company had recruited in England at various places including Newmarket. Everything in this distant country was strange to them – the trees, the plants, the birds, the insects. As if to emphasize the point a giant beetle scuttled across a massive tropical leaf and then disappeared from view.

'Come on, let's go to it', said the foreman and the men moved out.

Passage Two: Anticipating Christmas

The run-up to the Christmas period was always a very busy time for Judy but she loved every minute. Today would see the preparation of the Christmas puddings. The bowls lay waiting on the work surface in the kitchen. Judy was very fond of the traditional dishes – turkey, mince pies, sprouts, stuffing, Christmas cake and, most of all, the puddings soaked in Napoleon brandy.

The weather had already turned cold. Judy disturbed the fire with a poker. She watched the flames burst forth and she heard the snap of new wood as it was set alight. The house would have to be warm for the festive season. Her father was coming to stay and he was quick to complain about cold draughts.

Christmas was a time to be happy, families getting together and a change from the normal routine. Modern life was so busy and as the year came to a close it was time for more trivial pursuits. There might even be the chance for the occasional nap.

Judy opened the sideboard and pulled out a small red box. She opened it up and gleaming inside was a solitaire diamond ring. It was a piece of family history and this Christmas it was to be given to Judy's eldest daughter as a surprise. Judy took one last lingering look and shut the box.

Her mind drifted to Christmas day itself. The darts into the stockings to scrabble about among the waiting presents. The shopping leading up to the great day would be heavy. All the food that had to be loaded into the trolleys and then pushed to the checkers at the tills where hard-earned savings were turned into seasonal fare. It was to be hoped that nobody would make a pig of themselves.

Judy and her husband always went to a West End theatre as one of the Christmas treats. This year was to be no exception, with a performance by the Royal Shakespeare Company. What was it that they had tickets for on this occasion? Judy frowned as she thought hard. Was it Hamlet or Othello? She was not sure.

Solutions

Passage One: Rainforest Assignment

1	Pool	8	Monopoly
2	Brag	9	Boxes
3	Solo	10	Jacks
4	Pontoon	11	Donkey
5	Bridge	12	Newmarket
6	Hazard	13	Beetle
7	Patience	14	Go

Passage Two: Anticipating Christmas

1	Bowls	9	Nap
2	Sprouts	10	Solitaire
3	Napoleon	11	Shut the Box
4	Poker	12	Darts
5	Snap	13	Scrabble
6	Draughts	14	Checkers
7	Happy Families	15	Pig
8	Trivial Pursuit	16	Othello

N.B. There are 16 references but 15 different games as Nap (9) is a shortened name for Napoleon (3).

ROUND TWO: ALL IN THE GAME

Although children may not know all the games and terms, there are sensible strategies to be employed. If definite pairs are established first then common sense and intuitive thinking can be brought to bear upon the now-reduced choice. This is an important lesson to learn.

Sometimes we all have to make the best possible selection without having exact knowledge.

This is where character and effective working practices play a part.

1	Mah Jong	f	Fishing
2	Pool	g	Break
3	Dominoes	a	Knock
4	Chess	j	En passant
5	Bridge	p	One club
6	Whist	q	Trumps
7	Backgammon	m	Block
8	Bingo	b	Clickety-click
9	Nine Men's Morris	c	Mill
10	Draughts	r	Huff
11	Snooker	n	The colours
12	Darts	o	Oche
13	Mancala	h	Store
14	Monopoly	s	Community Chest
15	Scrabble	t	Double-letter score
16	Napoleon	e	Wellington
17	Cluedo	d	The murder bag
18	Trivial Pursuit	l	Category
19	Beetle	k	Body
20	UNO	i	Wild draw four card

NOTE

The term 'trumps' fits both Bridge and Whist but 'one club' must be linked to the former if all 20 pairs are to be matched correctly. Similarly a 'break' ocurrs in pool and snooker but 'the colours' is specific to snooker.

ROUND THREE: ARIAL NOUGHTS AND CROSSES
MERATC page 75

ROUND FOUR: GAMES TEASERS
MERATC page 259

Enrichment Activities for Able and Talented Children © Barry Teare (Network Educational Press, 2004)

Humanities/Thinking Skills Courses, Activities and Resources

Introduction

The humanities subjects provide vital opportunities to use the higher-order thinking skills of analysis, evaluation and synthesis which are of crucial importance to able children. Not only that, those opportunities are provided through interesting, enjoyable and challenging material which fires the imagination and touches the humanity within us all.

Perhaps the need for courses involving the humanities is particularly strong at present, given that the subjects involved have been squeezed for time in the curriculum by a number of recent initiatives, especially the introduction of literacy and numeracy projects.

The activities described below involve fascinating material from history and geography, and, to a lesser degree, religious education. However, content has been linked with a number of key elements so that the courses and activities can accurately be described as 'thinking skills and problem solving through the humanities'.

Possible Titles for Courses
'Travellers in Time and Place'
'Any Time, Any Place, Any Where'
'Where do We Come From? Where Are We Going To?'
'Voyages of Discovery'
'A Sense of History'
'Throwing down the Gauntlet'
'Going Up in the World'
'The World's your Oyster'
'In Good Faith'

Part One: Starters, Icebreakers

A: Lateral thinking problems
Starting courses with lateral thinking problems work well. All children can make a contribution and discussion work certainly 'breaks the ice'. They can be general or chosen particularly to fit the humanities theme. Try the following:

Paul Sloane, *Lateral Thinking Puzzles* (Sterling Publishing Company, 1992)

   'The Grateful Prisoner', page 22
   'The Woman on the Bridge I', page 25

Chris M. Dickson, *Mystery Puzzles* (Robinson Publishing, 1999)

'**The Snake and the Boat**', page 5
'**Samuel Pepys' Diary**', page 55

CRATC
'**School of Thought**', page 255
'**The Mary Celeste**', page 256
'**Fields Apart**', page 257

'Morton's Fork'
See page 218 in this book.

For the introduction to the method, allow five–six minutes. For each example, allow 15–20 minutes (depending upon the amount of discussion allowed).

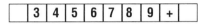

Instructions to the pupils

Lateral thinking problems have been used by many people in different ways. Described here is a method that works well with able children.

- Listen carefully to the short passage that will be read to you.
- Make notes if you wish, but the extract is short and you will probably remember the key points without any.
- Brainstorm possible ideas in your group concerning the question at the end of the passage.
- One person in the group should keep a record of your ideas.
- If you think of a good solution don't be satisfied with it but, rather, add alternative answers.
- You must not contradict any of the facts stated in the passage; for example, if a man wears a baseball cap in the story, then it is a baseball cap that he wears and not a top hat or a bowler.
- However, you can 'fill in gaps' by adding information that does not contradict the given facts. In this way, you can think 'laterally' to find a solution or solutions.
- Any suggestion must be realistic. A solution that Martians landed in Stockton/ Swansea/Rotherham/Aberdeen (and so on) and 'zapped' everybody with ray guns would not be acceptable.

Collecting the ideas

- In a moment, I/we shall ask for suggestions.
- Listening skills are not as good as they should be. Sometimes when children are waiting to give their own answers, they do not listen carefully to someone else's idea.
- So, listen carefully to suggestions from other groups and think critically about what is said.
- Put up your hands when you wish to support and approve the idea, or make criticisms of it.
- Think about the solution:
  - is it realistic?
  - does it fit the facts?
  - does it contradict any of the given facts?

- are the gaps filled in reasonably?
- is it a strong answer?
- are there weaknesses?
- If you suggest a solution do not be worried about criticisms. The criticisms are not of you personally, but of the idea.
- If somebody makes a criticism of your idea, you will then have a chance to answer it, either by explaining more fully or by adding to your story.
- Only when one idea has been properly explored will we move on to another one.

The skills involved

It is always worthwhile detailing the skills used and how they are important in real life. The problems used might not be very significant but the transferable skills are very important.

- Lateral thinking – going sideways to find solutions.
- Fluency – not being satisfied with one answer, but looking for alternatives.
- Handling data accurately – if in doubt go back to the text (using what is actually said is one of the keys to success in examinations and in life).
- Elaboration – when a criticism is made, the person who made the original suggestion can add details and elaborate upon the idea.
- Listening carefully.
- Thinking critically.
- Prioritizing – which solution is the best, and why?
- Making decisions in real-life situations – the principles followed here are the same as those employed in education, business, health, and so on. When a change is required the management team brainstorms possible solutions: comments are sought; weaknesses exposed; original ideas improved; some suggestions are thrown out; the number of possible solutions is reduced; the group decides which is best. A similar process is also very valuable to personal life.

A worked example: 'Use your Head'

There is a real-life example of lateral thinking, based upon the First World War, which is used by several people. The key point that the pupils need to decide upon is why head injuries actually increased when the metal helmet replaced the cloth cap as part of the British soldiers' uniform. It is clearly pointed out that this was not the consequence of a changed level of fighting.

Some answers from children:

1 The helmet was uncomfortable and soldiers, therefore, removed it entirely. However, this does not explain the increase in injuries.
2 Soldiers became more confident about their safety and, as a result, they took more chances than before.
3 As the helmet was heavy and cumbersome, the soldiers did not move as quickly or as nimbly as before.
4 When the sun was shining, it glinted on the metal helmet and identified the position of the target more clearly.
5 The number of head injuries increased but the number of deaths decreased. What would have been a fatality in the cloth cap sometimes now became an injury in the metal helmet.

NOTE: As this is a real-life example there is a known answer. It is, indeed, number 5. Some children are thrilled to have discovered that for themselves, but it does not negate the good thinking behind other suggestions that fit the facts, and children should be given credit for those ideas.

An advantage of starting with a lateral thinking problem is that everybody is immediately engaged. If children have come together from different schools they have a chance to get to know each other.

If many answers are forthcoming and the teacher wishes to move on, additional suggestions can be accepted on slips of paper. Good ideas can then be included later in the day.

B: Decision-making through discussion

Just as lateral thinking problems involve all the children and get them talking to each other, so do decision-making situations.

'Eyam'
ERATC

The pupils are given information on the outbreak of plague in the Derbyshire village of Eyam in 1665 (page 187). They have to explain how this isolated outbreak was caused and its possible links with the nursery rhyme 'Ring-a-ring-a-roses'. The most important part of the work is to put themselves in the shoes of the rector, William Mompesson, and to detail the problems facing him and what actions they would have taken given the then current state of medicine and understanding of the plague.

Forty-five minutes.

	4	5	6	7	8	9	

'Decision Makers'
ERATC

Two situations are used (page 184). The first is 'The Wisdom of Solomon' and is an RE example of decision-making. The second one, 'Life and Death', is a fictionalized problem based upon the position of Winston Churchill when he had advanced notice of German attacks as a consequence of the breaking of the Enigma Code.

Forty-five minutes each.

	4	5	6	7	8	9	+

Part Two: Logical Thinking Pieces

Developing the ability to think logically is very important and many able children enjoy the challenge presented by these problems. It is also important to develop spans of concentration, as some of these problems require persistence to solve.

A: Matrix Puzzles

The following examples present a particular type of logical thinking problem with a humanities theme. Some children may have met this type of problem before, others won't. Therefore, the teacher needs to explain the method (full details are given in Detective/Thinking Skills Courses and Activities, page 247).

'Royal Research'

It is sensible to do a worked example from the curriculum area. This does not need to be particularly difficult, nor be completed – the intention is to illustrate the way of working before a more complicated example is attempted.

The basic scenario is that five children have each been studying a different monarch of England for a special project. They are Elizabeth I, Victoria, Henry V, Henry VIII and Richard III. The pupils suggest five children's names, making sure that there is a mixture of girls and boys, two of whom have the same initials. This might then result in the children being, for example, Harry, Hubert, Lucy, Beth and Barbara.

A matrix is then drawn on the flip chart or board. Simple clues are then given to fill in most of the matrix, as follows:

1 The two queens were studied by two children of the opposite gender to these monarchs. (This clue puts crosses against Elizabeth I and Victoria for Lucy, Beth and Barbara. Also, crosses are placed against Harry and Hubert for the three kings.)

2 The most recent ruler was chosen by a child whose name contains a double consonant. (A tick is placed against Victoria for Harry, which automatically means that Hubert studied Elizabeth I.)

3 The ruler who belongs to the House of York was researched by the child whose name is an abbreviation of one of the rulers. (Beth – short for Elizabeth – worked on Richard III. This places a tick in the appropriate box and crosses for Lucy and Barbara.)

One more clue would be needed to separate Lucy and Barbara for Henry V and Henry VIII. Pupils are then asked for a clue to do that.

The clues can vary dramatically in terms of difficulty or, indeed, content. Teachers can substitute a different example to match a recently studied area.

	Harry	Hubert	Lucy	Beth	Barbara
Elizabeth I	✗	✓	✗	✗	✗
Victoria	✓	✗	✗	✗	✗
Henry V	✗	✗		✗	
Henry VIII	✗	✗		✗	
Richard III	✗	✗	✗	✓	✗

Fifteen minutes.

		4	5	6	7	8	9		

'County Living'

A logical thought exercise that has geographical content on primary, secondary and tertiary industries and also upon the map of England. People of differing occupations are matched to the counties where they live (page 220).

Forty minutes.

				6	7	8	9	+	

'In Good Faith'
CRATC

An RE problem that can be solved by a matrix or other methods (page 140). Twelve students have done assignments on six different religions. Who has studied what? This cannot be answered without knowledge of comparative religions.

Thirty minutes.

			6	7	8	9	+	

B: Longer Logical Piece

'The Tree of Life'

Family trees are at the heart of this piece (page 222). It is a useful tool as preliminary work to any units where claims to the throne are going to be important.

Thirty minutes allows able pupils to complete Parts One, Two and Three. Time for Part Four depends upon the balance between existing knowledge and the need to research.

		5	6	7	8	9		

C: Codes

'The Enigma Variations'
CRATC

A code is solved through using dates in history linked to famous people, events and places (page 134).

One hour to one hour 15 minutes

			6	7	8	9	+	

Pepi and the Secret Names

Frances Lincoln (1996) publishes this excellent book written by Jill Paton Walsh and beautifully illustrated by Fiona French. Set in ancient Egypt, *Pepi and the Secret Names* is a stunningly beautiful book to read and use. Pepi's father has the task of painting the Pharaoh's tomb. Dangerous creatures, such as Sebek the crocodile and Mertseger the deadly winged cobra, have to be included. Pepi tries to lure them to the tomb to make his father's job easier. To do so safely he has to work out the creatures' secret names by means of a cryptic clue and a hieroglyphics code. Children are asked to carry out the same task.

The clues and the hieroglyphics can be separated from the story and written up on a flipchart or board.

Forty-five to 50 minutes including reading out the story.

	4	5	6	7				

Part Three: Subject-Specific Vocabulary

All areas of the National Curriculum, and guidelines in other parts of Great Britain, require pupils to work extensively with subject-specific language. In the following pieces there is ample scope for able children to employ abstract thinking in exploring concepts within the humanities area.

'DEPICT'
ERATC

'DEPICT' stands for Data, Epigrams, Phrases, Images, Concepts, Thoughts (page 67). This piece encourages children to represent conceptual thinking through a variety of verbal and pictorial methods. 'Monarchy' and 'Volcano' are the particular examples used but any topic within history, geography or religious education could be included.

Posters or other outcomes can be employed. A response involving computer graphics is a rich potential route.

At least 30 minutes per item depending upon the amount of research and the sophistication of the response.

+	3	4	5	6	7	8	9		

'Quintessential Qualities'
ERATC

The form of speech, alliteration, is used in 'Quintessential Qualities' to define various terms (page 71). Wordplay is combined with conceptual thinking. Any curriculum area can be included. Specific examples are given of 'Hearing Heady History' and 'Generating Geographical Glossary'.

Added to this now is 'Researching Religious References' (page 227).

At least 30 minutes, but the time varies depending upon how many examples are required.

		5	6	7	8	9	+	

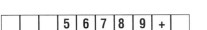

'Coming to Terms with Geography'
CRATC

Pupils match up the items from two lists that define 26 geographical terms. List A has alternative or cryptic clues and List B gives a more straightforward definition (page 131). Children can also write their own examples.

Forty-five minutes.

			6	7	8	9		

Part Four: Allegory, Speculation, Hypothesizing, Alternative Views

Working well in the abstract is a characteristic of many able children. Allegories provide very suitable material.

Aesop's Fables

There are many collections of Aesop's Fables available. The version referred to here is *Aesop's Fables* (Wordsworth Classics, illustrated by Arthur Rackham, 1994). A fable is read out and pupils discuss the message within the fable, trying to find an example of the meaning from within the humanities area.

One example is 'The Mice in Council' (page 4) where the mice meet to work out a plan to defend themselves from the attacks of the cat. All present are delighted by the idea of putting a bell on the cat until it is asked who is going to carry out the belling.

Pastor Niemöller comes to mind during the Nazi rule in Germany. He is quoted as saying that when various groups were persecuted others took no action as they were not members of those groups, so that when they were attacked no one defended them. The fable and this example are about taking responsibility, individually and collectively.

A second example is that of 'The Cage-Bird and the Bat' (page 149). When the singing-bird is asked by the bat why she is silent by day and sings only at night, she explains that a fowler was attracted by her voice in the daytime and caught her as a result.

This is a case of acting when it is too late, or 'closing the stable door after the horse has bolted'. Possible examples abound including geographical incidents where reforestation follows floods caused by deforestation.

Perhaps 20 minutes for each example, including the verbal collection of suggestions.

		5	6	7	8	9	+	

These could also be used as Starters' or 'Icebreakers.

Voices in the Park

Anthony Browne's wonderful book (Picture Corgi Books, 1999) tells, through typically surreal pictures and small paragraphs of text, the story of a walk in the park via four different voices. There are clear uses in English but this highly original presentation can provide the inspiration for an excellent piece of work in the humanities.

'As I See It' (page 229) is based upon Anthony Browne's work, *Voices in the Park*.

One hour.

	3	4	5	6	7	8		

'Conflict of Interests'
CRATC

This piece of work deals with the very important area of geography which concerns decisions and developments that affect people's lives (page 152). On separate pages there are ten newspaper headlines, a brief description of 40 people and comments made by them. Pupils are asked to put together groups of four people with their correct quotes and also the newspaper headline with which they are associated. The fact that people have contrasting opinions about proposals and actions is shown.

This can also be used as a piece of work on logical thinking.

One hour.

		5	6	7	8	9		

Part Five: Map-Related Work

Map work is an important element in all geography guidelines. Two challenging and absorbing activities follow that have produced high-quality responses from able children.

'On the Map'
ERATC

Pupils are required to create a map on a sheet of paper, marked out with a grid, by following a set of detailed instructions (page 190). Some of the features are positioned exactly and, at other times, there is some leeway as to location. Ordnance Survey symbols, six-figure grid references and working to scale are all key features. The extension task encourages pupils to add to the map appropriately. Able children have shown their ability and, sometimes, their sense of humour, for instance, by using the River Big so that the town on the estuary becomes Bigmouth.

One hour 30 minutes if the extension work is included.

		5	6	7	8	9		

This becomes a progressively simpler task after the initial features have been placed. Even able pupils need to concentrate hard at the start.

'Shipping Forecast'
MERATC

This piece starts with work on existing shipping areas around the British Isles and moves on to an activity involving an imaginary area, Tranland (page 106). Geographical vocabulary is also prominently featured.

Task One only needs some five minutes or so. Task Two also requires a very short time. Task Three is difficult to predict due to the research needed. Task Four can be completed in 45 minutes.

		5	6	7	8	9		

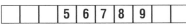

Part Six: Open-Ended Materials

As there is considerable content within the humanities subjects, facts can come to dominate. However, hypothesizing and being creative are beneficial features.

'The Question Is'
ERATC

This has been a very popular item for many years. Answers are given to which children set appropriate questions. There is a general version and science, history and geography versions (page 221).

A new RE version is on page 231.

The time needed is variable depending upon the number of examples attempted and the sophistication of response.

		4	5	6	7	8	9	+	

If the items included do not fit the content required, the teacher can write his or her own examples.

'Just Imagine'
ERATC

'Just Imagine' (page 235) encourages children to use their imagination to consider what would happen or what might happen if circumstances changed in one way or another. The 20 'imagines' cover many different areas.

Items have been restricted to the humanities area in 'Imagine That ...' (page 233).

The time needed will depend upon the number answered and the level of detail included.

		4	5	6	7	8	9		

Part Seven: Unusual, Interesting Content

One of the many forms of enrichment is to look at material that is not always covered in the normal syllabus.

'Groundwork'
MERATC

'Groundwork' is a short foray into the fascinating field of archaeology (page 119).

At least one hour 30 minutes is required.

		5	6	7	8	9	+	

'Finders Keepers ... Sometimes'
MERATC

Children work on a primary source linked to archaeology and metal-detecting, namely The Treasure Act (page 114).

Thirty minutes for the first part with, perhaps, 30 minutes for the 'Metal Detecting Code'.

		5	6	7	8	9	+	

'Dustbin Detectives'
This is a practical, kinesthetic activity that is very simple in concept but is very popular with children (page 235).

One hour 30 minutes is required for the setting-up, physical examination of evidence and the written report.

	3	4	5	6	7	8	9		

Able children, like all children, like to have variety in their work; therefore, written exercises need to be separated by other types of activities.

Part Eight: Longer Activities

'Throwing Down the Gauntlet' — A Tournament
This particular tournament has eight sections to it. Full details are given so that this activity could be run almost exactly. Teachers can, however, substitute any other themes that they wish.

Alternatively, units from the tournament can be used as short items in the classroom or for homework.

One method of operation
Each one of the eight sections is set out at a 'station'. At the end of each time period, the teams move from station to station in a clockwise direction. Six minutes are allocated for each station.

Movement breaks up the activity. The short time slots add an urgency and excitement to the tournament.

'Meaningful'
Children choose the correct one from four possible definitions (page 237).

'Hidden Britain'
Children are required to identify ten places from cryptic clues (page 239).

'Anachorisms'
MERATC
The task is to find the odd one out geographically and explain the reasoning in each of ten groups (page 112).

'The Passage of Time'

Ten events have to be placed in correct chronological order (page 240).

'Anachronisms'

Used here is the book *Parallel Universe* written by Nicola Baxter and illustrated by Mike Taylor (Franklin Watts, 1996). There is an interesting context: 'Your task is to trek through the dimensions of time and space and to track down the time-slipped objects. Briefing notes from the Controller of the Intergalactic Centre for Planetary Co-ordination will help you in your quest.'

Essentially there are 14 detailed pictures covering different periods of history and contrasting locations. The task is to locate all the anachronisms: the items that do not fit timewise.

In 'Throwing Down the Gauntlet' the illustration for Rome, AD 100 is used. Answers are given in the back of the book including details of when the anachronisms would have appeared.

If a teacher is keen to use this idea but is unable to get hold of a copy of the book, a way forward would be to create a picture of your own.

CRATC
'The Sounds of Rivers'

Children have to identify the names of rivers from cryptic clues (page 273).

This sheet asks the children to identify 20 rivers. In the original tournament piece there were ten rivers. If six-minute stations are used, ask the children to complete the first ten only.

'Inventors' Identities'

Inventors are to be identified from anagrams (page 241). Children are also asked to name the inventions for which the people are famous.

'Collectively Speaking'

The task is to find the collective names for ten groups of words from humanities subjects' content (page 242).

Fifteen minutes introduction, explanation and forming teams.
Fifty-two minutes for the eight stations and moving times between stations.
Twenty minutes to go over the answers.

		5	6	7	8	9		

'Travellers in Time and Place' – A Treasure Hunt

Children visit 26 locations spread out in as many spaces as are available. Each location has a card with a number of questions on it. There are also photographs and objects to increase interest and to bring variety. The materials cover history, geography and RE.

The objects used by the author are very particular and, therefore, the full details are not printed in the book. Examples are given on the following page to give a flavour of the treasure hunt. Teachers can use their own resources to establish a similar event.

Some examples to illustrate the organization

1. A jigsaw with a canal lock and a steam train going by. There are questions about when the picture would have been taken, how do you know this, what was happening in the locks and why this form of transport became popular.

2. A sheet with photographs of various places of worship. Children are asked to name them and state to which faith they belong.

3. Silhouette maps of 12 countries are provided. Children identify the countries from the shape and cryptic clues.

Some two hours are required for an introduction, the treasure hunt itself and feedback on the solutions.

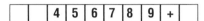

morton's fork

Henry VII, the first Tudor king, came to power with many problems. He realized that a strong financial position was important and that some of the previous rulers of England had struggled because of lack of money. That had made them too dependent upon other people.

One of Henry's ministers was John Morton, Cardinal and Archbishop of Canterbury. He was keen to fill Henry VII's coffers. Morton went on many visits to the homes of wealthy men. He took note of how he was entertained. No matter what treatment he received, Morton managed to tax all those he visited.

Your Task

Having taken note of the information about Cardinal Morton, work out why his taxing of the rich became known as 'Morton's Fork'. Try to make as many sensible suggestions as possible.

Extension Task

Find another suitable story in history, geography or religious education. Write it out as a lateral thinking problem with a key question at the end. Set it for other people to try to find an explanation or explanations.

Teaching Notes

'Morton's Fork' provides very suitable material for lateral thinking. As it is based upon real life, there is an actual solution, but that does not prevent other good answers being given after a brainstorming session by groups of children. The reason for this suitability is that the situation has a number of clues but then many possible routes to explore. There is, in other words, sufficient open-endedness with some parameters.

One of the keys to this suitability is the word 'fork' which is a homograph. 'Fork' has more than one meaning and that opens up a number of sensible possibilities.

The 'Real' Answer

Morton looked at how his hosts were living. If there was a display of wealth, then clearly they were capable of making a substantial contribution to the royal coffers. However, those who lived in a frugal way must be saving their money and be in possession of large assets. In that case, they also were capable of paying heavy taxes to the king.

The method was nicknamed 'Morton's Fork' because of its creator's name and because it was two-pronged by nature.

NOTE: The fact that there is an actual answer does not in any way detract from other good suggestions that fit the facts of the story. Even so, it would be particularly pleasing for a child to arrive at the real solution not from previous knowledge but because of their own thinking.

COUNTY LIVING

'Living' is one of many words that have alternative meanings. It could refer to 'location', or 'where you are living'. It could also describe your 'job' or 'occupation'.

Can you match correctly the places where eight people are living with their occupations?

Your Task

Look at the lists of eight counties and eight occupations. Use them, together with the clues below, to decide where each person lives.

THE COUNTIES	THE OCCUPATIONS
Buckinghamshire	Assembly worker in a furniture factory
Lancashire	Farmer
Yorkshire	Fisherman
Devon	Forestry worker
Suffolk	Machine operator in an engineering factory
Cornwall	Shop assistant
Staffordshire	Teacher
Warwickshire	Tourist guide

THE CLUES

1 The two people with secondary occupations live in counties that do not have a coastline.

2 The two northern cross-Pennine rivals and the most westerly of the counties are home to the three people who are involved in primary industries or occupations.

3 The teacher lives in the only county that has two separate, unconnected coastlines.

4 The two remaining tertiary industries' workers, or service workers, have never been north of Birmingham.

5 The fisherman lives in a county that only borders one neighbour.

6 The tourist guide has knowledge of many areas through her work, but she has only spent two days in East Anglia.

7 The machine operator lives in a county that borders Cheshire among others.

8 The furniture assembly worker likes to visit the theatre and she is lucky to live very close to Stratford-upon-Avon.

9 The farmer has never been to the western side of England.

COUNTY LIVING

Teaching Notes

'County Living' is a short logical thought exercise that has geographical content.

Key Elements

❖ logical thinking
❖ synthesis
❖ analysis of data

❖ primary, secondary and tertiary industries
❖ the map of England
❖ research.

Contexts

'County Living' can be used in the following ways:

❖ as extension material to work on occupations and/or England
❖ as enrichment material for those who have completed other tasks
❖ as differentiated homework
❖ as an activity during an enrichment session, cluster day or summer school
❖ as an activity for the Geography Club
❖ as an activity within a thinking skills course.

Even able pupils have a sketchy knowledge about the country in which they live. It is necessary, therefore, to have maps available that show the position of the counties. Knowledge of the locations of Birmingham and Stratford-upon-Avon is also needed and a separate map, that does not show the counties, is required. This adds an extra demand in that pupils have to recognize how the two places relate to county boundaries.

Solution

A variety of methods can be used including a written method, slips of paper or a matrix.

Clue 1 The machine operator and the furniture assembly worker live in Warwickshire or Buckinghamshire or Staffordshire. Other counties are eliminated.

Clue 2 Yorkshire, Lancashire and Cornwall are home to the farmer, fisherman and forestry worker but the exact links are not yet known. Other counties can be eliminated. Also, Yorkshire, Lancashire and Cornwall have to be eliminated for the other people.

Clue 3 The teacher lives in Devon where there are northern and southern coastlines that do not meet.

Clue 4 The people are the shop assistant and the tourist guide, for whom Staffordshire can be ruled out.

Clue 5 The fisherman must live in Cornwall.

Clue 6 Suffolk is part of East Anglia and, therefore, the tourist guide does not live there. By process of elimination it is the shop assistant who lives in Suffolk.

Clue 7 This county has to be Staffordshire, given what has already been ruled out, and it is home to the machine operator.

Clue 8 Stratford-upon-Avon is in Warwickshire, which is where the furniture assembly worker lives. By process of elimination, the tourist guide lives in Buckinghamshire.

Clue 9 Of the two remaining possibilities, the farmer must live in Yorkshire which also means that the forestry worker's home is in Lancashire.

	Buckinghamshire	Cornwall	Devon	Lancashire	Staffordshire	Suffolk	Warwickshire	Yorkshire
Farmer	✗	✗	✗	✗	✗	✗	✗	✓
Forestry worker	✗	✗	✗	✓	✗	✗	✗	✗
Fisherman	✗	✓	✗	✗	✗	✗	✗	✗
Furniture assembly worker	✗	✗	✗	✗	✗	✗	✓	✗
Machine operator	✗	✗	✗	✗	✓	✗	✗	✗
Shop assistant	✗	✗	✗	✗	✗	✓	✗	✗
Teacher	✗	✗	✓	✗	✗	✗	✗	✗
Tourist guide	✓	✗	✗	✗	✗	✗	✗	✗

THE TREE OF LIFE

You may be familiar with the idea of a family tree. Many people trace their ancestry for interest or as a hobby. Family trees are of particular interest to historians and archaeologists. Claims to the throne involve their study. In 'The Tree of Life', you are introduced to the conventions involved in the layout of family trees. Various tasks follow, including interpretation of information, creating your own 'tree', and an historical context.

PART ONE

Below is a small family tree showing three generations, starting with a marriage in 1937. Such a diagram is 'artificial' in that it starts with one marriage as though Dai and Serena have no parents. It is 'unfinished' in the other direction in the sense that new generations will be added unless all five children do not have children of their own when they grow up.

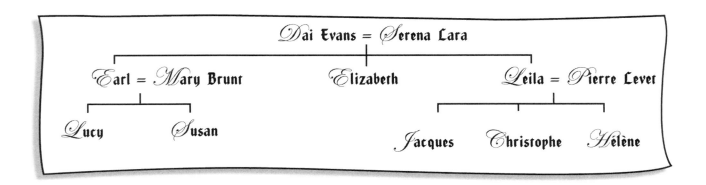

CONVENTIONS

The = sign denotes a marriage. People from a particular generation are shown on the same line running across. It is normal to show children of a marriage in order of the first born ('oldest') to the last born ('youngest') from left to right as the viewer looks at the tree, for example Jacques was born before Christophe and Hélène. The family shown followed the convention of the time, which was that the women adopt their husband's surname at the time of marriage.

Your Task

Answer the following questions based upon the family tree shown above, assuming that they are all still alive:

1 What is Christophe's surname?
2 What relation is Serena to Susan?
3 What relation is Earl to Hélène?
4 What is the name of Christophe's elder brother?
5 How many people shown in the tree have the surname Lara, by the time the tree was drawn?
6 What relation is Dai to Mary?
7 How many nieces has Elizabeth got?
8 How many cousins has Lucy got?
9 How many sisters has Hélène got?
10 How many grandsons has Serena got?
11 How many grandsons has Pierre got?
12 How many people in the tree have the surname Evans, by the time the tree was drawn?
13 What is the name of Serena's youngest child's youngest child?
14 By the time that the tree was drawn, whose initials are MB?

PART TWO – YOUR TASK

Let us now reverse the process in Part One.
Construct a family tree of three generations from the following information. Make up your own names.

a A couple had four children, three boys and a girl. One of the boys did not get married.
b Three of the children married.
c There were five children, in total, who made up the third generation.

PART THREE – YOUR TASK

You are asked to draw a family tree from the following information that is not necessarily given in the order that you wish to use it. Although the finished tree is more complicated, it can be drawn by building up the component parts from the various clues. You may need to do two versions, one rough and one neat, as the work may be difficult to organize.

a Five generations are shown.
b No first name is repeated.
c Of the seven children in the fifth generation only Carol and her younger sister, Shirley, continue the name Redmond.
d The tree 'begins' with the marriage of Harvey Redmond and Margaret Longford.
e Harvey and Margaret had four grandchildren, one of whom, Paul (the eldest), did not marry and another, Gillian (the third to be born), died when she was only 12 years old.
f Joy Bingley worked for Harvey Redmond before marrying his only child, Steven.
g Graham is the only child of Harvey and Margaret's youngest grandchild, Michael, who married Ann Murphy.
h Graham was a page boy at the wedding of his Aunt Valerie to David Barton.
i Michael's nephew Roy married Susan Hall and Roy's younger sister, Yvonne, married Andrew Hopgood.
j Ann's daughter-in-law was called Norma Davies before her marriage.
k Vernon Barton was born two years before his brother Roger and four years before his sister Hilary. There are no other brothers and sisters.
l Hilary goes to the same youth club as her cousin Mark and his younger brother Richard.

PART FOUR - YOUR TASKS

Having looked at family trees in a general way, let us now apply the principles to Henry Tudor's claim to the throne.

1 Study the simplified line of succession produced below. Also refer to research material.

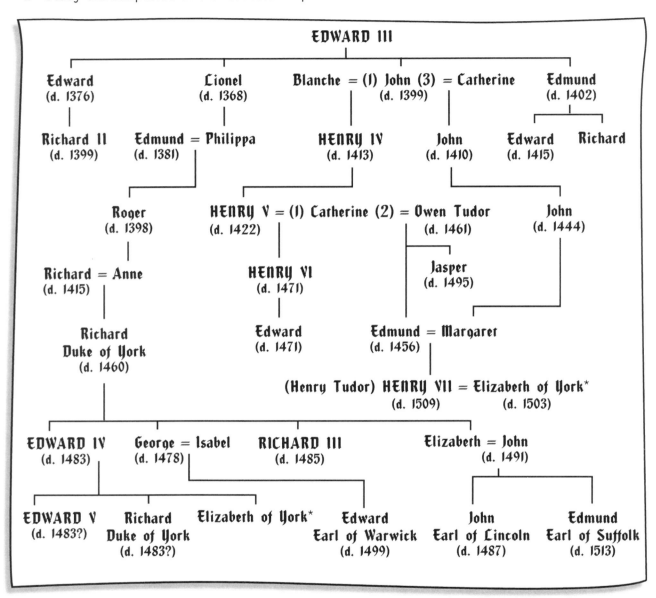

2 Answer the following questions:

a Why was Henry Tudor's own claim to the throne not particularly strong? He became king as Henry VII in 1485.

b If a woman could inherit the throne, who had a good claim? How did Henry Tudor deal with that threat?

c If only men were eligible, which three 'claimants' must be taken into consideration?

d What events removed the danger from these three male claimants?

NOTE: Only the information required to answer these questions has been given on the simplified line of succession, for example, the marriage of Henry VII to Elizabeth of York provided four children, one of whom became Henry VIII.

Teaching Notes

'The Tree of Life' will be of particular interest to historians, although the thinking skills involved are of a more general value. The parts become increasingly more complex as greater emphasis is placed upon the higher-order thinking skills.

Key Elements
- ❖ family trees
- ❖ Tudor history
- ❖ logical thinking
- ❖ careful handling of data
- ❖ progression from comprehension to application to synthesis
- ❖ research (in Part Four).

Contexts
'The Tree of Life' can be used in the following ways:
- ❖ as extension work to material on Henry VII
- ❖ as material for a thinking skills course
- ❖ as an enrichment activity for those who have completed other tasks
- ❖ as differentiated homework
- ❖ as an activity during an enrichment day, weekend, summer school or cluster day
- ❖ as an activity for the History Club.

1 The first three parts can be used separately from Part Four.
2 A 1937 start has been used for Part One to avoid a conflict with more modern views.
3 Part Two allows a more modern interpretation if teachers wish to encourage such an approach.

PART ONE
This is a comprehension exercise as all the questions can be answered separately.
1 Levet
2 Grandmother
3 Uncle
4 Jacques
5 None – Serena's surname is Evans by the time the tree is drawn
6 Father-in-law
7 Three – Lucy, Susan and Hélène
8 Three – Jacques, Christophe and Hélène
9 None
10 Two – Jacques and Christophe
11 None yet – none of his children have got children of their own
12 Seven – Dai, Serena, Earl, Mary, Elizabeth, Lucy and Susan
13 Hélène
14 Nobody's – Mary Brunt is known as Mary Evans

PART TWO
Application of existing knowledge is required in this part. Children will produce a variety of answers. Many variations can be used but the couple must be the first entry. From their marriage four children should be shown: two boys and a girl married, and one boy unmarried. A third generation is shown, consisting of five children. These five children can be distributed in a number of ways. Children used to more modern conventions may place a child or children as coming from the unmarried boy in the second generation.

PART THREE
This part involves considerable synthesis of data. It has been complicated deliberately by mixing up the order of the information and by including superfluous data. Sorting out the essential information is an important prerequisite. Writing out the individual names on slips of paper presents a kinesthetic method for solution. A diagrammatic method can also be adopted but it may need to be 'tidied up' to get different generations shown properly aligned.

a Five 'levels' can be mapped out roughly.
b This gives no immediate help.

---

c On level five, seven names will be placed. Two of these will be Carol and Shirley Redmond.

d The first level is Harvey Redmond = Margaret Longford.

e Level three shows the grandchildren of Harvey and Margaret. From left to right (oldest to youngest) they read Paul, unknown, Gillian, unknown. We know that there are no marriages or children to mark for Paul and Gillian.

f We now know that the second level shows simply Steven = Joy Bingley. This allows us to draw in the connecting lines between level one and two, and level two and three.

g On level three, Michael is the previously unnamed grandchild of Harvey and Margaret on the extreme right (as he was the youngest). Michael = Ann Murphy can be entered. Below that, on level four, we can write Graham.

h This completes level three, because we can now place Valerie = David Barton between Paul and Gillian.

i Any nephews and nieces of Michael must come from the marriage of Valerie to David Barton as neither Paul nor Gillian had any children. Therefore, on level four, beneath a line from Valerie and David's marriage, we can place two entries. Because he is the elder, Roy is on the left and Yvonne is on the right. The two entries are Roy = Susan Hall, and Yvonne = Andrew Hopgood.

j Graham = Norma Davies completes level four.

k The three Barton children come from the marriage of Roy Barton and Susan Hall. On level five the names Vernon, Richard and Hilary can be added (from left to right).

l The final entries can now be made. From clue **c** we know that Carol and younger sister Shirley have the surname, Redmond. They are, therefore, the children of Graham and Norma and can be placed. Hilary's cousins are the children of Yvonne and Andrew Hopgood, and so the names Mark and Richard complete the family tree.

The completed family tree is shown below:

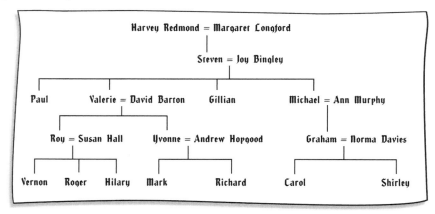

PART FOUR

This is very different from the previous work, as additional knowledge about Lancastrians, Yorkists and Tudors is essential. This may, or may not, be tackled alongside the other parts.

a His mother, Margaret, was the last of the Beauforts who were the illegitimate descendants of Edward III's son, John of Gaunt. This union was subsequently legitimized by the Pope and by Richard II but the line had been excluded from the succession. His grandmother, Catherine of France, had married her Welsh Clerk of the Wardrobe, Owen Tudor, but there were more substantial claimants.

b Edward IV's eldest daughter, Elizabeth of York, was the rightful heiress if a woman could inherit the throne. Henry Tudor married her but not until after his coronation and his recognition by Parliament, so that he staked his claim independently.

c Edward, Earl of Warwick, stood first as the son of Edward IV's brother, George, Duke of Clarence. Second would be John, Earl of Lincoln as the elder son of Elizabeth, Edward IV's sister. Third would be Lincoln's younger brother, Edmund de la Pole, Earl of Suffolk.

d Warwick was imprisoned in the Tower of London at the age of ten. Opponents used first Lambert Simnel and then Perkin Warbeck to impersonate Warwick. Henry decided that while Warwick lived there would always be a threat. In November 1499 Warwick was condemned and executed for treason. Lincoln was involved in a rebellion in 1487, supposedly on behalf of Warwick in the person of Lambert Simnel. He was killed on the battlefield of Stoke in June 1487. Edmund de la Pole fled abroad in 1501 and became the centre of a fresh Yorkist plot. He was surrendered to Henry by Philip of Burgundy and was imprisoned. In 1513 he was executed.

Researching Religious References

The title uses a particular figure of speech known as alliteration. This device is used a great deal to make writing more colourful and interesting. In this piece of work, alliteration is to be used to define the essential ingredients, or 'quintessential qualities', of aspects of religious studies.

Example:

Khalsa: kesh, kirpan, kangha, kara, kaccha

Explanation

Khalsa is an order of the Sikh religion. To operate within an alliterative framework, only words starting with the letter 'K' can be used. Kesh, kirpan, kangha, kara and kaccha are the five 'Ks' associated with the Khalsa, namely the long uncut hair, the short sword, the wooden comb, the steel bracelet and the shorts.

Task One

For each of the following religious references, make a list of at least four words that alliterate with the main term and that help to define that term, physically or spiritually.

1 Christianity
2 Muslims
3 Sabbath
4 Priest

Task Two

Create some 'Researching Religious References' examples of your own. Write down the term and follow it with at least four alliterative words that describe some of the key 'ingredients'.

Teaching Notes

'Researching Religious References' provides an unusual method of looking at content through one particular form of wordplay. All sections of the National Curriculum encourage subject-specific language.

Key Elements

- ❖ use of specialist dictionaries and reference material
- ❖ wordplay, especially alliteration
- ❖ open-endedness, thus promoting differentiation by outcome
- ❖ subject-specific vocabulary
- ❖ understanding and demonstration of key concepts and ideas
- ❖ application of knowledge in an unusual manner
- ❖ analysis of concepts
- ❖ vocabulary extension.

Contexts

'Researching Religious References' can be used in a variety of ways:

- ❖ as extension material for particular topics
- ❖ as enrichment material for those who have completed other work
- ❖ as differentiated homework
- ❖ as an activity within an enrichment day, weekend, summer school or cluster day
- ❖ as an activity for the RE Club
- ❖ as an open-access competition.

Some Answers

Task One

Some suggestions are given, but credit should be given for any terms that satisfy the requirements.

1 Christianity:	crucifixion, Christmas, creed, Catholic Church
2 Muslims:	Muhammad, Mecca, mosque, Medina, muezzin (the man who calls Muslims to prayer)
3 Sabbath:	Saturday, Sunday, separate, special, synagogue, service (as a Jewish term, the Sabbath is Saturday, but in the Christian faith, some people refer to Sunday as being the Sabbath. In either case, the Sabbath is supposed to be 'separate' and 'special' in that it is distinct from the rest of the week).
4 Priest:	praying, protecting, peaceful, pastoral

Task Two

Answers will be judged on the extent to which the alliterative words define the concepts within the main term or reference. This is a difficult task and necessitates careful study of texts and dictionaries.

Enrichment Activities for Able and Talented Children © Barry Teare (Network Educational Press, 2004)

s ee t

Voices in the Park is a wonderful picture book created by Anthony Browne. In the book we hear, and see, four different accounts of a walk in a park. They have contrasting views of what goes on there.

- First Voice is a wealthy woman with her son Charles and a pedigree Labrador dog.
- Second Voice is an unemployed man with his daughter Smudge and a mongrel dog.
- Third Voice is the little boy, Charles.
- Fourth Voice is the girl Smudge.

Voices in the Park is illustrated beautifully but in a strange way as the people are portrayed as monkeys or apes.

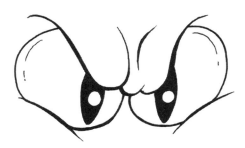 

Your Tasks

- Look at *Voices in the Park*.
- Describe the contrasting views of the four voices and explain why there are such differences
- Choose a situation from:
  - an episode in history where different people would have contrasting opinions
  - a development in geography where there are conflicting views
  - an issue involving differing religious perspectives.
- Write about your chosen topic, through four different voices, under the title 'As I See It'.

As I See It

Teaching Notes

Different interpretations of the same events or situations are at the heart of work in the humanities. Anthony Browne's *Voices in the Park* is a deceptively simple book that leads into that key area.

Key Elements

- ❖ engagement with text
- ❖ deduction and inference
- ❖ transfer of key features
- ❖ alternative interpretation of data.

Contexts

'As I See It' can be used in a variety of ways:

- ❖ as a piece of writing in a particular genre
- ❖ as an extension task from a module on conflict in the humanities
- ❖ as enrichment work for those ahead in the standard tasks
- ❖ as a differentiated homework
- ❖ as an activity within an enrichment session, cluster day, weekend or summer school
- ❖ as an activity for an after-school club in history, geography or religious studies
- ❖ as an open-access competition.

Success Criteria

- ❖ obvious understanding of the genre
- ❖ selection of a suitable example
- ❖ effective transfer of the principles
- ❖ the interplay between the four voices to illustrate the contrasting viewpoints
- ❖ the level of subtlety employed to draw out the differences.

Voices in the Park is a very well-known book. Even without the Anthony Browne story, 'As I See It' can be tackled, but clearly it is far better for children to see, and appreciate, his brilliant work for the lead-in.

THE QUESTION IS: RELIGIOUS STUDIES

You are used to giving answers to questions set in a variety of ways. For some questions there is only one correct answer but, on other occasions, a number of responses are considered as being correct, even though some answers could be regarded as stronger than others. This exercise reverses the normal process by giving you the answers. Your task is to provide suitable questions. Try to give as many questions as possible to each of the answers that are listed. Look for both the obvious and the less obvious questions. These 'questions' could be in a simple written form or presented as a diagram, puzzle or problem.

THE ANSWERS

1   prayer
2   an extremist
3   the Book of Genesis
4   inner peace
5   a deadly sin
6   five
7   Passover
8   unethical
9   care of the hair
10   the Ganges
11   ← ↑ →
12   salvation
13   the Noble Eightfold Path
14   only one God
15   meditation
16   in harmony with the environment
17   light
18   Mecca
19   a tragedy
20   a conflict of principles

Teaching Notes

This very open-ended exercise leads to a wide variety of answers, including some that could not have been predicted.

Differentiation by outcome or response is important here. Some children will feel disconcerted about being taken off familiar ground, given that they are provided with the answers and are asked, instead, to write the questions. Others will understand the concept but may not be capable of writing imaginative responses. They may settle for rather dull and straight responses. Here they need to be encouraged to 'fly'. Many able children will feel liberated to do exactly that and produce amazing questions in a variety of formats.

Differentiation by task will take place if children are given choice as to which of the 20 answers they tackle. They have been written to give a real mixture. Some are content-based answers that are likely to generate content-based questions, although an able pupil might go a very different route. Others have been included because many approaches could take place.

 All the 20, bar one, have been taken obviously, or less directly, from a number of religions. The symbol used as answer 11 is not, as far as the author knows, one that means something definite. It has been included to give an opportunity to use the imagination. Perhaps, as there are three arrows, a connection with the Holy Trinity will be made.

Key Elements

- ❖ creativity and imagination
- ❖ open-endedness
- ❖ interpretation of data
- ❖ alternative answers
- ❖ an unusual approach to knowledge
- ❖ differentiation by outcomes
- ❖ differentiation by task.

Contexts

'The Question Is: Religious Studies' can be used in the following ways:

- ❖ as a piece of general classroom work where differentiation by outcome will apply
- ❖ in sections, as 'starters' or 'icebreakers' in the classroom
- ❖ as normal homework
- ❖ as differentiated homework
- ❖ as an activity during an enrichment session, day, weekend, summer school or cluster day
- ❖ as an activity for the RE Club
- ❖ as an open-access competition.

Imagine That ...

People often speculate on what might have been. They often think back and say, 'What if a particular course of action had been taken?'

Much of their hypothesizing is idle speculation concerning them personally.

Now, let us consider applying this speculation to history, geography, religious education, politics, law, economics and civics where the consequences would affect many people.

Your Task

For each of the situations that follow, let your imagination run and write down the possible consequences. Remember, however, that hypothesizing often involves existing knowledge.

Now imagine that ...

1 Hitler had carried out a successful invasion of Britain.
2 the jury system was abolished.
3 it was compulsory to go to a place of worship once a week.
4 climate change altered the route of the Gulf Stream.
5 you could change the result of one major battle in European history.
6 the Ten Commandments actually became law.
7 nuclear weapons had never been developed.
8 a pond was a compulsory feature in every garden.
9 goods from the United States of America were banned by all European Union countries.
10 you could wave a wand and relocate any one foreign tourist attraction to this country.
11 the British election system switched to fixed four-year terms of office.
12 the Gunpowder Plot had been successful.
13 the whole population of Britain became vegetarian.
14 Tim Smit had been put in charge of the construction of the Millennium Dome.
15 a common minimum wage was established throughout the world.
16 Siddhartha Gautama had been born in Nottingham rather than Nepal.
17 an accused person could be brought to trial for the same crime five times.
18 you had the power to put a major historical figure of the past in charge of Britain now.
19 all the main world religious leaders and persons of great influence promised to exclude from their faiths anybody using violence against believers from a different faith.
20 no opinion polls were allowed to be carried out or published in the 12 months before a General Election.

Extension Task

Create some 'Imagine That ...' examples of your own from the areas of history, geography, religious education, politics, law, economics and civics.

Imagine That ...

Teaching Notes

Imagination does not rule out consideration of existing facts. Indeed, it is more potent when existing knowledge is taken into account. The amount of detail and depth of understanding in the answers can vary considerably.

Key Elements
- ❖ imagination
- ❖ logical thinking
- ❖ lateral thinking
- ❖ mind mapping
- ❖ hypothesizing
- ❖ analysis
- ❖ synthesis.

Contexts
'Imagine That ..' can be used in the following ways:
- ❖ individually as extension work to particular topics
- ❖ as discussion material in the classroom
- ❖ as enrichment material for those who have completed other work
- ❖ as differentiated homework
- ❖ as topics for the Debating Society
- ❖ as an activity during a humanities enrichment day, weekend, summer school or cluster day
- ❖ as an open-access competition.

Responses
Many of the situations play strongly to hypothesizing and, therefore, to synthesis. One of the factors that will determine the quality of the answers, will be the use made of existing knowledge.

Example
1 'Imagine that Hitler had carried out a successful invasion of Britain.'
    Part of the answer would refer to knowledge about Nazi occupations in general. Obvious elements would include a range of terrors, the use of secret police and informers, the executions or imprisonment of people who might lead any opposition, the banning of organizations such as trade unions, the takeover of the education system and compulsion upon teachers to present situations in a prescribed manner.

    The able child is likely to contrast other occupations and place Britain into context. Would an invasion of Britain be followed by a Danish-style occupation or a Polish-style occupation? The answer is the former because of Hitler's views on race and the relative values of people. Although unpleasant, a successful invasion of Britain was unlikely to have been followed by the same degree of terror as in Slav countries.

    Given enough time, the able child might then speculate on the changed course of European and world history.

- ❖ Some of the situations play more strongly to another higher-order thinking skill: that of evaluation. Numbers 5 and 18 stand out in this respect.

NOTE: For those unaware, in 14, Tim Smit is the man who redeveloped the Lost Gardens of Heligan and, more pertinently, established the incredibly successful Eden Project in Cornwall.

DUSTBIN DETECTIVES

The police were called to the house by a suspicious neighbour. They treated the property as though it was the scene of a crime, even though nobody was sure that a crime had been committed. The urgent departure added to the concerns. Most of the potential evidence had been removed carefully but the suspects had made one very significant mistake. They had left a black plastic sack full of rubbish in the dustbin by the back door. The contents were examined with enormous care.

Imagine that you and the other members of your team are in the position of the scene-of-crime officers. What can you learn about the suspects from the contents? How successful can you be as 'Dustbin Detectives'?

Your Tasks

1 Examine the contents of the dustbin spread out on the floor in the order in which they came out of the black bag. Carry out as much of the examination as you can with your eyes. You can pick items up, but put them back exactly where they came from.
2 Make full and detailed notes in the time allocated. Once the evidence has been removed, you will not be able to see items again.
3 Discuss the significance of the contents of the dustbin bag. What can you say about:
   ■ the number of suspects
   ■ the type of people
   ■ their lifestyle and habits
   ■ what is missing, what gaps there are in the evidence
   ■ the strength of the evidence and how sure you can be.
4 As a team, prepare and write a report based upon your discussion, with an eye carefully on the success criteria listed below.

The Success Criteria

The report on the suspects, who are responsible for the contents of the dustbin, will be judged by the following success criteria:

1 The detail in which the evidence has been examined.
2 The skill with which the evidence has been linked to support ideas.
3 The quality of the assessment of the strength of the various ideas.
4 The validity of the gaps, or missing evidence, identified.
5 The clarity of the presentation of the report in terms of the ideas expressed.
6 The credibility of the ideas about the suspects. The report should not be sensational but should, rather, be based upon hard fact and cold reasoning.

Extension Task

Write an account of the events that led to the police raiding the house and examining the contents of the dustbin.

Teaching Notes

'Dustbin Detectives' could be used during a detective course but it is included here as the piece of work plays very much to the humanities skills.

Key Elements

- ❖ observation
- ❖ analysis
- ❖ deduction and inference
- ❖ synthesis
- ❖ evaluation of evidence
- ❖ team collaboration
- ❖ writing for a particular purpose
- ❖ creative writing (in the extension task).

Contexts

'Dustbin Detectives' can be used in a number of ways:

- ❖ as a classroom activity during a thinking skills course
- ❖ as general work in humanities, where differentiation by outcome will apply
- ❖ as an activity during an enrichment day, weekend, summer school or cluster day
- ❖ as an activity for the Humanities Club.

Organization

1   The evidence is spread out carefully on the floor as a thin layer to aid observation. A reasonable area is needed to allow the teams to move around the contents. Masking tape is fastened around the perimeter of the evidence to give a more authentic feel and to mark the boundaries clearly. Children need to be encouraged to replace items in their original position.
2   Pupils are grouped into detective teams.
3   An introduction is given about the exercise and attention is drawn to the success criteria. The introduction can include references to archaeological methods if the teacher wishes.

For practicality of storage, and for hygiene reasons, items that rot have to be eliminated from the dustbin. This gives a lopsided slant to the evidence but it is clearly necessary. There are two ways of handling this situation. Either the teacher can 'come clean' and explain, in advance, what has been done, or this can be left as one of the gaps in the evidence to be explained.

THE CONTENTS

These can vary to suit the organizers. They can be tailored to produce particular comments about the suspects – for instance, deliberately excluding any items that would indicate the presence of children or pets. There needs to be irrelevant material, such as junk mail, and sufficient variety to promote open-endedness.

Some items used by the author include: TES (*Times Educational Supplement*), Quorn burgers box, three sea shells, an old pair of torn ladies trousers, butcher's receipts, supermarket receipts (all dates for receipts fell within a short time span – could be important evidence), old paintbrush, toothbrush, styptic pencil, coffee jar, washing-up liquid bottle, empty coleslaw tub, two free-range egg boxes, various plastic shopping bags, Tesco Club envelope, chicken stock-cube box, empty cough-sweet packet, golf ball, clothes peg, pizza base box, Marks and Spencer magazine, RSPB (Royal Society for the Protection of Birds) magazine, AOL (America on Line) CD, SAGA leaflet, used envelopes, spring water bottle, cinema leaflets and ticket stubs, old stamp booklet, energy-saving leaflets, Cotton Traders catalogue, box that held a telephone extension lead, WWF (World Wildlife Fund) information and so on.

Meaningful

For each of the ten highlighted words, name the correct definition from the four possibles.

1 Col

a   the highest peak in a range of mountains
b   the sheltered side of a mountain
c   a depression in the summit line of a chain of mountains
d   the favoured route up a mountain

2 Manifesto

a   a declaration of policy and aims by a political party
b   another name for the electoral register
c   the many ways in which voting can take place in an election
d   the programme for the parliamentary year, announced by the Queen

3 Despot

a   the next in line of succession
b   an absolute ruler
c   the government formed by a coalition of parties
d   a ruler who bases his decisions upon electoral promises

4 Anticyclone

a   a weather system with high pressure at its centre
b   a weather system with low pressure at its centre
c   the climate of a small area
d   when warm air has to rise over cold air

5 Sedile

a   a small stone basin in the wall of a chapel
b   a stone seat, often recessed, on the south side of a sanctuary
c   a square notch cut in the parapet of a stone wall
d   a length of stone parapet between two crenels

6 Contour

a the direction shown on a map by the points of the compass
b a square on a map representing an area of ground
c a pattern of routes that are linked together
d a line drawn on a map to join places at the same height above sea level

7 Blitzkrieg

a an intense military campaign
b a war fought on two fronts
c a siege of a city to starve the inhabitants
d a retreat, destroying property on the way

8 Biological Weathering

a the breakdown of rock by chemical action
b the breakdown of rock by plants and animals
c a form of weathering where water in cracks freezes and expands to split or shatter rock
d the wearing away and removal of rock by rivers, sea, ice and wind

9 Abdicate

a to change one's religion
b to change party allegiance
c to give up items for the period of Lent
d to give up or renounce the throne

10 Seismograph

a an instrument used to measure wind strength
b an instrument used to measure earthquakes
c an instrument used to measure rainfall
d an instrument used to measure minimum and maximum temperatures

Enrichment Activities for Able and Talented Children © Barry Teare (Network Educational Press, 2004)

Tournament: Throwing Down the Gauntlet

HIDDEN BRITAIN

Can you name the ten places in Britain from the clues below? The number of letters of the place is indicated in brackets.

1   Edible organ in the swim. (9)

2   Strong animal crosses the river. (6)

3   Treasure container hesitates. (7)

4   Farm building holds paper together. (10)

5   Male sheep at entrance to field. (8)

6   Easy speed for a horse should not put it under the ground. (10)

7   No peace in the middle of the candle. (7)

8   Following neither she casts her spell without any tea. (7)

9   Sounds as though it destroys them. (7)

10   The female parent is feeling fine. (10)

Tournament: Throwing Down the Gauntlet

The Passage of Time

Place these ten events in correct chronological order, starting with the earliest and finishing with the most recent.

THEN

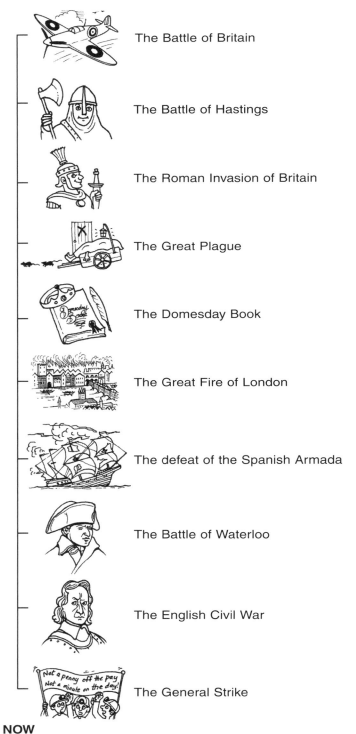

The Battle of Britain

The Battle of Hastings

The Roman Invasion of Britain

The Great Plague

The Domesday Book

The Great Fire of London

The defeat of the Spanish Armada

The Battle of Waterloo

The English Civil War

The General Strike

NOW

Tournament: Throwing Down the Gauntlet

INVENTORS' IDENTITIES

Sort out the following anagrams to name ten British inventors
and then try to name their inventions.

1 A T T W

2 L E B L

3 D M C A A M

4 P H S S O N T E E N

5 L U L T

6 N E L U R B

7 G H T K A R W R I

8 Y D V A

9 D R A B I

10 C K T H I V I T R E

Collectively Speaking

What word or words connects the four items in
each of the ten groups below?

1   mistral; chinook; sirocco; trade

2   Herschel; Copernicus; Kepler; Messier

3   trebuchet; cat; mangonel; mining

4   California; Utah; Montana; Nebraska

5   Jurassic; Cambrian; Devonian; Triassic

6   zloty; rupee; drachma; yen

7   low; isobars; front; high

8   Luke; Mark; John; Matthew

9   ammonites; trilobites; belemnites; amber

10 bailey; portcullis; drawbridge; keep

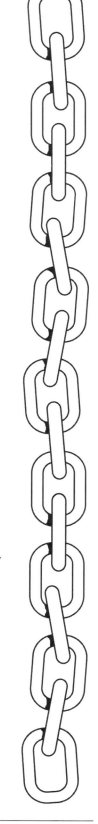

Enrichment Activities for Able and Talented Children © Barry Teare (Network Educational Press, 2004)

Teaching Notes

A Tournament causes excitement and it is a popular feature within enrichment courses. Nobody is going to get everything correct – a salutary lesson for able children to learn. There is considerable content involved but there are other key elements.

Key Elements

❖ knowledge

❖ word play

❖ teamwork

❖ collaboration

❖ chronology; correct and incorrect

❖ subject-specific vocabulary

❖ classification

❖ working at pace

❖ using common sense to narrow down choices.

Alternative Ways Of Working

In the main text the suggested method is to have eight stations for 6 minutes each.

1   The number of stations can be reduced or, indeed, increased if other material is added.

2   The 6-minute allocations can be extended.

3   The tournament can be amended to concentrate upon a single subject within the humanities.

4   All teams can tackle each section at the same time. Stations are therefore replaced by rounds. This does, of course, have implications for the number of each resource that needs to be available.

Solutions

Meaningful

1	Col	c	a depression in the summit line of a chain of mountains
2	Manifesto	a	a declaration of policy and aims by a political party
3	Despot	b	an absolute ruler
4	Anticyclone	a	a weather system with high pressure at its centre
5	Sedile	b	a stone seat often recessed, on the south side of the sanctuary
6	Contour	d	a line drawn on a map to join places at the same height above sea level
7	Blitzkrieg	a	an intense military campaign
8	Biological Weathering	b	the breakdown of rock by plants and animals
9	Abdicate	d	to give up or renounce the throne
10	Seismograph	b	an instrument used to measure earthquakes

HIDDEN BRITAIN

1	Liverpool	6	Canterbury
2	Oxford	7	Warwick
3	Chester	8	Norwich
4	Barnstaple	9	Wrexham
5	Ramsgate	10	Motherwell

Anachorisms

MERATC, page 113.

The Passage of Time

Earliest to most recent:

1 The Roman Invasion of Britain
2 The Battle of Hastings
3 The Domesday Book
4 The defeat of the Spanish Armada
5 The English Civil War
6 The Great Plague
7 The Great Fire of London
8 The Battle of Waterloo
9 The General Strike
10 The Battle of Britain

Anachronisms

See *Parallel Universe* or your own version.

'The Sounds of Rivers'

CRATC, page 273.

INVENTORS' IDENTITIES

1	Watt	the steam engine or unit of power
2	Bell	the telephone
3	McAdam	road surface
4	Stephenson	'The Rocket' or other railway developments
5	Tull	the seed drill
6	Brunel	bridges, steamships and so on
7	Arkwright	the spinning frame
8	Davy	the miner's lamp and chemical discoveries
9	Baird	television
10	Trevithick	railway developments

Collectively Speaking

1 winds
2 astronomers
3 siege weapons and tactics
4 states in the USA
5 geological periods
6 currencies
7 meteorological terms
8 gospels in the New Testament
9 fossils
10 parts of a castle

Enrichment Activities for Able and Talented Children © Barry Teare (Network Educational Press, 2004)

Detective/Thinking Skills Courses, Activities and Resources

Introduction

A high percentage of able children find detective material fascinating. Using titles that fit that genre attracts attention. However, there is much more to these courses and activities than that. They cover lateral thinking, logical thinking and code breaking as well as detective work. As a result, there is a high dependence on the higher-order thinking skills of analysis, evaluation and synthesis. The links with areas of the curriculum are very strong, especially with mathematics and English and, perhaps most of all, with the humanities. The varied outcomes also develop presentational skills and the capacity to work as part of a team.

Very serious objectives and outcomes can be delivered through activities that provide a high level of interest and enjoyment.

Possible Titles for Courses
'Elementary My Dear Watson'
'Exercising the Little Grey Cells'
'Super Sleuth'
'All Clued Up'
'The Mysteries of Gresham Grange'
'Cracking the Case'
'Quentin Questor Investigates'
'The Clued-in Detective Agency: Situation Vacant'
'Shreds of Evidence'

Part One: Starters, Icebreakers

A: Lateral Thinking Problems

These make excellent starters or 'icebreakers' as everybody can make a contribution and a variety of answers is possible. There is an early opportunity to talk and exchange ideas.

Very full details on how to use lateral thinking problems effectively are given on page 205 of this book.

Favourites that produce really good results can be found in the following titles:

Paul Sloane, *Lateral Thinking Puzzles* (Sterling Publishing Company, 1992)
    'The Men in the Hotel' (page 9)
    'In the Pet Shop' (page 11)
    'Trouble with Sons' (page 14)
    'The Two Barbers' (page 34)

Mind-Bending Lateral Thinking Puzzles (Lagoon Books, 1994)
  'The Petrol Station Attendant' (page 11)
  'Bankruptcy' (page 15)
  'The Lonely Man' (page 41)
  'Two Men at a Table' (page 45)
  'The Frail Neighbour' (page 52)

Chris Dickson, *Mystery Puzzles* (Robinson Publishing, 1999)
  'Cutting the Cake' (page 13)
  '1 to 100' (page 57)
  'Car Registration' (page 64)

'So ... Answer This!'
This piece consists of four intriguing situations that open up many possibilities: 'Plugged in', 'Families!', 'Going, Going, Gone' and 'Motorway Madness' (page 253).

'One Question Many Answers'
MERATC
'One Question Many Answers' has 12 examples (page 247). 'Blackbird' and 'Eden Delayed' have worked well on courses.

'Answers on a Postcard'
CRATC
Similarly, there are 11 lateral problems in 'Answers on a Postcard' (page 254). 'Such A Card', 'As Keen As Mustard' and, especially, 'Fields Apart' have been used with very pleasing results.

Fifteen to 20 minutes for each example used.

| 3 | 4 | 5 | 6 | 7 | 8 | 9 | + | |

You can collect and use lateral thinking problems of your own. When you come across a situation and wonder about it, it could probably be used. Unusual circumstances, that may have several explanations, are best.

B: Short Detective Cases

'Shreds of Evidence'
'Shreds of Evidence' (page 256) contains five short cases. Individually they provide appropriate material early in a course.

Fifteen other cases, from previous publications, can be used as individual units or collectively as longer pieces:

'Vital Evidence'
ERATC
'Vital Evidence' (page 213), consisting of 'Eye Spy', 'Paper Exercise', 'A Horse of a Different Colour', 'Turning the Tables' and 'On Second Thoughts'.

'Critical Clues'
MERATC
'Critical Clues' (page 221), consisting of 'Lady In Red', 'Suspected Suicide', 'Message Understood', 'Diamonds are Forever' and 'A Strange Confession'.

'Cracking the Case'
CRATC

'Cracking The Case' (page 214), consisting of 'Man's Best Friend', 'Initial Confusion', 'A Dangerous Brew', 'Pearls of Wisdom' and 'Story in the Snow'.

Twenty to 25 minutes per case, including discussion of various views.

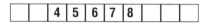

Quicksolve Whodunit Puzzles

Although an American book (you can 'anglicize' the stories), children like to spot the one, or at most two, giveaway clues at the heart of the mini-mysteries contained within *Quicksolve Whodunit Puzzles* (Sterling Publishing Company, 1995).

As a follow-up, or during 'Choice Time', children can write their own examples.

These have very little detail and five minutes, or so, are sufficient per puzzle.

Part Two: Logic Problems

It is useful to present a contrast to lateral problems with logic problems, both short and long.

'Canine Avenue'

This short logic problem concerns the correct pairing of houseowners and their dogs, who live in the appropriately-named 'Canine Avenue' (page 264).

Twenty minutes for the introduction and a solution by those who think quickly and accurately.

Teaching the Matrix Method

Most children will not have met the matrix method of solving this particular form of logic problem. 'Canine Avenue' (page 264) can be solved using a matrix, although some children will prefer an alternative method. They will need instruction to make the matrix method a possible route to use.

- The method works best when there are distinct and separate links between two variables. An example would be that six friends have a birthday in each of six different months.
- The size of the matrix depends upon the number of people or items – six on each side in the example quoted.
- One variable is placed horizontally and the other vertically, but it does not matter which way round.
- A matrix is established (as shown below, for the example described).

	April	May	June	August	September	December
Andrew						
Andrea						
Sue						
Peter						
Sebastian						
Monica						
Vladimir						

- A series of clues are then given that enable the matrix to be completed to reach the solution.
  - When a clue shows, for example, that Peter's birthday is not in December, a cross is placed in the correct box where Peter and December intersect.
  - When a clue shows that Sebastian's birthday is in August, a tick is placed in the intersecting box, and then the rest of Sebastian's row and August's column have crosses placed in the boxes.
  - There must eventually be one tick, and one tick only, in each row and column.
  - Sometimes a tick can be placed by a process of elimination. If April, June, August, September and December have been crossed out for Monica, then her birthday must be in May and a tick can be placed in that box.
  - In a more testing matrix problem, the information from more than one clue has to be used at the same time to reach a solution.
  - Watch out for 'either/or' clues. If a clue states that 'the child with the shortest name has a birthday in a month of 30 days in length', it means that Sue could have been born in April, June or September and all three must be kept open.
  - Don't place ticks until a pairing is a definite. Be patient and build up the number of crosses.

It is helpful to run through an example together unless all the children are experienced in the technique.

Writing their own Matrix Problems

Solving somebody else's problem is one thing, writing one of your own brings in new skills.

- Decide about the content of your problem. Choose variables that cover a subject you know something about, whether it be fashion, football, horses, pop music, or anything else.
- Construct a matrix and place the names of the two variables. Deliberately choose items that allow 'either/or' clues to be set.
- Either start with a completed matrix from which clues are set, or complete the matrix as the clues are set.
- Do not give away too much information too quickly. Make the solver work for their answers.
- When you have written the problem, draw up another blank matrix and go back through the clues, to make sure that it works.
- Give the written description (of the context of the puzzle) and set of clues to a friend and see if he or she can solve the problem. It is easy to overlook other interpretations when you create such a problem. Other people might take a different meaning from a clue.

Reversing a process and getting children to set a problem is a very challenging and worthwhile task.

Other Short Logic Problems
ERATC

'**Field and Track**' (page 150) matrix problem
'**Food for Thought**' (page 152) written solution
'**Radio Six**' (page 165) pure logic

MERATC
'The Votewell Election' (page 194) pure logic
'Just the Job' (page 200) simple matrix
'Case Histories' (page 202) two-variable detective matrix
'Detective Case Clues' (page 204) three-variable detective matrix extension

CRATC
'What Weather!?' (page 184) written solution

Times vary from 15–30 minutes.

		5	6	7	8	9		

Long Logic Problems

Four extensive pieces, from previous books, have been used on detective courses, producing excellent work and immense satisfaction for the children.

There is no long logical problem in this section of the book but there is one in the Games Section – 'What's Your Game?' (page 179).

ERATC
'Ruby Red' (page 133), a piece on the identification of mineral specimens.

MERATC
'Birds of a Feather' (page 207), involving mathematics, living processes and information about British birds.

CRATC
'The Barratt Trail' (page 197), concerns British mammals and map work.
'Detecting the Detectives' (page 226), links readers to their favourite fictional detectives.

Around one hour, including an introduction. Additional time is required for feedback (20-30 minutes).

		5	6	7	8	9		

Part Three: Codes

These can be of varying length and difficulty.

'Lucky the Cat'
ERATC
'Lucky the Cat' (page 169): a relatively short code that can be solved reasonably easily if the given data is given sufficient attention.

Twenty minutes, if the information is used properly.

	4	5	6	7	8	9		

'Cipherus'
This 'Star Trek' or 'Star Wars' type code puts a premium on using given data effectively (page 266).

Thirty minutes, or so, for those who take full advantage of the information given.

		5	6	7	8	9		

'A Gift from Cocklesea'

This is a much more complicated code, involving a considerable amount of data (page 270). There is a strong seaside 'fun and games' element.

At least one hour is required for this challenging code.

		5	6	7	8	9		

Able children often succeed too easily. They need to work for their success or there is a danger that they may become intellectually idle. Complicated codes provide a real challenge.

Codes Long and Short

A number of other codes have been key components of 'detective' courses, to great effect.

'A Capital Idea'
EPATC

This code is based upon the correct and incorrect use of capital letters, a vital skill (page 70).

One hour, including an introduction.

		5	6	7	8			

'Mosaic'
ERATC

'Mosaic' (page 172) provides a lengthy challenge on what looks like a mosaic pattern. Children often struggle all the way through it and then vote it their favourite piece!

One hour is required

		5	6	7	8	9	+	

'Crossedwords'
ERATC

'Crossedwords' (page 176) uses a 'suspect' crossword to deliver a coded message from a secret agent in trouble.

At least one hour is required.

		5	6	7	8	9	+	

'The Shapes'
MERATC

This piece (page 234) has a bright, cheerful format – a comic strip. This is very much a visual code.

Fifty minutes to one hour.

	4	5	6	7	8			

'The Hidden Will of Gresham Grange'
MERATC

This piece (page 237) makes use of a shelf of books and a sketch map of Gresham Grange itself.

One hour 30 minutes is needed, including an introduction.

| | | 5 | 6 | 7 | 8 | 9 | | |

Part Four: Detective Materials

Some materials have already been described under 'Shreds of Evidence' (page 246). Others will follow in Part Five: Longer Activities (page 252).

'According to the Evidence'
ERATC

This is a very popular 'country-house' murder (page 203). The emphasis here is upon finding all the supporting evidence, a skill that is required in good answers in many subjects.

One hour 15 minutes to one hour 30 minutes is required to get full value from the detailed evidence. This allows feedback time.

| | 4 | 5 | 6 | 7 | 8 | 9 | | |

'Cliffhanger'
MERATC

A kidnapping is the crime to be investigated (page 228). Synthesis of data, including a map, is a key feature. For courses, a Report Sheet to the Chief Constable of Devwall has been added to increase the drama.

One hour 15 minutes for a briefing at the start, the work itself, and feedback.

| | 4 | 5 | 6 | 7 | 8 | 9 | | |

'Who Nobbled the Racehorse?'

This problem is to be found in Brian Bolt's *Mathematical Funfair* (Cambridge University Press, 1989, page 2). Spatial awareness is important to solve the doping case.

There is considerable challenge involved and it is useful to keep adding clues at regular intervals:

1. The weather is critical to the solution.
2. Further snow did not cover the footprints.
3. Remember that their paths did not cross.
4. For people to 'meet' or see each other, their paths must come close together.
5. Nobody needed to go outside the racecourse.
6. The paths did not have to be direct.
7. Remember where the crime took place.

Able children do sometimes require additional help, but only after they have made a real effort themselves. Giving away clues too early destroys the challenge.

The quickest answers tend to take around 45 minutes.

| | | 5 | 6 | 7 | 8 | 9 | | |

'An Arresting Problem'
ERATC

A sketch map, scale and suspects with dog's names are key features in this case (page 211).

Fifteen to 20 minutes.

		4	5	6	7	8			

Detective work is not only enjoyable and popular, but also puts emphasis upon the higher-order thinking skills of analysis, synthesis and evaluation.

Part Five: Longer Activities

'Brief Case' – A Presentation
CRATC

This activity has been used most successfully with a wide range of ages (page 222). Creativity, urgency, teamwork, collaboration and presentational skills are exercised, as well as thinking skills.

One hour to one hour 15 minutes is required, depending upon the number of teams presenting.

		4	5	6	7	8	9	+	

'The Scene of the Crime' – An Investigation

This major piece of work starts off as an individual activity, and then changes into a team event and report (page 276). Children respond to it very favourably indeed.

Two hours 30 minutes covers the initial briefings, individual participation, team collaboration, the writing of the report and feedback.

		4	5	6	7	8	9		

'Silence in Court' – A Murder Trial
MERATC

As well as being regarded as detective material, 'Silence in Court' works well within history and civics (page 133). The dramatic appeal is heightened if court personnel wear wigs and gowns. It is exciting to play an acting role, but the children who form the jury say how responsible they feel, even though this is a piece of fiction with no real-life consequences.

Two hours 30 minutes gives time for a 30-minute introduction on court procedure, the acting out of the case, and 45 minutes deliberation for the jury. The work could be split, especially by dealing with court procedure on a previous occasion.

			5	6	7	8	9	+	

So ... Answer This!

When faced with mysterious or unusual circumstances, people sometimes say to others, in frustration, 'So ... answer this!', or, in other words, 'What do you make of this?'

Your Task

Read the four situations below. Try to find more than one answer to fit the evidence given. Use your imagination, but avoid unrealistic responses.

So ... Answer THIS!

Plugged in

A household consisted of only husband and wife, as their children were grown up and had moved away. The man was puzzled by what he started to see in the wash basin of the bathroom of the house. Unlike what had happened for many years previously, the husband found that on many occasions the plug had been left in the wash basin but that there was no water in the bowl. He could not understand why this situation had started to occur.

- What was the explanation for the plug often being left in the wash basin, even though no water was in there?

Families!

Mr and Mrs Logan have an apartment on the east side of town. Mrs Delgardo, the mother of Mrs Logan, has a house on the west side of town. Mr Logan visits his mother-in-law on a daily basis. Mrs Delgardo goes to see her daughter every day but she never enters the apartment. She stands in the courtyard and waves to her daughter who comes out onto the balcony. Sometimes, mother and daughter exchange written messages that are lowered one way, and pulled up the other way, using a basket. The three people never all come together.

- Can you suggest the reason for this strange family behaviour?

Going, Going, Gone

Two men went by car together to an auction. They chattered happily and laughed on more than one occasion. From the moment the two men entered the auction room they did not communicate with each other. Indeed, they sat in different parts of the room. When the auction was over, the two men left separately, but they met at the car, started to speak to each other again and drove home happily.

■ Why should the two men behave in this particular way?

Motorway Madness

Sheila Ferguson regularly travels between Slough in Berkshire and Exeter in Devon. Her normal route is along the M4 and then onto the M5 near Avonmouth. The total distance is some 173 miles. Sheila breaks the journey just once at either Leigh Delamere or Gordano Services. If traffic is very heavy, and therefore the journey takes longer, she might stop twice.

On one Thursday morning in August, Sheila made the Slough–Exeter trip but, on this particular occasion, she stopped at every service station *en route* – Reading, Membury, Leigh Delamere, Gordano, Sedgemoor, Bridgwater, Taunton Deane and Cullompton.

■ Why should Sheila have stopped at all eight service stations on that particular morning when her normal practice was one stop or, at most, two?

So ... Answer This!

Teaching Notes

The problems set play strongly to lateral thinking, as many answers are possible. Even so, logical thinking will also be involved as engagement with the text and analysis of the key points are necessary.

Methods of Working
Alternative methods of working with 'So ... Answer This!' are:
- ❖ individual pupils produce written responses
- ❖ groups of pupils discuss and then make a combined written response
- ❖ the answers from groups are given verbally and other groups consider them.

Contexts
'So ... Answer This!' can be used in a number of ways:
- ❖ individually, as 'starters' during form period
- ❖ as classroom work for all in thinking skills courses
- ❖ as an enrichment task for those who have completed other work
- ❖ as differentiated homework
- ❖ as an activity within an enrichment day, weekend or summer school
- ❖ as an open-access competition.

Some Answers
Some ideas are given as to what the answers might be, but these are only suggestions, and credit should be given for any answers that fit all the facts. Even if there is a real-life solution, good alternatives are valid. Lateral thinking aims to generate varied responses, some of them surprising and unexpected.

Plugged In
One factor that any answer needs to incorporate is that only recently has the situation occurred; therefore, some form of change must be part of the response. One reason for some people leaving a plug in is to prevent spiders getting into a basin. The phobia would have had to be newly acquired. This example is based upon a real-life scenario. Late in life, the wife had her ears pierced and started to wear earrings. As there was a mirror above the basin (an additional fact that does not contradict any of the given data), she put on and removed the earrings there. Concerned that an earring should not fall into the basin and be lost down the pipe, the wife put the plug in as a safety measure. Sometimes she forgot to remove the plug when she had finished.

Families!
This is not a situation taken from real life, but rather based upon the central mystery of Pirandello's 1917 play, 'Absolutely (perhaps)'. In this intriguing play, the situation caused much gossip. When Mr Logan or Mrs Delgardo made explanations to the townspeople, no more light was shed upon the real truth. This is an ideal lateral thinking problem as there is no actual answer and Pirandello delighted in leaving the audience to come to their own conclusions. This is, then, an exciting scenario to explore.

Going, Going, Gone
Among several possibilities, one explanation is that two friends were in collusion to affect the bidding, and they did not want others to know that they knew each other. Another suggestion is that one of the men was the auctioneer or somebody in an official position while his friend was going to bid for some of the lots.

Motorway Madness
There may well have been a problem with the car. Perhaps a tyre had been losing air or the radiator was losing water. As a consequence, Sheila stopped at every service station to check that the 'fault' was alright. An alternative could be that Sheila was waiting for important news and stopped to make a call on her mobile, as she knew that it was dangerous to use it while driving. A number of other routes are likely to be explored.

SHREDS OF EVIDENCE

Being a detective is often not the glamorous occupation that it seems from fiction and television. Routine investigations, including house-to-house enquiries, go on for months. However, there are occasions when a conclusion is reached more quickly and dramatically due to key clues. The five cases below fall into that category. Read the cases carefully and see if you can solve them by spotting the significance of the critical 'Shreds of Evidence'.

CASE ONE: A GAME OF CHESS

When Detective Constable Sinead O'Brien reached Grove Hall on a cold January evening, she found Antony Price in a state of high excitement. She took an initial statement from Antony Price who said:

'I came to Grove Hall at the invitation of the owner, Gerry Burns. I have known him for some time. We had a cup of coffee and then Gerry suggested a game of chess. I was very happy to play. We had reached a particular point when Gerry said that he had forgotten to close up a workshop at the bottom of the garden. He asked for a five-minute break while he went to lock up. When Gerry had been gone three or four minutes, I heard a cry from the garden. It didn't sound right to me so I went to take a look. It is a big garden, so at first I didn't find anything. Eventually, I found Gerry dead on the floor with a head wound. Somebody had obviously struck him down.

I came back into the house and met the housekeeper, Mrs Gladstone, who had just returned from a visit to her sister's. I explained what had happened and she telephoned the police.'

A few minutes later, Detective Inspector Larry Butler arrived at Grove Hall, muffled up with a scarf and a heavy overcoat to keep out the cold. Without delay, he went to view the body in the garden before it was removed. Larry looked thoughtfully down at Gerry Burns and at the blue T-shirt and black trousers that he was wearing. The detective exchanged a few words with the police doctor.

Detective Inspector Butler then returned to the house. He took off his outdoor clothing as the house was very warm from the central heating. He had a quick word with Sinead and read Antony Price's initial statement. Frowning, he looked down at the chess board that still showed the position of the unfinished game (see the following picture).

Detective Inspector Butler then asked Antony Price to accompany him to the police station. 'Whatever for?' asked Price. 'I've done nothing wrong. All I did was to play a game of chess.' Larry Butler responded, 'There are a number of discrepancies in your account. You have not been telling the truth.'

Your Tasks

1 Even at this early stage of the investigation, Detective Inspector Butler had five serious concerns about Price's statement. Write down what they were.

2 What might be inferred from these concerns?

3 If you had been the inspector, how would you follow up those particular concerns?

Burns (white)

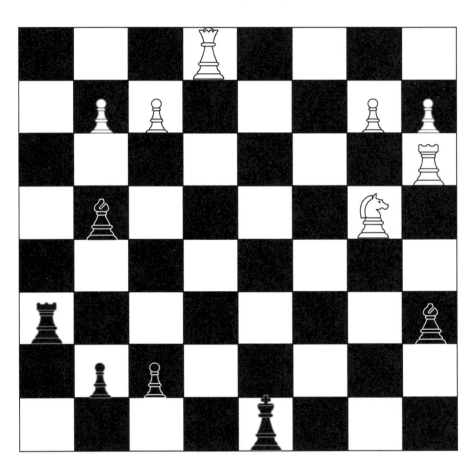

Price (black)

CASE TWO: AN UNSHAKEABLE ALIBI

The burglary of the Jenkins' property took place on Sunday 27th October 2002. A neighbour living on her own, Mrs Bentley, saw a man acting suspiciously and got a good look at him. When questioned by the police, she said that the time had been 11.25am. There was no doubt about that in her mind as, just after seeing the man, she had glanced at her clock as she was baking a cake and needed to know the time that the cake went into the oven.

In many ways Mrs Bentley's evidence was extremely helpful. She gave a detailed description of the man and it fitted that of Gordon Meek, a well-known local burglar. There was, however, a real stumbling block. Purely by chance, PC Davies had seen Meek at 11.20am on a housing estate some distance away from the Jenkins' property. He knew the burglar well from past dealings, and took note of the time.

Detective Sergeant Mary Murchison investigated the case. At first it seemed impossible to reconcile the two statements. Mrs Bentley had identified Gordon Meek at the scene of the crime but he seemed to have an unshakeable alibi, given to him, ironically, by PC Davies.

Your Tasks

Detective Sergeant Mary Murchison eventually worked out that the two, apparently conflicting, statements could be reconciled. Explain how this could be so. Describe how she could verify her theory.

CASE THREE: CASUAL TALK SAVES CRIME

Trevor Barnard is a very successful detective, who has made great progress in his chosen career. His cousin, Philip Barnard, has not been so fortunate. He has struggled to keep any job for very long. The two men met infrequently and such an occasion occurred only recently. Trevor asked Philip how life was treating him, and he was surprised to find that his cousin was very pleased with a couple of developments. First, he had taken in a lodger called Lionel Dickens, an acquaintance he had made in a local pub, who was also out of work. The rent came in very useful as Philip's finances were never particularly strong. Second, he

had put Philip in the way of a strange, but well-paid job. Trevor's job always made him rather cautious and, therefore, he asked Philip what he knew about Lionel Dickens. Philip had to admit that he knew very little. Trevor warned him to be careful, although Philip responded that Lionel's arrival had been a great stroke of fortune.

The two men chattered on, and Philip explained more about the job. Lionel Dickens had come home one evening to say that he had heard of a job that might suit Philip. Philip himself had been doubtful, but he had gone for an interview and had been successful. He was, however, rather baffled. The job consisted of sorting and cross-referencing a large number of press cuttings about sport. He couldn't quite see the point, but the pay was very good. The man who had hired him, Danny Regan, got rather 'snappy' when asked about the reasons. This Danny Regan was also a stickler for punctuality and good attendance. When Philip arrived, Danny was always there to check him in. He appeared 'out-of-the-blue' at odd times almost as though he didn't trust Philip. Once there had been a nasty scene. Philip had gone out from the work office to buy some cigarettes, and when he returned, Danny was there. He lost his temper with Philip for being absent. Philip thought that it was all rather strange, but as the work was very easy and the wages were really good, he had decided not to think too much about it.

Trevor was uneasy about what Philip had said. It didn't seem right. He kept an eye on Philip's ground-floor flat, without his cousin knowing. The detective put a few enquiries into place. A few days later, Lionel Dickens and Danny Regan were arrested as a serious crime had been detected.

Your Tasks

1. Explain why Trevor Barnard was uneasy about what his cousin Philip had said at their meeting.

2. Describe Trevor Barnard's enquiries.

3. Work out what you think was going on, including the crime that was detected.

CASE FOUR: ON SECOND THOUGHTS

Gary Lester's body had been found on the edge of woodland. The police doctor had said that the cause of death was a blow from a blunt instrument. He had been dead two days and the discovery of the body was made by chance by a walker. Gary Lester lived on his own in an isolated area and this accounted for him not being missed sooner. Detective Inspector Radley had organized a detailed search of the area.

Now back in his office, he went over things in his mind. He had the feeling that he had missed the significance of something that he had seen. The detective visualized the search again. There were pieces of branches from trees, following a recent storm. They had all been lifted carefully, the decayed area under them noted and then replaced. There were footprints still showing in the wet ground, for there had been plenty of rain recently. A largish stone had been lifted but, again, there had been nothing of note underneath in the lush green grass. A couple of spent matches and two cigarette ends suggested that either Gary Lester, or his attacker, had been smoking before the murder.

Then Detective Inspector Radley smiled. Now he knew what was wrong. He would return to the scene of the crime quickly.

Your Tasks

1. Explain what particular point had come into the inspector's mind when he gave the situation second thoughts.
2. Describe what would be the follow-up to his realization.
3. Make a comment about the need for a second visit to the scene of the crime.

CASE FIVE: THE CALENDAR KILLINGS

The Brinkshire police were worried, very worried: four murders and still no closer to finding the killer. First it was a shop assistant in her early twenties. An anonymous telephone call afterwards said, 'Happy New Year. This is your January murder.' Next was an unemployed youth, not long out of school. The accompanying message was, 'Not such a good Valentine's Day for the February victim.' The third murder was of a homeless person, living in care. His killing was followed by a call stating, 'The Mad March Hare has struck.'

There was little public attention at first, but by the time of the third murder the newspapers were headlining what they had christened 'The Calendar Killings'. The Brinkshire police force was put under more and more pressure. The main problem was that there was very little to go on. The killings appeared to be motiveless, other than there was a homicidal maniac loose who, for some reason or another, was linking his or her crimes with the months of the year.

April was nearly ended and the Brinkshire force was holding its collective breath when the fourth blow was struck. To make matters worse, in terms of publicity, the victim this time was a wealthy retired businessman. 'Not such a good start to spring,' was the taunting message.

At this stage an additional detective, Beryl Paine, joined the crime squad. During a meeting of the whole team, she apologized for jumping in as 'the new girl', but suggested that the previous approach had been mistaken and that a more traditional view should be taken as to the reason for the murders. Although rather doubtful at first, Beryl's colleagues gave her opinions serious consideration. The murder enquiries changed track and the killer was caught. There was no macabre message received in May.

Your Tasks

1   Explain what Beryl Paine meant by taking a more traditional view.

2   Give a detailed explanation of the motive behind the murders.

Teaching Notes

Detective mysteries are very popular with both adults and children. The particularly useful feature, as far as children are concerned, is that they have less previous experience and, therefore, they have to work things out for themselves rather more.

Key Elements

- ❖ analysis of data
- ❖ deduction and inference
- ❖ logical thinking
- ❖ hypothesizing
- ❖ synthesis
- ❖ lateral thinking
- ❖ an appreciation of genre
- ❖ enjoyment.

Contexts

'Shreds of Evidence' can be used in a number of ways:

- ❖ as individual written work where differentiation by outcome will apply
- ❖ as five separate cases
- ❖ as a total piece
- ❖ as discussion work in groups
- ❖ as enrichment work for those ahead in other tasks
- ❖ as differentiated homework
- ❖ as an activity during an enrichment day, weekend, summer school or cluster day.

Some Answers

There follow some specific interpretations of the five cases. They are only suggested answers. Both logical thinking and lateral thinking are involved. Alternative responses should be given credit providing that the key elements of the data have not been ignored.

Success Criteria

- ❖ The answer takes note of the information given in the case.
- ❖ There are no contradictions of key points.
- ❖ Imagination is displayed but within realistic possibilities.
- ❖ The solution is appropriate for the setting of the case.

CASE ONE: A GAME OF CHESS

Gerry Burns' body was dressed in light clothing, including a T-shirt. This would have been suitable for the warm house but it was very cold outside. If Antony Price's story was accurate, it would have been expected that the owner would have put on some outdoor clothing before locking up the workshop. It seems more likely, therefore, that he had been murdered inside the house and the body was then removed to provide an explanation. There is also some doubt that Antony Price would have heard a cry from the workshop, which was at the bottom of a large garden, when he was inside the house.

The other three pointers are all related to the game of chess itself. There are three, very wrong, features of the board:

1 for both players there should be a white square in the right-hand corner, not black as here;
2 white has no king on the board;
3 black has two bishops, both on the same colour of square.

Anybody who really did play chess would know that the board was incorrect. This, therefore, seems a clumsy attempt to give Price a reason for being in the house.

There are obvious follow-ups for the inspector, including:

❖ looking for evidence of an attack inside the house
❖ looking for evidence of the body being moved into the garden
❖ finding a motive
❖ involving Price in discussions about the setting up of a chess board and the playing of the game.

CASE TWO: AN UNSHAKEABLE ALIBI

It might be the case that either Mrs Bentley's clock or PC Davies' watch was not keeping accurate time. There is, however, a stronger indication in the evidence and that is related to the particular date. In the early hours of Sunday 27th October 2002, British Summer Time ended. The clocks go back one hour. Every year some people forget to change their clocks and watches, and find themselves 'an hour out'. Of the two, Mrs Bentley, living on her own, was the most likely. When she glanced at the clock and it said 11.25am it should really have been 10.25am. There would have been sufficient time for Gordon Meek to carry out the burglary and be seen on a housing estate some distance away at 11.20am.

CASE THREE: CASUAL TALK SAVES CRIME

Trevor was uneasy because of the nature of Philip's job. It was too well paid for what was involved. He couldn't see the purpose of the job. If it was such a good position, why hadn't Lionel Dickens taken it himself? Trevor was also intrigued by the behaviour of Danny Regan. Why was he so keen to keep a close check on Philip? The whole situation did not make sense. The enquiries were likely to include a check into the background of Lionel Dickens and Danny Regan, and whether there was a connection between the two men. A key element would be the watch on the flat and a look at the immediate neighbourhood.

There are various cases that could be constructed. Central to the explanation has to be Philip's absence from home during set hours. Danny Regan made spot checks to ensure Philip would be at work. The flat is being used for some illegal purpose. The examination of the neighbourhood might have shown the close proximity of a post office or bank, and the men were planning a raid through underground access. They might have needed premises to carry out drug-trading or illegal gambling. Whatever case is suggested, the crime must be highly profitable to justify the expenses laid out to keep Philip away.

CASE FOUR: ON SECOND THOUGHTS

The point that Inspector Radley realized was wrong, was that grass under a weight goes yellow and decays quite quickly. This was what was found under the pieces of branches. However, when the stone was lifted, the grass below was green and lush, indicating that the stone had not been in that particular position for very long. Given that the murder had been carried out with a blunt instrument, the stone deserves further examination. The police laboratory should examine it for hairs and blood from the dead man, and the pathologist should be asked if the stone could have caused the particular injury. Indeed, one might feel that this possibility should have been given serious consideration from the start. The initial search may be regarded as somewhat careless.

CASE FIVE: THE CALENDAR KILLINGS

This is a very open-ended situation and a variety of sensible responses may be made. Whatever they are, they need to find an alternative to the 'homicidal maniac' theory. A more traditional view of crime is that gain is a primary motive. As a consequence, one possible explanation is that only one of the murders was important as far as the killer was concerned, with the other three murders acting as a form of 'camouflage'. Looking at the four deaths, the one that draws attention is the fourth one, that in April. The victim was a wealthy businessman, whose death would benefit somebody financially. After Beryl Paine's intervention, the resources of the crime squad were directed solely to the April murder and to those who benefited from the death. This approach proved to be successful as the so-called 'calendar killer' had cold-bloodedly murdered three random people just to establish a misleading pattern.

NOTE: The names and events are fictional and any link to real people is accidental and coincidental.

CANINE AVENUE

There are only six houses in Canine Avenue and, amazingly, all but one household owns a dog. The five dogs are a Labrador, a spaniel, a boxer, a corgi and an Alsatian. As you enter the avenue, on your left are situated the odd-numbered houses inhabited in ascending number order by Mrs Tail, Mr and Mrs Paw, and Mr and Mrs Muzzle. If you cross the avenue at the house belonging to Mr and Mrs Muzzle and walk back along the even-numbered side, you pass the houses of Mr Bark, Mr and Mrs Yelp, and Mr and Mrs Woof, in that order, before you come out of Canine Avenue and back into Feline Road – where the pet situation is rather different.

From the information above and the clues below, can you say which dog belongs to which people and which is the house where there is no dog?

A A person living on his/her own has a dog with a name of five letters.

B A house with an odd number does not have a dog.

C Mr and Mrs Paw once owned a spaniel but their present pet is a different breed.

D The highest even-numbered house has a dog whose initial letter is the letter immediately preceding the initial letter of the owner, in the alphabet.

E The boxer has a house on either side of its own. Each of these two neighbouring houses has a dog but, of the two, the boxer much prefers to visit the property where the spaniel lives.

CANINE AVENUE

Teaching Notes

This piece demands that children have their wits about them. Establishing who lives where is an essential first step. Reading the clues carefully involves proper use of the word 'preceding'. The silly names play to the particular sense of humour that many able children possess. They can be overheard saying, 'Look, the odd numbers refer to parts of a dog'; 'Yes, and the even numbers involve different noises made by dogs'; 'I bet Mrs Whiskers lives on Feline Road'.

Key Elements
- ❖ simple map work
- ❖ handling data carefully
- ❖ synthesis
- ❖ word humour
- ❖ alternative ways of working
- ❖ logical thinking.

Contexts
'Canine Avenue' can be used in the following ways:
- ❖ as classwork within a thinking skills lesson
- ❖ as enrichment work for those who have completed other tasks
- ❖ as differentiated homework
- ❖ as an activity during an enrichment day, weekend, summer school or cluster day.

Methods of Working
Children may tackle the problem in different ways. The important point is that it suits them personally, as long as it is not uneconomic in terms of time. A written method, a map on which information is written and then crossed out, or the use of slips of paper are all possible and sensible. A matrix also works well for this problem (see page 208 for a full explanation of the method).

Solution
A The two people living on their own are Mrs Tail and Mr Bark. Therefore, one of them owns the boxer or the corgi.

B The house with no dog is Number One (Mrs Tail) or Number Three (Mr and Mrs Paw) or Number Five (Mr and Mrs Muzzle).

C Mr and Mrs Paw can be eliminated for both the spaniel and no dog. From B the house with no dog is narrowed down to Number One or Number Five.

D The highest even number house is Number Six and it is where Mr Bark lives. The dog's name therefore starts with an 'A' and has to be the Alsatian. From A it is Mrs Tail who owns the boxer or the corgi (eliminating the Labrador, spaniel and no dog). Mrs Tail lives at Number One and therefore from B and C it is Number Five (Mr and Mrs Muzzle) where there is no dog.

E A dog with houses on either side must live at Number Three or Number Four. It is not Number Three because Number Five has no dog. Therefore, the boxer lives at Number Four with Mr and Mrs Yelp and it likes to visit the spaniel at Number Two where Mr and Mrs Woof live (as Number Six is already allocated). Mrs Tail must, therefore, own the corgi, and the Labrador must live with Mr and Mrs Paw at Number Three.

	Mrs Tail (1)	Mr and Mrs Paw (3)	Mr and Mrs Muzzle (5)	Mr Bark (6)	Mr and Mrs Yelp (4)	Mr and Mrs Woof (2)
Labrador	✗	✓	✗	✗	✗	✗
Spaniel	✗	✗	✗	✗	✗	✓
Boxer	✗	✗	✗	✗	✓	✗
Corgi	✓	✗	✗	✗	✗	✗
Alsatian	✗	✗	✗	✓	✗	✗
None	✗	✗	✓	✗	✗	✗

Cipherus

You are captain of the spaceship Investigatory. The latest mission for your crew is to stop the aggressive actions of the planet Cipherus. Progress so far has been slow but now the tide has turned, for your communications officer has intercepted a coded message from Cipherus. Breaking that code could be a crucial development. Your work may well be assisted by an intelligence report that has been compiled about Cipherus.

Your Tasks

1 Study the intelligence report about Cipherus and look for any clues that will assist your mission.

2 Apply those clues, and your intelligence, to the intercepted coded message and work out what it says.

3 Decide upon a course of action, informed by the contents of the coded message.

Get to work quickly.
You need to preserve interplanetary peace.

The Intercepted Message

```
17 – 23 – 9 – 13 – 24 – 10 – 1   19 – 9 – 17 – 17 – 10 – 3 – 9
   22 – 12   22 – 15 – 9   3 – 25 – 12 – 8 – 23.   22 – 15 – 9
            17 – 23 – 10 – 13 – 9 – 17 – 15 – 24 – 23
    24 – 5 – 26 – 9 – 17 – 22 – 24 – 3 – 10 – 22 – 12 – 25 – 11
     24 – 17   12 – 5   24 – 22 – 17   21 – 10 – 11.   21 – 9
  10 – 25 – 9   5 – 12 – 22   25 – 9 – 10 – 20 – 11   11 – 9 – 22.
    24 – 22   24 – 17   24 – 19 – 23 – 12 – 25 – 22 – 10 – 5 – 22
         22 – 15 – 9 – 25 – 9 – 18 – 12 – 25 – 9   22 – 12
       23 – 1 – 10 – 11   18 – 12 – 25   22- 24 – 19 – 9.
          22 – 21 – 12   12 – 25   22 – 15 – 25 – 9 – 9
       19 – 12 – 25 – 9   20 – 10 – 11 – 17   21 – 24 – 1 – 1
      10 – 1 – 1 – 12 – 21   15 – 9 – 1 – 23   18 – 25 – 12 – 19
     12 – 8 – 25   10 – 1 – 1 – 24 – 9 – 17   12 – 5   22 – 15 – 9
  23 – 1 – 10 – 5 – 9 – 22   16 – 10 – 16 – 9 – 17.   1 – 12 – 5 – 3
       1 – 24 – 26 – 9   6 – 24 – 5 – 13 – 12 – 5 – 6.
```

Extension Task

Assuming that the spaceship can transmit to Cipherus, send an appropriate message, in the same code, to the people there.

The Intelligence Report about Cipherus

The people are normally peaceful but recently they have come under the power of Zinconz, a very belligerent woman, who wishes to extend her influence and that of the planet Cipherus. They are very frightened of Zinconz and her supporters, and do not do anything that might incur her anger. It is normal, therefore, to wish Zinconz well in all messages and communications, often as a parting greeting. These goodwill sentiments are not sincere, but the people are frightened for their lives.

Cipherus is militarily strong, but probably needs the help of others if a successful campaign of aggression is to be launched. Some neighbouring planets are hostile to Cipherus and would certainly refuse aid. Help to Zinconz is most likely to come from one or more of three planets – Radux, Xaxes or Lux.

Cipherus uses the same basic language as we do with the same alphabet. This is a real boost when dealing with messages and communications. One particular point that our agents have noticed is that communications tend to be addressed early in the message 'to the sector' or 'to the group'.

Cipherus

Teaching Notes

Codes test mental agility and the ability to deal with the abstract. Their solution can be assisted, as here, with full use of the available data. 'Cipherus' uses a science fiction-fantasy setting for interest and enjoyment. Presentation, such as this, adds an extra element, capturing the imagination and engaging able children in the task.

Key Elements

- abstract
- following instructions
- deduction and inference
- engagement with text

- synthesis
- logical thinking
- systematic approach
- code-breaking.

Contexts

'Cipherus' can be used in a number of ways:

- as part of a thinking skills course
- as enrichment work for those ahead on other tasks
- as differentiated homework
- as an activity during an enrichment day, weekend, summer school or cluster day
- as an activity for the Spy Club
- as an open-access competition where the extension task acts as a discriminator.

Solution

A long-winded way would be to use letter frequency and then common sense. The five most common letters are E, T, A, O and N. Combinations such as TH are also helpful.

However, the intelligence report gives a short cut. Messages tend to be addressed 'to the sector' or 'to the group' and it is the second of these that can be located early on. There is a strong suggestion that the name Zinconz will appear late in the communication, with some sort of well-wishing. Children should quickly see the name as the final word, especially as it has to begin and end with the same letter. 'Long live' is a phrase that is very likely to precede the name of the ruler. The third useful aid from the intelligence report is about the three planets that are most likely to help Cipherus. It turns out to be Xaxes that is named and the two 'X's' assist decoding. With three words or phrases known, progress should be fairly rapid. The letters from those words and phrases can be used elsewhere in the message and then context and common sense take over.

The Decoded Message

17 – 23 – 9 – 13 – 24 – 10 – 1   19 – 9 – 17 – 17 – 10 – 3 – 9
S P E C I A L   M E S S A G E

22 – 12   22 – 15 – 9   3 – 25 – 12 – 8 – 23.   22 – 15 – 9
T O   T H E   G R O U P.   T H E

17 – 23 – 10 – 13 – 9 – 17 – 15 – 24 – 23
S P A C E S H I P

24 – 5 – 26 – 9 – 17 – 22 – 24 – 3 – 10 – 22 – 12 – 25 – 11
I N V E S T I G A T O R Y

24 – 17   12 – 5   24 – 22 – 17   21 – 10 – 11.   21 – 9
I S   O N   I T S   W A Y.   W E

10 – 25 – 9   5 – 12 – 22   25 – 9 – 10 – 20 – 11   11 – 9 – 22.
A R E   N O T   R E A D Y   Y E T.

24 – 22   24 – 17   24 – 19 – 23 – 12 – 25 – 22 – 10 – 5 – 22
I T   I S   I M P O R T A N T

22 – 15 – 9 – 25 – 9 – 18 – 12 – 25 – 9   22 – 12
T H E R E F O R E   T O

23 – 1 – 10 – 11   18 – 12 – 25   22- 24 – 19 – 9.
P L A Y   F O R   T I M E.

22 – 21 – 12   12 – 25   22 – 15 – 25 – 9 – 9
T W O   O R   T H R E E

19 – 12 – 25 – 9   20 – 10 – 11 – 17   21 – 24 – 1 – 1
M O R E   D A Y S   W I L L

10 – 1 – 1 – 12 – 21   15 – 9 – 1 – 23   18 – 25 – 12 – 19
A L L O W   H E L P   F R O M

12 – 8 – 25   10 – 1 – 1 – 24 – 9 – 17   12 – 5   22 – 15 – 9
O U R   A L L I E S   O N   T H E

23 – 1 – 10 – 5 – 9 – 22   16 – 10 – 16 – 9 – 17.   1 – 12 – 5 – 3
P L A N E T   X A X E S.   L O N G

1 – 24 – 26 – 9   6 – 24 – 5 – 13 – 12 – 5 – 6.
L I V E Z I N C O N Z.

Special Note

Aids from an intelligence report are known as 'cribs'. They were of great importance for the breakers of the Enigma Code in the Second World War. Indeed, 'to the group' was an actual phrase that was used at the start of messages. Children would be fascinated to see how their work was fitting into a vital episode from history.

Course of Action

The decoded message places emphasis upon speedy action before Cipherus has the assistance of Xaxes.

Extension Task

Various messages are possible, but a clever one would be to suggest that the spaceship 'Investigatory' had changed course away from Cipherus.

All seaside resorts are constantly trying to add attractions to entertain their visitors. The south-coast town of Cocklesea is no exception and, as Festival Week drew closer, a meeting was held of the many people working for the local council in one capacity or another.

Sid Stebbings was at the meeting. He reminded those present that some years ago a competition was run during the summer by a national newspaper in which holidaymakers could win a sum of money by recognizing a newspaper employee from a photograph of part of his or her face, and then challenging that person with a suitable rhyme. Sid offered to design a similar competition for Festival Week. His offer was accepted readily by the town representatives and it was agreed that the competition, to be called 'A Gift from Cocklesea', would be printed inside the brochure for Festival Week.

However, when the brochure was ready, many of those who had been at the meeting were dismayed at the difficulty of Sid's competition. The general feeling was that the money would be unclaimed. Despite the misgivings it was too late to make changes in the brochure. The townspeople had not, however, taken account of the determination of one Jamila Singh. She was among the holidaymakers who arrived for Festival Week. She solved Sid's competition and won the money.

Your Tasks

Imagine that you have just arrived in Cocklesea for Festival Week. You obtain a free brochure of the events for the week and you see Sid's competition, 'A Gift from Cocklesea'.

- Read the instructions and work out the keyword from the 'Spot the Difference' pictures and the coding system.
- Look at the list of public buildings and decide which to visit to find 'Cockle Sid'.
- Write down what you would say to 'Cockle Sid' to claim the £50 prize.

The sun is shining, the gulls are crying, the sea is glittering in the bay. Go on, have a try. Wouldn't you like to take home 'A Gift from Cocklesea'?

Competition Instructions

Look at the two 'Spot the Difference' pictures. Write down two lists to show 12 differences of number. Now use that information together with the following coding system.

The Coding System

1 The following 26 numbers are to be used in the order given, against letters in alphabetical order.

1	21	19	16	17	12	14	10	11	4
2	26	20	15	25	8	9	6	23	13
3	24	18	5	7	22				

2 The date of the competition claim will determine at which place the letter 'a' is to be positioned, with the other letters following in alphabetical order, until there is a letter against each number (for example on July 13th the 'a' would be placed against the number 20 as that is 13th in the list of numbers).

3 Both pictures of the puzzle are important and need to be used together at first, but then one picture will play a greater role in the decoding whereas the other picture will assist the placement or order.

A word will be spelled out.

Now look at the list of public buildings. Decide which one fits best with the keyword.

The List of Public Buildings

Council Offices   Leisure Centre   Floral Hall
Library   Tourist Information Office   Town Hall
Citizens Advice Bureau   Bus Station   Swimming Pool

Making your Claim

A competition claim can only be made on the Thursday of Festival Week. Go to the building that fits the coded word best. Ask for 'Cockle Sid' and, when he appears, say this rhyme to him with the missing word filled in:

'Cockle Sid, I feel so sad,
But your 50 quid will make me glad.
Your word is _____!'

If you are the first person to make a correct claim, 'Cockle Sid' will hand you £50.

Festival Week

This year, Festival Week starts on Saturday 5th August.

Spot the Difference

Picture One

Look carefully at the two pictures.

Write down two lists to show 12 differences of number.

Spot the Difference

Picture Two

Teaching Notes

This involved code takes a good deal of thought to sort out. It involves a number of important thinking skills.

Key Elements

❖ following instructions

❖ logical thinking

❖ synthesis

❖ using data carefully

❖ observation

❖ abstract – in a code, something stands for something else.

Contexts

'A Gift from Cocklesea' can be used in the following ways:

❖ as an enrichment item for those ahead in normal classwork

❖ as classwork in a thinking skills course

❖ as differentiated homework

❖ as an activity during an enrichment day, weekend, summer school or cluster day.

The Solution

To be able to use the number code provided, the first task is to find the numbers themselves. This is achieved by careful observation of the two pictures that show 12 differences, all of which involve numbers. Children should be encouraged to look for differences overall, not just in one section of the picture.

Picture one	Object	Picture two
11	Kite	9
12	Bucket and spade	10
6	Beach ball	5
2	Camera	6
8	Sun	1
9	Sunglasses	4
10	Ice cream	7
7	Windmill	8
5	Anchor	6
4	Balloon	3
3	Boat	2
1	Surfer	2

NOTE:

1 The children may use different names to identify the objects.
2 The order of noting the differences does not matter.

There are now two sets of numbers to use. The instructions explained that one picture would be used for decoding and the other for replacement. Some children may decode both sets of numbers and see which is the more likely to form a word. Careful scrutiny of the two lists shows, however, that picture one provides the numbers 1–12 inclusive, and therefore shows what order to use the letters to form a 12-letter word. The second picture thus provides the numbers to be decoded using the system described.

The next task is to place the letters of the alphabet against the number code given in the instructions. As the competition claim date is 10th August, the 'A' is to be placed in the 10th position – that is, against the number 4. The code can now be written out:

1	21	19	16	17	12	14	10	11	4
R	**S**	**T**	**U**	**V**	**W**	**X**	**Y**	**Z**	**A**

2	26	20	15	25	8	9	6	23	13
B	**C**	**D**	**E**	**F**	**G**	**H**	**I**	**J**	**K**

3	24	18	5	7	22
L	**M**	**N**	**O**	**P**	**Q**

The numbers from picture two decoded give the following letters: H, Y, O, I, R, A, P, G, I, L, B, B. From picture one, the numbers give the order in which to use these letters. For example, H (9 kites in picture two) is positioned eleventh in the word (11 kites in picture one). When each letter is placed correctly, the word BIBLIOGRAPHY is produced.

In the 'List of Public Buildings', there is the library, and that is the place best linked with the word BIBLIOGRAPHY.

On Thursday 10th August, Jamila Singh went to the library and confronted Sid Stebbings with the immortal words:

'Cockle Sid, I feel so sad,
But your 50 quid will make me glad.
Your word is bibliography.'
She won the £50.

Hints

A difficult code is supposed to be exactly that. Giving away too much information too quickly reduces the challenge and prevents able children having to work hard for their success. However, it is also damaging to allow frustration to become too great. The skilled teacher gradually adds in hints, not too helpful to start with, but becoming more and more useful. A gap is left between hints so that children always think for themselves.

the scene of the crime

How many times have you watched fictional detectives on television or at the cinema? How often have you seen real-life cases be covered during news programmes or documentaries? Perhaps you have wondered what it is like to be a detective investigating a serious crime. Now is your chance to find out because you are going to be placed at 'The Scene of the Crime'.

Your Tasks

1 You will be taken to the scene of a murder. Before you enter the area, you will hear a short statement from PC Allan, who is on duty. Listen carefully to your instructions.

2 At the scene of the crime, you will see certain areas of the room marked off with tape. There is space to move around outside these areas. Do not enter the taped areas and do not touch any evidence other than indicated by PC Allan's instructions. Make detailed notes, as individual detectives, on all that you see. At this stage, do not think about what the evidence suggests.

3 You will then be put into crime squads. Members of each squad compare notes and observations. Look for common ground and differences of opinion.

4 Each crime squad then compiles a report on the scene of the crime. This consists of:
   A The name of the crime squad
   B The names of the members of the squad
   C A description of the scene. This is the very factual reporting of what you have seen: detailing and describing both the general scene and specific items. The first stage in any investigation is to collect evidence.
   D An action plan. The crime squad is required to explain what they would do with individual items of evidence, and what might be learned from those actions.
   E An initial or working model of the crime. These are still 'early days' for the investigation, but you are asked to present a theory of what you think might have occurred and why. It is important to link all suggestions and theories with actual evidence.

Success Criteria

Your reports will be judged by the following criteria:

- ? the detail of the observation
- ? the quality of the action plan in terms of what results could be obtained
- ? the degree to which pieces of evidence are seen to be connected
- ? the clarity of the written report
- ? the degree to which the working theory is based upon evidence
- ? the level of creativity and imagination displayed without a loss of realism.

POLICE · DO NOT ENTER · SCENE OF CRIME

POLICE · DO NOT ENTER · SCENE OF CRIME

the scene of the crime

Teaching Notes

This is a dramatic event that provides children with great enjoyment but, at the same time, plays to a number of important skills. It is particularly suited to a lengthy time-scale.

Key Elements

- ❖ analysis
- ❖ synthesis
- ❖ evaluation
- ❖ observation
- ❖ individual work
- ❖ teamwork
- ❖ collaboration
- ❖ hypothesizing
- ❖ producing a clear report.

Organization

The silhouette figure of a person is laid out in one part of the room. This is where the body was found. Other areas, containing furniture, are taped off and various items of evidence are placed in appropriate positions. These can be chosen for convenience by the teacher but they must allow connections and possibilities (while remaining very open). A suggested layout is given below, based upon the author's own set up for this activity. For the preliminary investigation of the room the children will need clipboards and paper. To add authenticity, and to help the children, a supply of magnifying glasses and tape measures are provided at the scene.

It is important to stress that the children will only have one chance to view the evidence, so they need to record their observations carefully and in detail (in real life a crime scene has to be returned to normal life after it has been examined).

pc allan

A member of staff (preferably wearing a plastic police helmet) announces to the children, before they enter the scene of the crime (at this point hidden, with a 'KEEP OUT – CRIME SCENE' notice on the door), the following statement:

❝ The initial examination has taken place. The body has been removed to the mortuary for further examination. An outline of the body shows where the body was found. There are sets of equipment available to help you with your investigations – tape measures and magnifying glasses. Do not enter the taped-off areas, as you may contaminate the evidence. There is space to move around without going into the taped sections. Do not touch the evidence, just look from outside the tapes. There is one exception: a waste-paper basket containing a number of items. You may remove these items but then please return them as they were. Keep your eyes peeled. Look for detail. Good luck with your investigation. ❞

the children

Work starts on an individual basis for the observation of the scene. When that stage is complete, the children are put into small crime squads of four, five or six people. They exchange information and theories before putting together a team report.

a possible layout

Area One
The silhouette figure of the body, lying in a particular position. This can be produced by getting a real person to lie on a large sheet of paper, or on wallpaper, and draw round him or her. If preferred, an outline could be drawn around a person on the floor *in situ* using chalk. A medal or piece of jewellery lies close by.

Area Two
This section is dominated by overturned furniture. A golf tee lies on the floor. There is also a button and one earring. Strands of blue wool are caught on one of the overturned chairs.

Area Three
Central is a table, on top of which there are several items – an audio cassette, a glass with obvious fingerprints, a key, a foreign coin and two rail tickets.

Area Four
This is dominated by a desk on top of which there are: a white pad with two strands of human hair on it; the photograph of a horse, sticking out from a photographer's packet, with the words 'Remember him' written on it ; and a hotel memo pad with the words 'Robert 9.30am' written on the top sheet. Beside the desk is a waste-paper basket containing a crumpled blackmail or threatening letter, a torn fishing licence, a cigarette packet, a receipt, a torn appointment card with writing on the back and a spent match.

Area Five
A small table or bureau has upon it a reference book, opened at a page describing poisonous mushrooms. An open tin contains a white powder (salt or sugar is easy and safe to use).

Area Six
Near a French window or door (any window will do) a 'bloodstained' handkerchief lies on the floor (red ink prevents health concerns) and there is also soil and plant debris. The window/door can be open or closed.

the action plan

This will depend very much on the items used by the teacher. For the objects above, some suggestions would be:

Cassette	play it
Hotel memo pad	contact the hotel
Handkerchief	analyse the blood for comparison
Post-mortem report	await
Fingerprints on glass	try to match
Soil and plant debris	analyse and try to locate its origin
Threatening letter	get a handwriting expert to look at it, try to trace materials
Wool and button	try to match to original garments
Earring	trace the other earring
Documents	follow up rail tickets, appointment card, receipt, fishing licence, horse photograph
White powder	analyse to establish its identity
Key	see what it opens

Enrichment Activities for Able and Talented Children © Barry Teare (Network Educational Press, 2004)

Titles from Network Educational Press

Accelerated Learning in the Classroom by Alistair Smith
Effective Learning Activities by Chris Dickinson
Effective Heads of Department by Phil Jones & Nick Sparks
Lessons are for Learning by Mike Hughes
Effective Learning in Science by Keith Bishop & Paul Denley
Raising Boys' Achievement by Jon Pickering
Effective Provision for Able & Talented Children by Barry Teare
Effective Careers Education & Guidance by Andrew Edwards & Anthony Barnes
Best behaviour and Best behaviour FIRST AID by Peter Relf, Rod Hirst, Jan Richardson
    & Georgina Youdell
    Best behaviour FIRST AID also available separately
The Effective School Governor by David Marriott (including audio tape)
Improving Personal Effectiveness for Managers in Schools by James Johnston
Making Pupil Data Powerful by Maggie Pringle & Tony Cobb
Closing the Learning Gap by Mike Hughes
Getting Started by Henry Liebling
Leading the Learning School by Colin Weatherley
Adventures in Learning by Mike Tilling
Strategies for Closing the Learning Gap by Mike Hughes with Andy Vass
Classroom Management by Philip Waterhouse & Chris Dickinson
Effective Teachers by Tony Swainston
Transforming Teaching & Learning by Colin Weatherley with Bruce Bonney, John Kerr
    & Jo Morrison
Effective Teachers in Primary Schools by Tony Swainston

ACCELERATED LEARNING SERIES   General Editor: **Alistair Smith**

Accelerated Learning: A User's Guide by Alistair Smith, Mark Lovatt & Derek Wise
Accelerated Learning in Practice by Alistair Smith
The ALPS Approach: Accelerated Learning in Primary Schools by Alistair Smith
    & Nicola Call
MapWise by Oliver Caviglioli & Ian Harris
The ALPS Approach Resource Book by Alistair Smith & Nicola Call
Creating an Accelerated Learning School by Mark Lovatt & Derek Wise
ALPS StoryMaker by Stephen Bowkett
Thinking for Learning by Mel Rockett & Simon Percival
Reaching out to all learners by Cheshire LEA
Leading Learning by Alistair Smith
Bright Sparks by Alistair Smith
More Bright Sparks by Alistair Smith
Move It by Alistair Smith

EDUCATION PERSONNEL MANAGEMENT SERIES

The Well Teacher – management strategies for beating stress, promoting staff health & reducing absence by Maureen Cooper

Managing Challenging People – dealing with staff conduct by Maureen Cooper & Bev Curtis

Managing Poor Performance – handling staff capability issues by Maureen Cooper & Bev Curtis

Managing Allegations Against Staff – personnel and child protection issues in schools by Maureen Cooper & Bev Curtis

Managing Recruitment and Selection – appointing the best staff by Maureen Cooper & Bev Curtis

Managing Redundancies – dealing with reduction and reorganisation of staff by Maureen Cooper & Bev Curtis

Paying Staff in Schools – performance management and pay in schools by Bev Curtis

VISIONS OF EDUCATION SERIES

The Power of Diversity by Barbara Prashnig
The Unfinished Revolution by John Abbott & Terry Ryan
The Learning Revolution by Gordon Dryden & Jeannette Vos
Wise Up by Guy Claxton

ABLE AND TALENTED CHILDREN COLLECTION

Effective Resources for Able and Talented Children by Barry Teare
More Effective Resources for Able and Talented Children by Barry Teare
Challenging Resources for Able and Talented Children by Barry Teare

MODEL LEARNING

Thinking Skills & Eye Q by Oliver Caviglioli, Ian Harris & Bill Tindall
Think it–Map it! by Ian Harris & Oliver Caviglioli
Reaching out to all thinkers by Ian Harris & Oliver Caviglioli

OTHER TITLES FROM NEP

The Thinking Child by Nicola Call with Sally Featherstone

The Thinking Child Resource Book by Nicola Call with Sally Featherstone

Foundations of Literacy by Sue Palmer & Ros Bayley

StoryMaker Catch Pack by Stephen Bowkett

Becoming Emotionally Intelligent by Catherine Corrie

That's Science! by Tim Harding

That's Maths! by Tim Harding

The Brain's Behind It by Alistair Smith

Help Your Child To Succeed by Bill Lucas & Alistair Smith

Help Your Child To Succeed – Toolkit by Bill Lucas & Alistair Smith

Tweak to Transform by Mike Hughes

Brain Friendly Revision by UFA National Team

Numeracy Activities Key Stage 2 by Afzal Ahmed & Honor Williams

Numeracy Activities Key Stage 3 by Afzal Ahmed, Honor Williams
    & George Wickham

Teaching Pupils How to Learn by Bill Lucas, Toby Greany, Jill Rodd & Ray Wicks

Creating a Learning to Learn School by Toby Greany & Jill Rodd

Basics for School Governors by Joan Sallis

Questions School Governors Ask by Joan Sallis

Imagine That... by Stephen Bowkett

Self-Intelligence by Stephen Bowkett

Class Talk by Rosemary Sage

Lend Us Your Ears by Rosemary Sage

A World of Difference by Rosemary Sage

With Drama in Mind by Patrice Baldwin

For more information and ordering details, please consult our website
www.networkpress.co.uk

Notes

Notes

Notes

Notes

Notes